The Zen of MLM
Second Edition, Revised and Expanded

Also by John David Mann

You Call the Shots (with Cameron Johnson, 2007)
The Go-Giver (with Bob Burg, 2008)
A Deadly Misunderstanding (with Mark Siljander, 2008)
The Secret Language of Money
(with David Krueger, MD, 2009)
Go-Givers Sell More (with Bob Burg, 2010)
Flash Foresight (with Daniel Burrus, 2011)
Take the Lead (with Betsy Myers, 2011)
It's Not About You (with Bob Burg, 2011)
Code to Joy (with George Pratt, PhD,
and Peter Lambrou, PhD, 2012)
The Red Circle (with Brandon Webb, 2012)
Funny Side Up (with Rita Davenport, 2012)
The Slight Edge (with Jeff Olson, 2013)
Among Heroes (with Brandon Webb, 2015)

The Zen of MLM

Legacy, Leadership and the
Network Marketing Experience

Essays and Editorials, 1991-2013

Second Edition, Revised and Expanded

John David Mann

Owens & Alfred Press

Some of the articles appearing in this collection were first published
elsewhere. A list of original publication and permission to reprint,
constituting a continuation of this copyright page, appears on pages
xiii–xviii.

Cover photo by Getty Images, design by Mia Inderbitzen
Text set in Janson

Second Edition: 2014
ISBN 978-0-9796081-1-7
Library of Congress Control number: 2014910601

Owens & Alfred Press
6 University Drive, Suite 206-227
Amherst MA 01002
www.owensandalfredpress.com

Visit the author at
www.johndavidmann.com

Owens & Alfred Press

Contents

Zen

n. 1. the pursuit of enlightenment, often through the vehicle of paradoxical statements. **2.** a loosely defined set of esthetic and philosophical values, including simplicity, understatement and careful economy of expression, aimed at achieving maximum effect with minimum means or effort. **3.** the application of those values to a specific discipline: *the Zen of archery*, *the Zen of design*.

MLM

abbr. of MULTILEVEL MARKETING (also: NETWORK MARKETING): **n.** a form of distribution of goods and services through a self-generating network of independent representatives structured and compensated in a cascading series of multiple tiers or levels.

Prologue
What *Is* This Thing Called Network Marketing?
April '07

In the winter of 1986, after devoting years to a career as a concert musician and teacher, I came to this sobering realization: I wasn't making it financially, and it was time to do something about it. Do what, exactly? I had no idea. But *something*. A few weeks later, a friend and fellow teacher called me on the phone to tell me about this thing he was doing called network marketing, or *multilevel* marketing. "MLM," he called it. I was intrigued.

It's twenty-one years later, and after more than two decades of witnessing first-hand the growth and maturation of this emerging economic powerhouse, I'm more intrigued than ever.

What *is* this thing called network marketing?

In the more than sixty years it has been around, it has grown to become a $100 billion-plus worldwide enterprise, making it an economic bloc roughly the size of New Zealand, Pakistan or the Philippines. Yet for much of that sixty-year history, mainstream culture has tended to regard network marketing, when regarding it at all, as the butt of jokes.

In the film *Edward Scissorhands*, the tragically weird figure of

Edward is orphaned by the demise of Vincent Price, left alone in a castle and isolated from the world until he is discovered by ... *ding dong*: the Avon lady. During the Soviet coup attempt in 1991, David Letterman observed on his show one night that the military had the Kremlin completely sealed off and neither journalists nor soldiers could penetrate the lockdown—"Although," he added, "one Amway salesman did get through."

Network marketing has for decades been the Rodney Dangerfield of business models: *it don't get no respect*. (Little known fact: Dangerfield actually spent time in his youth supporting his family as an aluminum siding salesman. Life imitates art.)

Funny thing, though: despite the easy punch lines, people's actual experience of the business is not necessarily what they *think* their experience of the business is.

In 1976, Lou Harris conducted a poll to measure American attitudes about the direct selling industry. (In those days, network marketing represented but a minority portion of the "direct selling" world; today it has grown to the point where the two terms are practically synonymous.) What Harris found was a classic schism between perception and reality: close to 100 percent of the people polled who had ever had any contact at all with the business had a positive experience—yet those same people had an overwhelmingly negative image of the industry itself. It was as if network marketing were a new food people still thought they hated—even though they'd actually tried it and found it tasted pretty good.

Things have changed since 1976, and especially since the mid-nineties. Mainstream acceptance, that elusive holy grail for so many network marketers, has been slow in coming, yet there are signs suggesting it may have finally arrived. For example, *Fortune* magazine has in the past few years published several multi-page supplements on the profession, citing involvement in the business by billionaires Warren Buffett and Richard Branson and such household brands as Citigroup, Sara Lee and Time Warner. According to statistics compiled from national surveys by the Direct Selling Association (DSA), the profession's gross revenue has increased every single year for the past fifteen, which is as far back as DSA web site (www.dsa.org) figures go. From 1999 to 2002, as U.S. retail sales overall suffered through a steep decline, the direct selling sector posted a marked *increase* in total sales. [For an update, see "Preface to the Second Edition."]

In *The Next Millionaires* (2006), two-time presidential economic advisor and *New York Times* best-selling author Paul Zane Pilzer points out that as the institution of the modern corporation begins to falter and collapse, we are seeing a vast emigration from corporate employment to home-based business. "The twenty-first century we have just begun will be known as the Age of the Entrepreneur," writes Pilzer. He goes on to forecast that a significant portion of new fortunes made among entrepreneurs in the years ahead will arise from the field of network marketing.

Over the decade and a half that this volume of essays covers, the profession has done some serious growing up. The self-policing efforts of the DSA and the network marketing companies themselves have helped to curb abuses of the system and establish profession-wide standards. As the profession's ranks have continued to swell, it has been fascinating to watch the shifting demographics of those leaving behind traditional employment for the 1099 world of the work-at-home networking professional: college professors and coaches, bankers and surgeons, engineers and pro athletes. They range from twenty-somethings to ninety-somethings and hail from quite literally all walks of life.

And there are now 55 *million* of them worldwide.

What are all these people looking for? The answers are almost as diverse as the people, but they boil down to three.

As I describe them, I'll also explain what has happened since that 1986 phone conversation, and how the essays in this book came to be.

First, the obvious reason: people come to network marketing to make money. Here's what is not so obvious: how *much* money are they looking to make? And, do they succeed?

Despite popular images of pinky rings, Cadillacs and million-dollar checks, the great majority of network marketers are in the business to make a *little* extra money.

Thomas J. Stanley and William D. Danko's best-selling 1996 book *The Millionaire Next Door: The Surprising Secrets of America's Wealthy* blew the reading public's mind with its revelation that many of the wealthy in our midst got that way not by hitting some jackpot, but by persistently earning modest money and leveraging it through scrupulous saving and cautious investments. It was a message that hit home especially powerfully for network marketers.

While the big check may have more sizzle from the stage and be a more sensational draw, more and more network marketers have come to realize that the *little* check is really where the action is. As the profession matures, its practitioners are coming to it with an increasingly realistic—and attainable—set of expectations: that they will earn a modest supplemental "passive" income stream they can then parlay into more time with family, the pursuit of personal interests, a better quality of life, perhaps some appreciating assets and, yes, even long-term financial security. And a surprising number of them succeed in doing just that.[1]

Here's how Jim Turner, a consumer-advocacy attorney in Washington, D.C. who has followed the profession for decades, put it in a recent interview I conducted with him:

Run the numbers on what goes through multilevel marketing companies and how many people there are, and you get
up into the $30,000 to $40,000 annual range pretty easily
for a very large number of people, which puts you above the
national mean income. You could easily become a major part
of a majority of households in America.[2]

Critics of the business sometimes cite its supposedly steep
attrition figures, claiming that 90-plus percent of the networking population quits every year after failing miserably. What
they never seem to mention is that many of those who leave
the business recycle themselves back in again, joining a second
organization, perhaps a third, even a fourth and fifth, learning
and improving their success rate as they go. Network marketers
are fond of describing this as a business where you "earn while
you learn," and experience bears this out: most of the successful
network marketers I've met over these past two decades achieved
their success only with their third or fourth (or fifth, or sixth) go
at it. Thus, while a given statistic might suggest that, say, only
one out of five networkers achieved her financial goals, the reality
might be that *all five of them were the same person*, simply refining
and deepening her skills as she went. What is presented as an 80
percent failure rate is in fact a 100 percent success story.

This was exactly my case.

When I first encountered network marketing in 1986, I was
a classical cellist, composer and educator with no experience
or training in business, but a powerfully motivating desire to
become unbroke. When my friend explained to me the concept
at the core of the business—that it is essentially a teaching
business, a model where you succeed to the degree that you
help other people succeed, and that it is dedicated consumers
of a product who benefit from its promulgation throughout
their sphere of acquaintance—I dubbed it "the Robin Hood

Principle" (redistributing wealth along more just channels) and fell instantly in love with it.

In the six months that followed I participated in four different network marketing organizations at the same time, figuring that if one was good, hey, four was better. I eventually realized that this bit of wisdom might be seriously flawed, and in fact, if I had any hope of learning how to ride this horse, I'd be better off holding onto one and letting go of the others. And that's exactly what I did: I chose one company to stick with, and quit the other three.

Now follow this: statistically, I represented a 75 percent "attrition rate" for the profession that year, "failing" in three out of the four companies I'd joined. But with the fourth, I went on to earn several million dollars over the following decade. Today, more than twenty years later, I still earn a substantial residual income from that same company—an income stream I anticipate handing down to my children when I shuffle off to the next editorial assignment in the sky.

While earning an income is the most obvious reason to start a network marketing business, it is not necessarily the most universal. Millions of people who earn little or no money above the cost of their own product use continue to participate in their company events year after year. Why? Because they *belong* to something and more than any club or other social constellation, it is a *something* that provides them with significant development not only as businesspeople but also as people, period.

Personal development, within which I include the acquisition of skills, the growth of a web of relationships, and the peer recognition that comes with achievement, is a compelling reward of the business—so compelling in its own right that it often rivals and even outranks the reward of financial gain.

For many, a given company's network is not simply a business organization one joins but a culture to which one *belongs*, a community of people with shared values, and one of the strongest values among them is self-improvement. Robert Kiyosaki, author of the *New York Times* best-selling *Rich Dad Poor Dad* series, encourages entrepreneurs to join the network marketing company of their choice for the sake of the training they'll receive.

> School prepares you for a job in a major corporation, government or teaching, but it doesn't prepare you for the real world. That's what network marketing does. Network marketing teaches people basic, critical life skills. I tell people, "Stay with it for five years and you'll be better equipped to survive in the real world of business—and you'll be a better person."[3]

For many, becoming "a better person" is all about that ultimate fruit of self-development, *leadership*. Richard Brooke, a network marketing CEO and frequent industry spokesperson, has said for years that leadership is the profession's principal product offering.

One reason for this is that network marketing is at its core a volunteer movement. In contrast to the "mother company," which is structured as a traditional corporation, the field of reps—which can easily grow to include hundreds of thousands and even millions—is composed 100 percent of independent contractors. There is no authority, no power structure, no hierarchy. Nobody *has* to show up to work. In a business environment that networkers often describe as "herding cats," leadership becomes a precious commodity.

I became aware of the larger network marketing community starting in January 1990, when two friends, John Milton Fogg and Randolph Byrd, and I began publishing a monthly journal called *MLM Success*, soon renamed *Upline*.

Having learned the business from the inside, now I began to learn about it as an external observer and commentator. In 1991 I wrote a piece for *Upline* to help network marketers explain the concept of *residual income*. "Residual Income, Residual Impact" was widely excerpted, photocopied and passed around, and is still kicking around the Internet today; it appears in this volume as the first in a series of seventy-one articles that span the years 1991 through 2007. [In this Second Edition, that's now 101 articles spanning from 1991 through 2013.]

Within a few years *Upline* had become the leading trade journal and *de facto* standard-bearer for the profession. In 1996 my partners and I sold the publication to new owners and I left the firm to devote my time to my own burgeoning organization. A few years later *Upline*'s new owners launched a glossy bimonthly newsstand magazine called *Network Marketing Lifestyles* (*NML*) and hired me to come back as editor in chief, a position I filled until the magazine's demise—which alas was not long in coming. In 2000 and 2001 the dot.com speculation bubble burst, and *NML* popped with it. At the close of 2001, after printing fifteen issues, the umbrella company that now owned both *NML* and *Upline* closed its doors.

But the world continued after 9/11, and so did network marketing journalism. Within less than half a year, my friends Chris and Josephine Gross, a seasoned entrepreneur and a Stanford-educated Ph.D., decided to fill the void left behind by the evaporation of *Upline* and *Lifestyles*. Chris and Josephine envisioned a publication that would raise the bar and, echoing our original mission at *Upline* twelve years earlier, champion all that was noblest in the profession.

While *NML* evoked comparisons to *People* magazine, the Grosses' new journal *Networking Times* was modeled more on *The Harvard Business Review*. I was hired on as senior editor for the inaugural issue and soon took the post of editor in chief.

From this position, I had the opportunity to explore still more far-reaching dimensions and implications of this thing called network marketing.

The third reason people join a network marketing company is the opportunity it affords them to make a difference in other people's lives. For many, in fact, this is the most compelling reason of the three.

Sit down and talk with a seasoned network marketer about her business for longer than ten minutes and you'll start hearing stories about the people whose lives have been transformed. Most network marketing companies have significant charitable and humanitarian arms, outreach efforts that often grow into grassroots missions of fervent activity, sweeping scope and astonishing impact. Network marketers are promiscuously philanthropic.

But the biggest place where "making a difference" makes a difference to network marketers is in their own back yards: that is, in the lives of the people in their organizations. That core idea that so excited me when I first heard it in 1986—that you succeed only to the degree that you help others succeed—is in fact one of the prime movers of the business. For example, many network marketers join the business in order to help one spouse (or both) stay at home, and they often find that even a fairly modest supplemental income can often effect a startling transformation in a family's quality of life. Seeing that kind of shift happen for other people whom they bring into the business becomes a reward beyond any price tag.

As much as networking reps love success, they often become even more motivated by the cause that drives it. Drawn by the promise of lifestyle, they become captivated by the opportunities of leadership and legacy.

During my tenure at *Networking Times*, I've had the opportunity to deepen my inquiry, going outside the profession itself to talk about network marketing with a wide range of authors, educators, business leaders and others, including:

Scott Allen (*The Virtual Handshake*), David Bach (*The Automatic Millionaire*), Ori Brafman and Rod A. Beckstrom (*The Spider and the Starfish*), Bob Burg (*Endless Referrals*), S. Truett Cathy (founder, Chick-fil-A), Dr. Henry Cloud (*Integrity*), Ben Cohen (cofounder, Ben & Jerry's), Vic Conant (president, Nightingale-Conant), Stephen R. Covey (7 *Habits of Highly Effective People*), Stephen M.R. Covey (*The Speed of Trust*), Michael Gerber (*The E-Myth*), Sen. Orrin Hatch (R-Utah), Tom Hopkins (*How to Master the Art of Selling*), A.E. Hotchner (*Shameless Exploitation in Pursuit of the Common Good*), Robert Kiyosaki (*Rich Dad Poor Dad*), Dr. Bruce Lipton (*The Biology of Belief*), Frank Maguire (past senior VP, FedEx and KFC), Howard Martin (*The HeartMath Solution*), Dr. Ivan Misner (founder, BNI), Neil Offen (president, Direct Selling Association), Paul Zane Pilzer (*Unlimited Wealth*), Nido Qubein (president, High Point University), Dr. Martha Rogers (*The One to One Future*), Hyrum Smith (cofounder, Franklin Quest), Brian Tracy (*The Psychology of Achievement*), Jim Turner, Esq. (*The Chemical Feast*), and Dr. Denis Waitley (*The Psychology of Winning*).

[Update: Interviews in the years since the first edition of Zen appeared have included: Shawn Achor (*The Happiness Advantage*), Jeffrey Arnett, Ph.D. (*Emerging Adulthood*), Colleen Barrett (president emerita, Southwest Airlines), Jack Canfield (*The Success Principles*), Kathy Cloninger (CEO, Girl Scouts of America), June Cohen (executive producer, TED Talks), Ken Dychtwald, Ph.D. (*Age Wave*), Maddy

Dychtwald (*Influence: How Women's Soaring Economic Power Will Transform Our World for the Better*), Matt Flannery (co-founder, Kiva), Dr. Barbara Fredrickson (*Positivity*), Michelle Gielan (CBS News), Seth Godin (*Permission Marketing*), François Gossieaux (*The Hyper-Social Organization*), Gay Hendricks, Ph.D. and Kathlyn Hendricks, Ph.D. (The Hendricks Institute), Tony Hsieh (CEO, Zappos), Kathy Ireland (CEO, kathy ireland worldwide), Larry Jones (cofounder, Feed The Children), Anya Kamanetz (*DIY U: Edupunks, Edupreneurs and the Coming Transformation of Higher Education*), David Krueger, M.D. (*The Secret Language of Money*), Joe Mariano (president, Direct Selling Association), Daniel Pink (*Drive: The Surprising Truth about What Motivates Us*), Terry Savage (*The Savage Number*), Marshall Thurber (cofounder, Burklyn Business School), Gary Vaynerchuk (*Crush It!*), and Marianne Williamson (*The Age of Miracles*).]

I've come to all these conversations with the issues of leadership and legacy in the forefront of my mind. In many cases, I've had the chance to ask these opinion leaders for their particular views of this profession and of what impact it may have on the world in the years ahead. Here is a tiny sampling of their responses:

I went into my research [on network marketing] with a "No way!" attitude. I'd avoided this profession like the plague for twenty years. I ended up devoting an entire chapter to it in my book [*Start Late Finish Rich*]. . . . Network marketing is a vehicle where you can make a little extra money, and with that, buy your freedom. Do that, and you'll spend the rest of your life doing what you were put here to do.[4]

—David Bach, author of the #1 *New York Times* best-sellers *The Automatic Millionaire* and *Start Late, Finish Rich*

To some extent, our world has lost trust. At a time when people have serious reservations about business, when they are shaken by the misuse of people's trust and poor ethics in business and government, we tend to go back to the basics. That's what network marketing is all about. The microcosmic essence of network marketing is trust, built one person at a time; once you have established trust, then the geometric progression takes over.[5]

—Nido Qubein, president High Point University, North Carolina

Young people in droves are getting interested in network marketing; we've been bombarded by so many network marketers asking us so many questions [at Young & Successful Media Corp.] that we're now considering forming another division specifically to meet those needs. ... After getting involved with network marketing and attending some of the big conferences, I became a voracious reader. I can't think of anything else I've done that's given me better exposure to the skill sets it takes to be successful in the real world.[6]

—Scott Kaufman, CEO of the Young & Successful Media Corp. and coauthor of the *New York Times* best-seller *Secrets of the Young and Successful*

Network marketing is a critically important way of helping people to use high-quality products [and] to give people an opportunity to sell those products and earn a good living from it. I see it playing a very important role in the twenty-first century.[7]

—Senator Orrin Hatch (R-Utah)

Network marketing is in the vanguard of a major consumer movement . . . I'd say you could have perhaps 150 million households successfully involved in network marketing, at least part-time.[8]

—Jim Turner, Esq., founding partner, Swankin & Turner

I think [network marketing] is potentially the greatest economic opportunity that has ever existed. You're creating an opportunity to affect the self-esteem of many, many people. You're giving people hope and providing a launching pad for people to discover their own greatness. You *are* the future.[9]

—Frank Maguire, former senior vice president of FedEx and KFC, former director at ABC and American Airlines

I included the remarks of these last three individuals— Hatch, Turner and Maguire—in a 2007 article on the evolution of the profession, entitled "Cutting a New Path," which (along with "Residual Income, Residual Impact," the 1991 essay that begins this collection) is one of the few pieces in *The Zen of MLM* that runs more than two or three pages. Mostly what you'll read here are very short pieces, written to fit the single-page parameters of magazine editorials. (All but a dozen of them originally ran as one-page pieces in my regular columns: "The Last Word" in *Upline*, "The Big Picture" in *Network Marketing Lifestyles*, and "The Close" in *Networking Times*.)

They are also mostly quite short because they were intended as concise bits of practical material, meant to be useful to in-the-trenches network marketers in the everyday pursuit of their businesses.

And that, finally, is the point of this book.

For the reader who is a curious observer of this business, perhaps investigating it for the first time and hoping to gain insight into what makes it tick, I hope it serves your purpose well. But I offer it mainly for those of you who are practicing network marketers yourselves, in hopes that you will find something among these pages that will inform, refine and animate your business—that they will be of some help as you go about cutting your own path.

A friend once told me he went to a workshop where he was directed to create a clear set of personal goals—for one hundred years in the future. "Sure puts things in perspective," was his comment.

It sure does.

"How will the world be different as a result of my being here?" is a sobering question, and it's one that serves us all the better the earlier in life we ask it. It's a question network marketers tend to take quite seriously, and one the network marketing model itself tends to put front and center. Over and above its function as a means of distribution for its high-quality goods and services and as a resonable, flexible, lifestyle-friendly income opportunity, network marketing provides a forum for the individual to have a positive impact on dozens, hundreds, thousands, potentially even millions of lives.

So, what is this thing called network marketing?

From what I've been able to see these past twenty-one years, it's an opportunity to do three things: to make a decent living; to make a good life; and to create a legacy worth leaving.

John David Mann
April 2007

Preface to the Second Edition

June '14

When *The Zen of MLM* appeared in the summer of 2007, cracks were already spider-webbing their way through the foundations of the mortgage, housing and banking industries. Then the walls caved in and the whole building collapsed in a dusty heap. Months inched by, then years, and still the much-hoped-for recovery struggled to get to its feet, like a wasted New Years Eve partygoer suffering the mother of all hangovers.

And what happened to network marketing during this same time? It exploded.

Just before the economic meltdown began, network marketing was at $117 billion worldwide. When the big hit came it staggered for a moment, then rallied, and in the next few years shot to *more than $166 billion*. That's a jump of over 40 percent.

Why? Some are quick to point out that the network marketing business always tends to be countercyclical, surging forward when the economy at large declines. But that argument's a little too pat. For one thing, when the worst of the crash happened networking sales took a hit too at first, albeit a fairly small one. What's more, the networking world doesn't recede during sunnier economic times, it continues to build. The business just keeps growing, regardless of what the larger economic climate is doing. It's growing because more and more people are finding that it's working for them. And it's working for the three reasons I summed up at the end of the prologue you just read: because more and more people see in it an opportunity "to make a decent living; to make a good life; and to create a legacy worth leaving."

In three words: *income, growth, impact.*

It's as true today as it was in 1991, when the first article in this collection originally appeared. Maybe truer.

In 2013, after writing for network marketing periodicals continuously for twenty-four years, I hung up my journalist spurs in order to devote full time to writing books. It seemed a good time to gather up some of the pieces penned in the interim and add them to this collection. This Second Edition includes all 73 of the essays from the original 2007 edition, plus another 28 that have appeared in the years since: 101 in all.

For me during these years, some things have changed, and some have remained the same. When *Zen* first appeared I was just starting out as a published author and had a single published title to my name (*You Call the Shots*); today it's more than a dozen. The woman I name on page 132 as "my friend Ana McClellan" ("Your Words," September '00) has by page 270 become "my sweet wife Ana Gabriel Mann" ("Compassion," June '09).

But one thing hasn't changed. That check, the one that was coming in every month and had been for twenty-one years when this book first appeared? Still coming, every month, like the planets in their courses, and it's going on thirty years now. You may love this business or hate it, laud it or fault it, idolize it or criticize it, but in my experience there is one thing about it that is inarguable and undeniable: *It works.*

JDM
June 10, 2014

Residual Income,
Residual Impact
The Reason This Business Works
September '91

One of the great promises of network marketing is something called "residual income." What does this arcane phrase mean, and why does this business give it to us?

The word *residual* means "left over." Residual income is that income which is the *residue* of one's initial efforts, the results that are left behind after the doing is done. A more familiar expression of this concept is *royalties*.

The concept of residual income originated with the monarchy. Kings and queens were paid *in residue* for a variety of things: land they owned, use of resources under their control, services they provided (armies, for instance) . . . or, hey, just for being the monarchy.

In these democratic days, royalties are a bit less high-handed. A "royalty" is income paid for a duplicated effort. Authors, inventors, actors and performers of many kinds earn ongoing residuals from their work. Create a popular song, and every time a CD is sold or your song is publicly performed, you'll receive a royalty payment. Even long after your initial effort in creating the song is expended, so long as it's being sold—through performance,

CD sales, use on movie soundtracks or TV commercials, you name it—you earn the royalty.

RESIDUAL INCOME: FREE AT LAST

The residual income in network marketing is income you continue to earn based on the productivity of your initial business-building efforts. In a legitimate network marketing program, this income is a reflection of (i.e., commission on) actual sales of products or services generated by the network organization you helped create and develop.

In a sense, it *is* a royalty—and you're the king or queen who's being compensated for the profits of your far-flung king- or queendom.

Residual income is desirable because, like the songwriter's or author's earnings, it is an income stream that continues flowing long after you've completed your initial efforts. In other words, you no longer have to do anything new to generate it. As long as sales are being made, the checks keep coming.

In a word: freedom.

Of course, there are some conditions that must exist in order for you to actually enter such a blissful state of residual keep. First and foremost, the company that issues your "royalty" checks must remain in business. (As the ancient knight says in *Indiana Jones and the Last Crusade*, "Choose wisely.")

What's more, the products or services must be of a sort that will continuously generate repeat sales. Historically, the favored choice for residual income in network marketing is a consumable product of exceptional quality and in great demand. (I use the word "product" to include services, which are every bit as much a product as a skin cream or nutritional beverage.)

Understand this distinction: we are not compensated for the sheer act of recruiting. It doesn't work to try to build your future income stream on more and more new people coming into the program. An unhealthily focused emphasis on recruiting (especially with hefty buy-ins or high-commission "startup packages") and large-volume purchases (the infamous "front-loading" ploy) are classic symptoms of poor repeat-sales potential. Neither dodge works, at least not for long. Genuine residual income comes from legitimate purchases and repeat consumption of products by the men and women in your group.

A third condition upon which your royalties rely is the strength—that is, the *enduring* strength—of the network you build. This is a function of leadership . . . which brings us to residual impact.

RESIDUAL IMPACT: MAKING A DIFFERENCE

Residual impact is just like the residual income that writers, artists, inventors and performers have, except here we're talking about the impact their work creates rather than the income it generates.

To have an impact, one must influence with power and velocity. The impact of the industrial revolution is an example. The influence of the Internet is another. The impact of a Gandhi, a Schweitzer, or a Chaplin is yet another.

Residual impact is impact that reverberates long after your initial efforts have ceased. For a writer, it would be authoring a best-selling book or even a classic. Bach, Beethoven, Brahms and the Beatles have all given us the residual impact of their music. There are numerous examples of great performances (Bogart and Bergman in *Casablanca*) and great inventions (the light bulb and the home computer) that have had and will continue to have an enduring residual impact on billions of people.

You create residual impact the same way you earn residual income: investing your time, energy and effort in other people.

What's the primary benefit of network marketing over conventional sales channels? Residual income. The same is true of residual impact. By enrolling, training and leading a network of men and women to success, you have a direct residual impact on their lives, the lives of their families and friends, the lives of countless consumers who benefit from their products, and the lives of all the future generations of men and women they will sponsor—and those whose lives *they* will influence, and so on.

Residual impact takes many forms. Each one serves by making a positive, sometimes even *life-changing* difference in people's lives. What's more, as the network marketing industry expands and prospers, you are playing a part in bringing to light a major shift in the way of life and work in our world.

Imagine the powerful model of "can-do-ness" President Kennedy thrust into the American consciousness when he declared the country's intention to put a man on the moon within ten years. *Everybody* enrolled in that dream; the entire nation watched its progress with interest and ownership. When the deed was done, we felt the pride of our own accomplishment.

That's residual impact on a national, even global scale.

Showing the world how network marketing honors people's values and purpose as no other business model in history has, proving that ordinary people can live extraordinary lives, offering the world a formula for personal and financial freedom, smashing the "glass ceiling" once and for all, providing much-needed leadership for the future—these are all powerful pieces of a model of possibility for a world in great need of all that is good and true about our profession.

Again, residual impact—on a very big scale.

TURN TIME INTO MONEY, MONEY INTO TIME

Benjamin Franklin once observed that he had spent his first forty years turning his time into money and his second forty years turning his money back into time. Franklin built a large enough asset base in his first four decades to supply sufficient residual income to allow him to spend his next four decades doing whatever he wanted to do. And it's a good thing for all of us that he did.

We all know of the remarkable contributions Franklin made that still affect our lives today. If Ben hadn't been free to mess with his kites, would I be typing on a Mac Powerbook at a coffeeshop right now? And what about his role in drafting the United States' Declaration of Independence? What would your life and my life be like right now if Franklin *hadn't* created four decades worth of residual income? Imagine what residual impact America and the world would have lost!

Now, imagine this one: where will our grandchildren's lives be tomorrow because you and I have created residual income today? Where will our grandchildren's lives be because you and I are free to play with our own kites—to discover, invent, create, refine, improve and play to our hearts' content on the world stage? When the ledgers are all totaled, what kind of impact will we have had?

What kind of legacy?

Residual impact generates residual income, which allows you to generate greater residual impact, which gives you more residual income . . .

To some people, network marketing is about making a lot of *money*. To some people, network marketing is about making a lot of *difference*. But the truth is, it is impossible to separate the two: front and back of the same coin. Both are legal tender in network marketing; both are your reason *and* your reward.

The One-Minute Networker
Build Your Business in Sixty Seconds
April '92

"Just a minute!" How often have you heard that? "I'll be off the phone in a minute . . . This'll take just a minute to explain . . . We'll be finished here in just a minute . . . ." How nice (albeit rare) when it's actually true. A minute seems so, well, convenient. So considerate. So complete.

So, let's do that. How to build your network marketing business in just one minute.

Okay: in a *series* of "just one minutes."

You might be familiar with the "One Minute" bestsellers, *The One Minute Manager*, *The One Minute Sales Person* and the rest. One reason for their success is that they pack their essential themes into bite-sized, delectably useful pieces. We do live in a *USA Today*, snapshot world—not because we're becoming morons, but because the world is moving and changing so *fast*. Your analyst has time for your life story. Your prospect doesn't.

ONE-MINUTE PRODUCT STORY

Most network marketed products are "information-rich" and their full story is integral to their value, which you want to share with new consumers. But unloading all that, all at once, has turned off many a prospect. People don't need fifteen or twenty reasons to try a product—just one or two good ones. Besides, how long can you hold people's interest before they start feeling they're being "sold"?

Enter the One-Minute Product Story.

You've established rapport with your new person and reached the magic point where she is curious enough to ask about your product. Give yourself a sixty-second window of opportunity to show and tell her what your product is, what you've experienced with it, or what someone else close to you has, and why (and how much) you love it. Sixty seconds—and your story's told.

Sound tough? For some of us, it's murder. Personally, it's easier for me to talk for twenty minutes than for one. We need a system.

Electronics outlets sell sixty-second cassette tapes for recording the outgoing message (OGM) on your answering machine. Buy one—or better, a half dozen. (Your key people will want to know how to become One-Minute Networkers, too.) Then go tell your story—to your cassette recorder.[10]

Think you'll have a hard time keeping it to sixty seconds? Naw, now it's a snap: on the sixty-first second, your machine goes "click!" and you're done. (Remember that "click!"—that's the sound your prospect's attention span makes when it starts to unravel.)

Will prospects be so wowed by your compelling one-minute rap that they grab your product—presto!—to buy and try?

Sometimes. And of course, sometimes not. But either way, it doesn't matter. Your One-Minute Product Story doesn't have to complete the encounter. It just needs to create a positive spark that leads to action.

ONE-MINUTE "WHY"

When do you tell customers about your opportunity? If you're waiting till people are committed product users and only then looking for "the right time" to tell them about the business opportunity . . . you're waiting too long.

Sure, you want people to be convinced about the product, to get its benefits. And it may not feel appropriate to tell them all about the opportunity just yet. But it's a lot harder to create a whole new dimension to your product-based relationship weeks or months down the road than it is to plant that seed *right now*. As early as you can, even in your very first conversation, give 'em a One-Minute Business Story.

No flip charts. No brochures, booklets, black- or whiteboards. Just you, them and One Minute. Don't rush; don't cram; just be concise and hit the bull's eye. Tell your prospect (or your cassette recorder) about your network marketing business—what it is, what it's like for you, and what about it is of greatest value to you.

That is, tell them your One-Minute "Why."

"How on earth could I explain all that in one minute!"

You can't. But you *can* tell them a few key things that convey the whole picture. You simply have to choose those aspects of your opportunity that will convey your offering with impact. And to do that, you need to have a sense of where *they're* coming from.

Which brings us to . . .

ONE-MINUTE LISTENING

How do you find out about another person—his or her situation, concerns, desires, wants, needs, dreams, values and purpose with a One-Minute Listening?

"No way. I may be able to control my own mouth with a sixty-second cassette—but I can't control theirs. How do I get people to tell me about themselves on a stopwatch timetable?"

You're right. This is one you can't practice on a cassette, because it's mostly not you doing the talking. The trick to One-Minute Listening is to apply the 80/20 Rule: 80 percent of your time you listen while they talk. Use the 20 percent talk-time to ask questions that guide your inquiry.

This means: for every five minutes of conversation, they have the floor for four and you have one—max!—to keep it on track and focused. You get one minute in every five. That's it.

When you're that focused, you'll pretty quickly hear a concise expression of what matters most to them. Even if they don't consciously identify it that way, that's *their* One-Minute "Why."

ONE-MINUTE GOALS AND ONE-MINUTE STRATEGIES
How do you work effectively with your leaders as One-Minute Network Marketers? Ask them:

"When you reach the level of success that you're shooting for in your business, what will that look like and feel like to you? What will you have, do and be?"

Then have them answer that question on—you got it—a sixty-second cassette tape.

Support them to make that a regular practice. Sure, it may take longer to spell out all the gorgeous details of one's success dreams—but a goal that fits on a 3 x 5 card (the visual version of the sixty-second audiotape) is easier to keep in mind and in action.

Brevity is the soul of wit—and of one's "Why."

One-Minute Strategies? Simple: have your leaders take a brief look first at their goals, and then at where they are right now with their businesses. Then ask the question:

"What's the next step? What is the single most significant thing you need to start doing to move you from this place to the next place on the path to your goals?"

People typically respond to this question with not one step but a whole laundry list. If you hear them going down that road, hold up one finger and say, "Hang on—not a whole list. Just one. What is your *single* most significant next step?"

And then—sixty-second cassette tape time.

ONE-MINUTE INSIGHT

At the end of every coaching call or session I do, I practice something I call the One-Minute Insight. It's like taking a high-lighter to your life. Here's how it works:

At the end of your call, conversation or coaching session, have everyone present take up to one minute (and no more) to say what was, for them, the single most significant insight they got from the call. "What is the one concept, idea, discovery, suggestion, theme, plan or other element that characterizes the value you've gotten from this call?"

In some cases, this will be frustrating—you can't really identify any one "most significant element." That's valuable right there: why can't you? What was missing in that call?

Every good story has a point, a punch line. Every symphony has a central theme. Every great film has a core message. Every effective coaching call has a Single Most Significant Insight, and developing the habit of always pausing at the end to articulate it—in One Minute or less—is a critical skill.

It is the skill of identifying *the heart of the matter*.

It's the exact same skill you're using to pinpoint the key ingredients for your One-Minute Product Story . . . One-Minute "Why" . . . One-Minute Listening . . . One-Minute Goals and One-Minute Strategies . . . and every other effective communication you have.

And that's a skill you can duplicate.

The Tortoise and the Hare
The Fast and Slow of Successful Networking
August '93

Upline's astute publisher Randolph Byrd has penned an article titled "The $300 Solution," which points out that once someone starts earning monthly commission checks of $300-plus, they're probably in this business for the long haul. Why? Because when income reaches that point, you've not only got momentum, you've got *concrete evidence* of that momentum.[11]

Typically, the $300-plus mark comes with reaching the first major achievement level in the pay plan—Executive, Director, Chieftain or whatever. Another way of describing this achievement level is *escape velocity*.

So here's a critical question: does it matter how fast you do that? The answer turns out to be, "Actually, yes."

VELOCITY COUNTS
In *Julius Caesar*, Shakespeare wrote: "There is a tide in the affairs of men / Which, taken at the flood, leads on to fortune." He was oh so right. Problem is, most times you have to *create* that flood.

Have you ever heard the expression, "Slow and steady wins the race"? Nice idea. Doesn't work. "Slow and steady" doesn't make any waves, doesn't create a tide. No tide, no flood. No flood, no fortune. In network marketing, "slow and steady" usually winds up looking like a lot of people standing on the banks of the river of success, waiting ever so patiently for the tide to come in. Aesop's fable of the careless hare and surefooted tortoise is something wonderful I learned in kindergarten—and it's not really that simple.

But neither is its opposite, the more cynical adage, "Nice guys finish last." You *can* be a nice guy or gal *and* a sure-footed hare. In fact, in the network marketing decathlon, that's the only way to win.

Back to the $300 question. Now ultimately, it doesn't matter—$300 is $300, whether it took you sixty days or sixteen months to get there. But let's say it took you one year to reach the Chieftain level: you'll tend to see that twelve-months-to-Chieftain paradigm replay itself throughout your organization unless you consciously act to change it. (Remember, this is the duplication business. What you do duplicates.)

Again, there's nothing *wrong* with that.

Except for one thing.

When you have a whole group of people s-l-o-w-l-y moving towards escape velocity, it takes a lot of effort to maintain a belief system that you're all actually going to get there. And that's energy you all need to be putting into your businesses—not into convincing yourselves that this business is eventually going to work. I've seen the Tortoise paradigm slowly suffocate entire legs of networks.

WAY OF THE HARE

In Randolph's article, the directive was to reach the $300 mark within six to nine months, one year being the max. To which I add: thirty to ninety days is even better. (We're counting from the day you really decide you're going to grow a network, not the day you signed a piece of paper.)

Everyone's got a program like this. It goes by different names: "Ninety-Day Blitz," "Ninety-Day Sprint," "Quicksilver Club" or "Fast Start Program." My brilliant friend Gilles Arbour used to teach a program he called "Create a Storm." The plan is thorough and quite complete, and it boils down to the same thing that all such programs boil down to:

For ninety days, you go bananas!

Talk to everyone. Go all out. Make major waves. Go nuts. Kick ass and take names. (Only we usually do that in reverse order: start with a names list, *then* go kick ass.)

I've read and heard so many different, fine, excellent formulas and recipes for succeeding in this business. Here's a quick look through a roster of *Upline* Special Reports from the last two years: *Five-Step Sponsoring, The $300 Solution, Sponsor a Ten, Look for Leaders, The Critical Factor, The Power of Teambuilding, Prospecting for Pearls, It's All in the Cards (Looking for Aces)* . . .

Now, these are all, every one of them, superb formulas, powerful models, proven recipes for success. They are all methodical, logical ways of describing a set of actions that leads to success. But bottom line? The truth?

The truth is, following a great recipe doesn't bake a great cake unless you turn on the oven. And we're not talking 130° or 165°. You've got to *turn up the heat.*

The truth is, every network marketer I've ever known who created serious success did these two things: 1) they decided to do it, and 2) then went bananas.

"But what if I've already been at this for twelve months, eighteen months, three years?" Well, you can't market spilt milk. What you *can* do is make creating your first thirty-, sixty- or ninety-day Executive/Director/Chieftain your next and most critical goal. Establish the hare paradigm in your own network—especially with those you directly sponsor. How far away you are from that escape velocity doesn't matter, because once it happens, your whole group will be affected.

In the company I work with, we just had two people reach the highest position in the compensation plan faster than anyone ever has before (in less than *half* the time it took me to do the same thing)—and the entire company has been powerfully energized by it.

What does a hare look like? All kinds. A hare won't necessarily be outgoing, love public speaking, or exude charisma.

What's more, not every hare in this business started out that way. Two major hares I know, Richard Brooke and Tom "Big Al" Schreiter, describe their first few years in networking as a time when they plodded along at a classic tortoise pace. So what happened? At one point, they just took off.

"But what if I'm shy, unsure of myself, uneasy talking about the business to people . . . what if I am truly a tortoise?" Well, one thing you can do is to sponsor a hare. (That's what happened to Brooke.)

What else?

When I ask groups, "How many of you would say you are tortoises?" over 90 percent of the hands go up. But being a tortoise isn't a congenital characteristic. It's a choice.

So make a different choice. Acknowledge your tortoiseness—and *decide* to tap into your own hareitage. (Don't forget, we *all* started out in life as hares—there's nothing "slow and steady" about shooting down the birth canal.)

The amazing thing is, everyone has got some hare in them. Yes, everyone. You, too.

WAY OF THE TORTOISE

Now, here's the twist: everyone is also a tortoise—and needs to be, too.

The qualities of the tortoise are patience, listening, long-term supportiveness. Nurturing. Waiting. Quiet championing.

There's a balance here. It takes momentum to raise the barn that is your business—but it takes all those slower, quieter, more reflective traits to effectively lead the people who will come to populate it.

The truth is, it's not really a question of "the tortoise *or* the hare." It's an *and* thing. (Hence the title of this article.)

Something I especially like about Gilles's "Storm" program is that after ninety days of going bananas, you devote the *next* ninety days to careful follow-through with all the people you brought in over the first ninety days. Then evaluate: do I turn up the heat again, or do we need more simmer while my new hares catch up?

Create a storm—and then secure its aftermath. If you don't, you've just got high winds and no foundations.

Just as pure tortoisity can grind momentum to a halt, un-relenting hareness has caused many a would-be networker to crash and burn. A hare with no tortoise qualities may win foot races, but in network marketing he'll be . . .

Well, hare today, and gone tomorrow.

Point, Click, Success!
The Business for the Rest of Us
December '93

It was exactly ten years ago. They claimed it was going to change how we work, how we play, even how we think.

Gone were the Greek-to-me "A>:" prompts, and in their place were a smiling face, little "icons" of familiar objects, and a thing they called a "mouse." All you had to do, they said, was "point and click," and it would let you draw, write, calculate—and create!

It was, they said, the computer "for the rest of us."

They called it "Macintosh."

It took a few years and a friend to cosign the note—we were dirt poor then—but eventually I got my first Mac.

That same year (1986), I got tired of being poor. I spent a week in Siddhartha-like contemplation and then wrote down a goal: *"In five years, I will be a millionaire."* I believed it, committed to it—and had no idea what to do next. I knew less in 1986 about earning money than I had known in 1983 about computers.

Soon after writing that eight-word sentence, I learned about network marketing. I knew I liked to talk and teach; this sounded like a way to achieve my goal doing that.

Fast-forward . . .

Well, I don't have a million dollars in the bank; and I don't yet earn an annual million. But I *feel* like a millionaire, and that's not all: I *live* like one, too. Why? Watch this: at today's rates of return, for a piece of real estate, a CD in the bank, or a good mutual fund to earn my family and me the generous six-figure annual income that our commission checks are currently bringing into the household, those assets would need to be worth not a million bucks, but more than *three* million.

So: I'm a *residual* millionaire, thrice over.

Now, simply having a Mac doesn't automatically make you productive. Likewise, a good network marketing opportunity doesn't make you a success. Those achievements take what they've always taken: determination, persistence, focus and hard work. What the Mac and MLM do is make this sort of success *accessible*.

To anyone.

Ten years ago, I couldn't draw. (In truth, even my handwriting was on the edge of illegible.) And I had but little business sense, with no gift at all for making or managing money. Today, I am well paid for producing good-looking book covers, brochures and more—on my Mac. I produce *Upline*—on my Mac.

And through my networking opportunity, I've become a "residual multimillionaire."

Ordinary abilities—extraordinary results.

Point ... click ... —success!

Network marketing: the business "for the rest of us."

P.S. Happy Birthday, Mac!

The Ultimate Secret to Handling Objections
Five Steps to Mastery
February '94

"I've tried a lot of different approaches to 'handling objections,' but try as I might, I keep getting slammed with the same few objections. What am I doing wrong?"

One reason network marketing is a "numbers game" is that it takes many encounters with different people to develop the communication skills of a good networker. Five or ten conversations won't do it. There's a natural progression here, of five steps: from Survival, to Knowledge, to Skill, to Listening, to ... well, let's hold off peeking at the fifth until we've first climbed through the other four. (The fifth one, after all, is *the ultimate secret to handling objections*, and we don't want to spoil the surprise.)

1) SURVIVAL
The first time you take your newfound enthusiasm, offer it excitedly to someone and get "slammed with an objection," chances are you handle the experience the way people usually react to criticism: get defensive, retreat and disappear, or fight back.

That's familiar, isn't it? It's the famous "fright, flight or fight" response. It's hardwired human behavior; comes with the equipment. This approach is operating out of *survival mode*: handling objections with your adrenal glands. Exhausting, and not all that effective.

2) KNOWLEDGE
Soon you start using your brain to control your adrenaline and emotions. You learn to counter objections with facts: you step up into *knowledge mode*.

"Well, it might *seem* expensive, but do you realize that this is a three-month supply, and on a per-day basis, that's only seventy-five cents . . ."

"Actually, Jim, network marketing has been around for over fifty years, and there are even quite a few Fortune 500 companies that employ its methods, including . . ."

The information-based approach lets you feel more in control, which certainly feels better—to you. But soon you notice a problem: it's not getting great results.

Why not? Because people don't really care about *facts*. (And they care about them even less when you are using those facts to prove them wrong.) Facts are *features*; what people want is *benefits*. Every year, millions of drill bits are purchased; what all those drill-bit-buyers want are not drill bits—they want *holes*. Besides, in this information-saturated age, people are bombarded with way too much information, anyway.

3) SKILL
Time and experience make you wiser. You start tempering your eagerness to dump information all over people and learn to focus on benefits. You learn to anticipate certain objections and "handle" them before they even come up. For example, after you've had a bunch of people say, "I don't have the free time to do something like that," you start including a most-people-do-this-part-time, ten-hours-per-week benefit in your initial pre-

sentation. You start developing more skillful ways of responding to people's questions and concerns, perhaps adopting the famous "feel, felt, found" formula ("I know how you feel, that's what I felt, but here's what I found . . .").

The *skill mode* is a big step up, and it gets better results.

But after a while, you sense that it's still limited. You're still not getting the results you believe you could and should. Why not? Because this approach, while more skillful and therefore less abrasive, still tends to be more you-based than them-based.

4) LISTENING

The next dimension of communication comes with listening—really listening—to the other person. When you do, you start hearing through and beyond the content of their "objection." What you start hearing is *them*—how and what they are feeling.

Most people's objections are 10 percent (at most) about what they're *saying*, and 90 percent or more about what they're *feeling*. When you get into listening mode and respond to the person, you're ten times more effective than if you simply respond to the information in the question.

Do you see what's really happening here as you move through this progression? What's changing here?

You are.

You're becoming not simply excited and enthusiastic about your products, company and profession, but truly confident. The more grounded you feel in your own opportunity, the less you feel the need to defend, attack, escape, out-logic or out-maneuver. Because you yourself no longer buy into these objections, they don't frighten or rattle you. You're becoming free to simply be with the person.

Aha—there's a clue to the final phase of the progression. Let's take one last step up this particular mountain, to . . .

5) MASTERY

As you become more and more secure with the *listening mode*, you gain access to the *mastery mode*, where you find The Ultimate Secret to Handling Objections, which is this:

Handle your own.

Handle your own objections. Get really, truly clear on what you're doing and how you feel about what you're doing, and the world will respond to you differently. The truth is, the objections that people bring you that most challenge you turn out to be projections of your own objections.

A quick example.

Years ago there was a woman in my network who complained that everyone she worked with was having problems "reacting" to one specific product. She got some coaching on how to help people use that product, on what they might do to get better results. Then someone asked her, "How do you like that product?"

Oh, she didn't use it herself, she told us—that particular one "always gave her reactions."

It's not always that obvious. Here's another, somewhat subtler example:

There are entire legs in my organization that routinely get "price objections," and entire legs that seldom get that objection. Can you guess which groups are comfortable charging the suggested retail price for the product, and which ones don't like to retail but prefer instead to give away products at wholesale cost—or for free?

And another:

The people who seem to have the most trouble finding serious business-builders are those who *are themselves* not yet totally comfortable with the idea of having their own business.

And another:

Several years ago, a friend and associate complained loudly that he couldn't attract serious people to do this business professionally. Our company, he said, was simply not behaving professionally, and that was the problem. Today, this same company is prospering. And my friend? He's gone. He left the company in a dispute over some allegations of distinctly unprofessional behavior—his.

My friend was the victim of his own objection.

As metaphysical as this may sound, it's true: the objections people most consistently offer you as gifts for your development and ultimate success are precise expressions of those objections you hold most fiercely yourself—no more, no less.

That's why objections are such a blessing—and why it's a waste to attempt to crush, quell or conquer them.

Love thine objecting prospects as thyself. They are exquisitely accurate mirrors.

In Praise of Quesfirmations
I Seem to Be a Question
March '94

"Every day, in every way, I am getting fatter and fatter . . . ." No, wait, that's not right. Try again.

"I *will* live my convictions and honor my commitments, because, gosh darn it, I *deserve* to be convicted, and then committed . . . ." No, something's off there, too.

I just can't get these affirmations right. The only thing I have pasted onto my bathroom mirror is my reflection. (I should reflect on that.)

I've never been comfortable with the practice of repeating affirmative statements about myself, to myself. Telling myself about myself, over and over, seems to me somehow self-indulgent, presumptuous. And it makes me silly, too. When I stare at myself saying, *"You are handsome, you are brilliant, you are a millionaire, you floss with amazing regularity . . ."* another voice inside wants to say, *"Excuse me, Miss Crabtree—are we gonna be tested on this?"*

Maybe it's because of this recalcitrant little flaw in my character: I don't like being told what to do. Not even by me. It makes me want to argue.

It doesn't work.

But I've discovered what does: *questions.*

I don't like being *told* what to do, but I'm fine with being *asked*, "What do you want to do?" (Even by me.)

Questions invite a response. Therefore, they also invite thought, which I think is generally a good thing to invite. The better the question, the better the thought in response.

A few months ago, while struggling one morning of a very busy day to prioritize my task list, an inspiring question just popped out: *"What can I do TODAY to make the world a better place?"* It stopped me in my task-list tracks. Led to all sorts of thoughtful thoughts-in-response. Now, I start every day with that question. My life literally hasn't been the same since.

Here are a few other powerful quesfirmations I've learned: From John Fogg, "What was the very best thing that happened for you today (this week, this month, etc.)?" And from Brian Biro, "What's my most powerful next step?"

An affirmation is the same statement every time you repeat it. I get bored. (But then, I always got bored with meditation and George Winston, too.) A *quesfirmation* invites a different response each and every time you ask it. Isn't that amazing? Questions are powerful creative forces.

Buckminster Fuller once wrote a book entitled, *I Seem to Be a Verb*. Nouns, explained Bucky, are things; verbs *move*. For me, I guess, affirmations are nouns.

I seem to be a question.

So: what question would you most like to start each day asking yourself?

Selling You on You
Your Single Most Important Sale
June '94

*"My single most important sale? But . . . this isn't really a sales busi-
ness, is it? I mean, I thought this was the business where teachers and
moms and coaches and clergy and all kinds of non-sales types could excel.
Isn't this the 'person-to-person' business, where the thrust of our networking effort is on relationships, on coaching and supporting people?
Isn't sales really just a minor, insignificant part of what we do?"*

Hmm. Yes, everything you just said is certainly true . . . except
for that last part. Because to be successful here, you must in fact
become very good at selling.

Now, don't wince. I don't necessarily mean the literal "mer-
chant's sell": the retailing of products to customers. Certainly,
sharing your enthusiasm for and personal experience of products
you love, and putting those products in the hands of others (at
least a few others) you care about, is something anyone in this
business could do and should do—but that's not what I mean.

The selling you need to master (or at least, to practice) is
a much broader matter than simply handing over a product
and getting back cash. This broader-sense selling is at the very
heart of what makes network marketing tick. The good news
is, it is also precisely that kind of selling at which "teachers and
moms and coaches and clergy" *already* excel. What we're talking

about here is perhaps the successful sponsor's most critical and important action.

It is Your Single Most Important Sale.

"Do you lead with the product, or with the opportunity?" Networkers ask each other this question with all the earnest sincerity of divinity students debating the nature of the Infinite.

Some say it's a classic chicken-and-egg dilemma; that a more powerful approach is to skip the question completely and "lead" with the benefits of network marketing itself (tax advantages of a home-based business, creating an income-generating asset, and so forth) before even getting to the particulars of your company and product. A good and powerful approach.

Others say that what you're really selling in this business is yourself; that what you really have to offer people is the resource that you are, or could be, to them. Brilliant insight, and true.

But I believe there's a yet deeper, more vital sell. When I first talk with you about my opportunity . . . when I answer your questions and sponsor you . . . when I help you get oriented and do your first "getting started" training . . . when I do three-ways with your best leads, show you all the ropes, work with you right up through the various achievement levels and help you help your people do the same—my Most Important Sale is at the core of what I need to do with you at every turn.

What I'm really doing is *selling you on you.*

I am selling you on your worth; on the validity and achievability of your dreams; on your ability to do this business successfully; and on the things *you do right* every step of the way.

I love this definition I once heard from Gilles Arbour:

> *Your job description as a sponsor is to be the steward of other people's dreams.*

That's your Most Important Sale.

To be an effective sponsor, you need to believe in the people you're coaching. Often, you need to believe in them *even when they don't*, to take their dreams even more seriously than they do themselves.

This is sometimes not so easy. It involves two steps. First you need to create a picture in your own mind's eye of that person being successful—a vivid, detailed, Technicolor®, holographic sort of picture. And then you need to *sell them* that picture.

By the way, we are not speaking here only of people who freely confess their lack of confidence, people who are quite up front about not being sure of themselves. Sometimes you sponsor someone who tells you:

> *Look out! I'm on fire . . . I'm serious . . . I'm going for it . . . I'll be at that top achievement level in five months! I'm in, I'm committed and nothing's gonna stop me!*

Well . . . maybe. He certainly is putting out a lot of effort to sell you on him. But what is so often true is that this sort of talk is really the sound of one lip flapping—the sound of someone trying like the dickens to sell himself (and you) on his own success *because he doesn't really believe it.* Most people, remember, have had that kind of belief beaten out of them long before they were old enough to sign your company's distributor application.

Red-hot, bonfire-o'-passion enthusiasm is fine, at times. The real job of selling others on their own eventual success is more often a quieter, less dramatic job—a slow bed of coals, not a fireworks display. It's a matter of being there, week in and month out, firm in your vision of what's possible inside them, while they go through the ups and downs, wins and disappointments of their initial network-building efforts.

In time, when the size of their group, the level of their

income and (especially) the appearance of true leaders in *their* network all reach a certain point, their dreams start looking real to them, too. At that point, they take off the training wheels of your belief and fly on the wings of their own.

Then, you've closed the sale.

Houses of Straw, Houses of Brick

Offering Shelter to Refugees
from the Economic Storm

September '94

It is still light out. I've just returned from the West Coast, and I'm standing in front of my home town's little airport, waiting for a cab.

As I wait, a pleasant, business-looking fellow appears next to me at the curb. I actually called for a cab. Jim hasn't, he tells me, he's just hoping there'll be an extra one there waiting. There isn't, so I offer to share mine.

Ninety seconds into the taxi ride, we've swapped information on the best restaurants in Charlottesville, and I've learned that Jim used to live here. Likes it here, went to college here, UVA. Moved to Georgia, terrific house there, low cost of living, can get an incredible property for a song. Two kids, wonderful wife . . . daughter's getting ready to go off to college now.

I ask, what is he doing back in town?

Visiting. Clears his throat. Actually, job interview. Never really done that before, he confesses. Fresh out of UVA, he took the first job offer that came along, and it was a good job. That was, oh, some thirty years ago.

We've clocked about a mile and a half.

So . . . ? I gently prod.

Well, the past eighteen months have been a rough ride. A restructuring and two LBO's later, Jim has suddenly found himself out of a job. Jim offers a quiet, shaky laugh. To tell the truth, he's a little nervous about this job interview. Feels like a freshman.

Yep, I volunteer, *the business world sure is shaking up.*

He nods. *That's for sure.*

We go a few hundred yards in pensive silence.

"You know," I say, "if someone ten years ago had told me that I'd be involved in network marketing and earning a good living at it, I *know* I would have thought they were crazy."

By this time, we've pulled into my driveway. He looks around briefly as he digests that last statement, with a look that says, *Nice neighborhood. Nice car. Nice house. Nice guy. Seems real.* Then he says, "Yeah, network marketing . . . that industry's really taking off, isn't it?"

I ask for his business card, say I'll send him something on what I do. He asks for mine. The cab driver gets out and retrieves my luggage for me. He hands me my bags—and then he gives me *his* business card, too.

People are taking us seriously. Because of the technological explosion in networking that author Richard Poe talks about in his new book *Wave 3*, we now have the technologies we can put into people's hands that make success in this business truly available to them.

Five years ago, I knew I had made it in my company; I wouldn't have been as sure that Jim, if he decided to give my opportunity a try, would have had the same success. Today, I don't have to think twice.

The business world—the corporate employment world, the world of pensions and lifelong job security, Jim's world—is falling apart. That world is a house of straw, a house of sticks, and the wolf of change is blowing it down.

We've got the house of brick, and Jim knows it.

You could call this "prospecting," but that's not what it feels like. It feels like we're opening our doors to take in refugees from an economic storm.

Paying for Lunch
When You See Someone Who "Got Lucky," Look Closer
December '94

I am on the phone, listening.

"...Why is it that some people seem to get into this network and take off like a speeding bullet, and I feel like there's so much personal growth that has to happen first that it's taking a snail's age for me? What's going on?"

I understand. My company's been hit by that magical force called "momentum," and it brings with it some serious soul-searching and reflection. This friend of mine has been in for years and now she's watching people come in and zip past her achievement in a matter of months or even weeks.

What, indeed, is going on?

I replay the entire voice mail message again, just to let it sink in, then press "6" to reply.

"It only looks like these folks are creating success in ninety days. But that's not real. What's real is that you're right: to create a large network means undertaking a massive program in self-development. This is the personal growth business, no question. The course you're taking is real; it's solid, it's good and it's valuable: you're earning the right to have not only residual income but also a powerful level of self-knowledge, which is perhaps the most precious resource and reward there is.

"When people shoot to the top in record time, it means one of two things.

"One: what goes up must come down. They're on a roller coaster, rapid growth without a strong underpinning. It simply won't last—rocketing up, rocketing down, riding an oh-so-ephemeral wave of temporal success.

"Or two: they're creating a huge organization that's for real, that will indeed last. And if that's the case, even though we can't always see it from the sidelines, I can promise you they're doing so on the back of years of struggle and hard-won insights into who they are and how they operate.

"Take my sponsor, Steve: people in our company often say, 'He's such a lucky guy . . . just signed up two hot players, and now he's pulling down a high six figures every year and hardly has to do a thing for it.' (Of course, when they say, '. . . such a lucky guy . . .' chances are good what they're really saying is, 'That's so unfair! How come that doesn't happen to me?!')

"Well, that may be what it looks like. But it's not what it *is*.

"When I look at Steve, what I see is all the years he put in before we ever got involved in network marketing—years of traveling, doing lectures and seminars on health and nutrition, years of long drives and fitful nights on people's couches, of coming home with less money than he left with . . . building his—that's right, his *network*.

"So many of these 'lucky' folks actually labored long and hard to create their networks—often with little or no compensation at the time—but their struggles go unnoticed because they went through them before getting involved in their current opportunity.

"When they come on board and are able to plug *our* company into *their* achievement, it looks like magic. It's not. We just don't see the epic spiral of personal history that wound up over the years to bring them to this point."

I press "1" to end, "1" again to send. I hope that when she gets my message, she will get my message.

In the film *A League of Their Own*, Geena Davis is going through a wrenching decision about whether or not to quit her baseball team, and she complains to Tom Hanks, "Why does it have to be so hard?" Hanks growls: "It's supposed to be hard. The hard is what makes it great."

Networking is hard and it's true: in network marketing, there's no free lunch. Everyone pays. And when it comes, it is one seriously delicious and satisfying meal.

Getting Stretched
It's the Only Way You'll Fit into Your Dreams
March '95

"Hi, you don't know me, but I'm on your fourth level—and I was wondering if you could work with me. I'm really going for it, but I just can't get along with my sponsor, or her sponsor, or his sponsor, either. Do you have some time for me?"

I can't tell you how many times I've heard someone say this. We like to say that one of the benefits of network marketing is that you get to "work with the people you want to work with."

Hmm. Sort of. Sometimes.

It's true, to an extent. But what also happens is that we get the opportunity to work with people who are "good for us"—something like having our teeth cleaned, eating our spinach and cleaning out our garages are "good for us." Not necessarily the top of our "fun things to do on a Saturday" list.

Shakespeare uttered these immortal lines in *A Midsummer Night's Dream*: "The course of true love never did run smooth." So it is at times for the course of true sponsorship. Sometimes we get along famously with those we sponsor, or those who sponsor us. Sometimes it is . . . a challenge.

There are three choices at this particular fork in the road.

One: do nothing. The path of least resistance. Ignore the

person and "track upline" (or downline) till you find someone who seems easier to work with . . . and that way lies attrition, resentment and downlines with weakening holes in them—incomplete relationships that tend to spread tendrils of ennui and dysfunctionality all about.

Two: complain. Call your entire upline to talk about it, then go to your company to request a transfer. Hint: in the army, soldiers who request transfers aren't popular. Networkers who request transfers generally are not loved by corporate, either. Here again, the stain tends to spread.

Three: work on it. The road less traveled. And sometimes that's quite a stretch.

If there is one thing network marketing assuredly offers, it's the opportunity to be the best person you can possibly be. And if there's one thing that stepping into that opportunity requires, it is that you stretch. And yes, it's often a stretch to break through shyness, to get self-disciplined, to shift to an abundant mentality, and so forth. But the situation that I most often see truly stretch people is finding yourself as the sponsor of someone with whom you truly, honestly, profoundly feel you cannot get along with. (Or worse, having that person as *your* sponsor.)

I don't want to get too cosmic here, but what I've seen happen again and again is that when you take Road #3, *it works itself out, in the long run, and usually reveals a higher purpose.* Options #1 and #2 (ignoring or transferring) rarely produce the fulfillment of toughing it out and transforming in the process.

It's the challenge of getting along with people.

Scott Ohlgren, a friend and training partner, wrote a superb training manual with a chapter he'd originally entitled, "Follow-Through: Phone Skills." Scott says he decided to change the title to more accurately reflect what that section is really teaching. Now he calls it, "How to Communicate with Human Beings."

It's exhilarating to have a big dream, a big goal, a big vision. Only thing is, you may find that you don't fully fit into it—until you stretch.

The Treacherous Dichotomy
Beware the Networker's Jabberwock!
June '95

> "Beware the Jabberwock, my son!
>   The jaws that bite, the claws that catch!
>   Beware the Jubjub bird, and shun
>   The frumious Bandersnatch!"
>   — from *Through the Looking-Glass, and What*
>   *Alice Found There*, by Lewis Carroll

Philanthropy. Giving. Altruism. Networking. It's what we do; it's who we are. We are all heroes in our own minds, and that's a good thing.

But if we're Luke Skywalker, does that also mean our dad is Darth Vader?

That's why I've got to write about the Treacherous Dichotomy. It's the networker's Jabberwock, the dark shadow that our greatest ambitions cast upon our souls at day's end—and it can throw a monkey wrench into your ability to grow your business.

> *Beware the Jabberwock, my son!*
> *The jaws that bite, the claws that catch! . . .*

Most of us live with an assumption: there is a fundamental contradiction between self-interest and altruism. You may be acting for others' benefit, or for your own—*but not both at once.* If you accept this Treacherous Dichotomy, then every time you pick up the phone to talk with a prospect, your subconscious has to conclude either:

> *a) I am greedy, manipulative and focused purely on my own personal gain at this poor slob's expense;*

or:

> *b) I am big-hearted and generous, on a mission to help this person—and must studiously avoid any hint of a result that could actually improve my own lot in life.*

Has the frumious shadow of this inner conflict never graced your thoughts? (Think loud, labored breathing and James Earl Jones: "Search your heart, Luke: you know it to be true . . .")

So: before you next climb onto the phone, take an attitude check, and remind yourself:

In network marketing, there is no distinction between effective self-interest and effective altruism. In the pursuit of this noble mission, these dualistic interests both disappear, and in their place there is simply *focused purpose*: making sure you do your best to let the people you talk with discover the possibilities that are here for them.

And they won't do this on their own, by the way: they're counting on you. Keep these two facts in mind on your next business call:

> *1) Your success does not depend on this particular person saying "Yes" . . .*

To be successful, you need people to join your business. But you don't need this particular person to be one of them. So relax. Go for clarity: find out whether they are interested, or they are not.

> *2) . . . but their getting the benefits you're offering does.*

You also know the phenomenal benefits this particular person stands to gain from what you are offering. And if you don't give them an opportunity to find out for themselves—a really good opportunity, the best you can possibly give—you also know what they stand to lose.

So, breathe; banish the Treacherous Dichotomy—and give it your best shot. There's not a lot riding on the outcome of this call *for you*—but there could be *for them*.

The High Road
Badmouthing the Competition
Is a Loser's Strategy
September '95

Last week, I had the chance to be a prospect.

Someone in my downline complained that I was embarrassing her by showing up to meetings at her house in the homely clunker I'd been driving for years. I thought she was kidding, but upon reflection realized, maybe not. Okay. It was time to get a real car. So I read a little in *Consumer Reports*, perused what we've written about cars in *Upline*, and set out to visit three dealers in my area.

First was the local BMW man, Mike.

I'd been there before, checking out Beamers. He remembered me, took my kids and me for a test spin and gave me a car to try overnight. No hard sell: on our drive, we chatted about network marketing, a bit about family, and I left liking Mike a lot—not knowing a whole lot about the car, but enjoying it.

Next was Lexus.

Now, the nearest Lexus dealer is a good hour and a half away, and I wasn't about to go clunking ninety minutes down the road. No problem. Tink Doyle from Lexus of Richmond called, asked me right away what I was looking for in a car, what interested me about Lexus, what else was I looking at. I told her: BMW,

Lexus, Mercedes. All three very good cars, she acknowledged cheerfully. Had to confess, she personally loved the Lex—obviously, that's why she worked there. But they were all excellent. What was I looking for in a car, how would I be using it? Ended up, she brought a car all the way out to Charlottesville for me to try—and the next day, a different model. And then another. For the next week, Tink made sure I didn't pass a day without a Lexus to drive.

Finally, I got to Mercedes.

Ed, like Tink, wanted to know what else I was driving. He had no comment on BMW, but the moment I mentioned the word "Lexus" he gave an unmistakable snort of derision. "Not much of a car, really," opined Ed, and he launched into a friendly lecture about how many ways the Benz eats the Lex for breakfast. What problems I'd have getting service all the way from Richmond. How it was essentially a Camry body with a higher price tag. How its airbag might not be as safe . . .

By the time I left the Mercedes dealership, Ed had sold me, all right. I got the Lexus.

I'm sure I don't need to point out all the fascinating lessons in the behavior of the three auto reps. But here's just one: *Don't knock the competition.*

Of course, there were features about each car that helped direct my decision. But it's true: *the nature of the three people's words and actions* had a powerful impact.

Tink's open respect for the competition warmed me up to her right away. Mike was pleasant, but stayed pretty much in neutral. Ed's eagerly disdainful Lex-bashing drove me off his lot in fifth gear.

Recently, a high-ranking distributor from a very well-known company had a fine slapped on him in civil court because he had publicly accused a competitor (Procter & Gamble, no less) of being satanically influenced—literally. Most of us don't take badmouthing the competition to quite that extreme, and don't get taken to court over it either—but we still suffer penalties. It's a shoddy way of doing business, and a classic dodge of prospectors who suffer low professional self-esteem, or hold their prospects in same, or both. Or, who simply don't know any better. Ignorance at best, cowardice and arrogance at worst.

The lesson I learned: follow Tink's example.

Take the high road.

Wemen
The X and Y of Networking
October '95

"How do women do network marketing differently than men?"

My first impulse is to answer, "Not nearly as differently as some seem to think." One of the fundamental values, benefits and joys of this jewel of free enterprise is that by its intrinsic nature, it is not a genderly partisan beast. Getting results from a product you love, sharing the story with your sphere of influence, enrolling others and coaching people to grow big dreams and follow them with big actions . . . it's an X-*and*-Y-chromosome-friendly way of working and living.

I've noticed virtually identical tendencies among both male and female networkers. Just as many men are timid about declaring their own goals as women; just as many women are as sky's-the-limitish about theirs. Statistically, there are more women doing the business than men. But as far as how they're doing it, I don't really see many glaring distinctions between the genders in their attitudes, strategies or results.

Hence the title. Did I misspell "Women," or misspace "We men"? Neither. Both.

That said, I do see one major difference. To generalize (and it's generally true, so I will): the women networkers I know are better listeners. And while the men are not nece: talkers, they do seem to *want* to talk more, to pl: value on talking about what they're doing.

Theoretically, "better listener" should mean a better ability to grow deeper roots; that is, a group with staying power and greater genealogical depth and cohesion. If you listen to people well, they'll feel it, get more emotionally invested in your group and, in the long run, drive that leg deeper.

If men are more committed to talking, then they will be—again, as a broad generality—stronger at growing wide front lines. More talking, more comfort with being "out in front of people," especially strangers, means more personal recruiting. And you know what? I find this to be exactly so. I've known more men than women who grow huge first levels with lots of breadth but less depth.

Question: if the women in this business accomplish at least as much as the men, and most likely more (since there seem to be more of them here in network marketing, and I'll bet they create longer-lasting network relationships overall), why don't we see more woman-authored books on networking? Why aren't there more female "generic" trainers and consultants? Is it that men are more inclined to spread the word, telling everyone what they've done and giving how-to advice in a public forum, while women tend more to keep out of the limelight and focus on helping individual people, up close and personal? I think so.

Men and women both make great networkers. Men like to talk about it more. Women listen better.

Time for me to shut up.

You Are Not a Dinosaur
Digital Technology Is Impressive—But It's All about the Characters
November '95

Whenever you hear a "latest buzz" in network marketing, it usually comes down to the same thing: some hot new approach to prospecting. A new and better way of getting more people in the door.

Getting more people in the door is an important topic, no question. Perhaps not as hot or exciting, but in a very real way far more important, is *retention*: once you bring people in, how do you *keep* them in?

The company I'm with recently witnessed earth-shaking proof of the power of a spanking new tool. Having loped along with modest, stable growth for a good decade, in the past few years we have suddenly taken off into the heady, thin atmosphere of hypergrowth. What fueled this sudden liftoff? More than anything else, it was the humble audiocassette.

It isn't the cassette itself, of course. It's what the cassette does. It provides the ordinary person with a systematic, massively duplicable process for making that otherwise scary, rejection-courting, dream-threatening entity: the Presentation.

Before the advent of the cassette tape method, most people in my company were trying to grow large networks with as much success as I'd have getting the lug nuts off my car's tires with my fingers. What was missing? The wrench. Cut to 1995. Finally, a systematized way to prospect, one that anyone can duplicate! The world is suddenly awash with deceased physicians who eschew prevarication . . .[12]

And yes, it works. But there's prospecting, and then there's sponsoring. Not the same thing.

Prospecting is bringing people in; *sponsoring* is taking care of them once they're here. If prospecting is giving birth (to a fully grown adult—ouch!), then sponsoring is bonding with the peach-fuzzy brand-new inductee.

I recently watched a "Making of . . ." video about how they produced the 1993 film *Jurassic Park*. When they started pre-production, they still planned to shoot many of the dinosaurs with old-fashioned stop-action animation; the fully staffed department had built their complex animatronic models and everything. Halfway through the process, they realized that CGI (Computer-Generated Image) technology had come so far, they could shoot all their *f/x* via computer.

CGI has come of age—in a film about dinosaurs.

Were the robot guys obsolete now? They thought so, at first. Said one, "These new tools were so sophisticated, we thought it might be like you just sit at a console and push the 'D' button for dinosaur." Instead, they discovered, they had *even more* work to do. CGI was a tool that did its job better than any human could, but it didn't (couldn't) do the humans' job. Its job: make dinosaurs. Their job: make movies.

Tell stories.

That's you. The tool's job: make a presentation. Your job: make a connection. Your job is to do the stuff that only people can do. Ask questions—and really listen to the answers. Find out what people want most, what they enjoy most, what they value most. Find out what's working in their lives, what's missing in their lives, and what's the most important next step for them to take *today*. Help them use the tools you've got to create the movie that is their lives.

Your new-fangled, CGI-quality network marketing tools are a better brush; the canvas is people's lives.

You're the artist.

Paint.

Dancin' Check to Check
Thoughts on the Shock of Having Enough
December '95

Heaven, I'm in Heaven
And my heart beats so that I can barely speak
And I think I'll find the happiness I seek
When we're out together dancing . . .[13]

—check to check?!

Wait. That wasn't right. That last line was supposed to be, "cheek to cheek." But for some reason, whenever I'd try singing it, it'd come out the same way: *Dancin' check to check . . . .*

There must be some sort of mysterious natural principle operating here, I suspected, a sort of fiscal Murphy's Law: *No matter how much your check grows, it will never, ever suffice: something, some unforeseen event, emergency or unexpected need, will invariably arise to take that burdensome monetary excess off your hands.*

What was wrong with me? Was I just greedy, slothful, pecuniarily cursed . . . or what?

Have you ever had thoughts like this? I have. And I still remember the feeling of mild (and quite pleasant) shock when one day, upon attaining a certain livelihoodinous level, I realized that the feeling was gone.

We had enough.

It took a while to break old habits of thought. Even after having well more than adequate income, I'd still hold onto bills when they came, as if I needed to wait for the next check to pay them. And I continued to experience an occasional mild panic if the commission check was a day later than expected.

What intrigues me is the psychology, the underlying mindset that keeps whispering in so many of our ears, "You're kidding yourself, it'll never work. No matter how much it grows, it'll never be enough . . . ." *Never.*

It's the habit of living check to check: a deeply ingrained sense that there is simply not enough to go around—that no matter what, a vicious circle of scarcity will always appear in our dreams to snatch them away.

Thomas Malthus, meet Freddy Krueger.

I once heard Buckminster Fuller say that if we divided up the world's wealth among every man, woman and child, we'd each have over $10 million. Contrast: as of this writing, the average annual income for the working stiff in the United States is well under $25,000. In other words, what is average, and what we therefore tend to hold as "normal," is to earn *less than one quarter of one percent* of the $10 million Fuller says we ought to have access to.

Put another way: we each expect to work for four centuries to accrue our "normal" share of wealth. (That's four centuries *before* expenses.) Aesop called it "the ant and the grasshopper." The ant was responsible and secured a decent living. The grasshopper knew only how to *live.* What a drag. Because who wants to be an ant?

The truth is, Aesop's moral notwithstanding, now we get to do both. For most of us, this is a whole new way of thinking.

Hey, Thomas? Freddy? Scram. No time to play your games any more.

I'm too busy dancing—cheek to cheek.

The Eighth Day of the Week
Someday: The Day That Never Comes
January '96

"Someday, when I have the time, I'm going to . . ."
"Someday, when I have the money, I'm going to . . ."

Have you ever said that? *"Someday . . ."* It's a way we have of reinforcing the illusion that the future is safely far removed, that it doesn't really touch us. It's a lie. Not a willful, intentional deception, but a lie nonetheless.

Let's say that, "someday," you're going to travel around the world. If that's really true, if you genuinely intend for that to happen, then here's how that looks: *you're making plans*. If it's not practical today for you to just up and circumnavigate the globe this instant, you are looking at what needs to happen first, and second, and third, to end up with that result. You're at the drawing board, making genuine preparation, excited and ready to go.

When you set that process in motion, the word "someday" disappears. You're making it happen today, right now. In a very real sense, you are *already taking* that trip. It may be six months or five years before you actually do the physical traveling, but the word "someday" no longer applies—so you stop using it.

When we say "someday," we're not really talking about our future. Our future is a concrete reality that we're connected to by what we're doing *right now*. "Someday" is about some vague possibility that we're not taking seriously.

"Someday" is not a vision of my future. "Someday" is a fantasy—nothing more.

Here's the damage we do with this illusion. When we give weight to our "someday" fantasies, we squeeze some sense of enjoyment from them *as if they were real*—and in so doing, we give ourselves permission to take no practical action whatsoever while we swim in the comforting sense that those someday scenarios will somehow, on their own, move closer to the unfolding present . . . eventually.

But they won't. The wistful, wouldn't-it-be-nice pretendings of maybe-futures do not insert themselves into your reality of their own accord.

You've got to go claim them.

You've got to grab hold of those practical steps you can take *today* to move the dream of financial freedom from the realm of *someday* to the world of *right now*.

I am talking about your prospective business partners, the people you know and those whom you'll soon meet. About introducing them to a vehicle whereby their "somedays" can be shifted into being real, I'm-already-doing-it futures.

And I'm also talking about you. Ask yourself, "What is there in my life that I hold as *someday* . . . ?"

Someday . . . the eighth day of the week. The day that never comes.

There is no eighth day. This is the day—*this* one. Right here. Right now.

Stop, Look, Listen
A Three-Word Leadership Commandment
February '96

What does a leader in network marketing do? I'll bet you've read and heard hundreds of answers to that question. Answers like these:

> Always be available for your people . . . Show people simple systems they can use to create successful actions . . . Help people set their goals, and keep them accountable . . . Help people stay focused and avoid unproductive actions . . . Always be positive: when you're up, talk to your downline; when you're down, talk to your upline . . . Be on the cutting edge: leaders are pioneers: be the first to use new technologies and pass the most useful ones down the line . . . Be a good example: the speed of the leader is the speed of the pack . . . Write newsletters to your people; keep them informed, involved and inspired . . . Offer your help—but don't help so much that you end up doing their work for them; don't just give them a fish for a meal, teach them how to fish for a lifetime . . . Put your people first; frame your goals in terms of *their* goals: helping others succeed is the only way you succeed . . . Hold yourself to a higher standard: whatever you want your people to do, make sure you are doing it first . . . Leadership is what you do . . .

> Leadership is what you show others how to do ... Leadership
> is who you are ...

Yikes! That's a lot to remember. Isn't there some way to simplify this business of leadership?

The first-century church inherited from the Mosaic tradition a host of directives on correct behavior; in John's Gospel record, the carpenter from Nazareth boiled it all down to three words: "Love one another." (Actually, it's even simpler in the original Greek: just two words, *agapao allenon*.)

The logic is brilliant: if you keep that one commandment, if you *really* keep it, then guess what? You'll automatically be keeping all the others, too.

So, is there one commandment of network marketing leadership? One directive which, if you follow it thoroughly and consistently, will result in your automatically also doing everything else you need to do? If there is one, my guess is that it would be this, which I learned in kindergarten from a sign on the railroad tracks:

STOP, LOOK and LISTEN.

STOP what you're doing; stop thinking about yourself, your situation, your business, your life, what's on your plate at the moment—hold everything, and

LOOK at what's happening; look at what your people are doing, at who they are and at what's actually going on for them—and then

LISTEN, *really listen*, to the person you're talking with.

You've probably heard this last one before. That's because it's so singularly powerful: it is probably the most important leadership trait, bar none. The way you listen to your people not only tells you what they need from you as the leader, it also reveals to you where *their* leadership resides.

In fact, the way you listen can actually make a shift in them.

Listen well, and the rest of the script will follow.

No listening—no leading.

STOP, LOOK *and* LISTEN. When you do, you're being a leader.

It's about the Product . . . and It's Not about the Product

If You Want to Grow Carrots, Why Would You Plant Celery Seeds?

March '96

As exciting and interesting as it is to learn how this business works, I've always found it even more fascinating to observe how it sometimes doesn't—where and how people get stuck or stopped. One of the most common stumbling blocks I've noticed is the *celery seed syndrome*.

Let's say your product is a powerful, health-supporting nutritional supplement; or it could be a line of beauty products, a gizmo that eliminates back pain, a wonderful insurance or financial services package—whatever. It helps people improve their lives, and you love it.

I call it "celery."

New networkers often come to a point (often fairly early on) where they say, "I've learned how to get people to try and love my celery. I've got no problem creating celery-eaters. But nobody in my group is doing what I do—how do I get business builders?" Often, the problem is this:

You're trying to grow carrots by planting celery seeds.

Business builders are different than plain produc
They love the celery, too—but they are carrots. There's a difference. Carrots are rooted in something *beyond* the product.

There comes a point where the aspiring entrepreneur needs
to come clean and fully embrace this fact: "I am an entrepreneur." Your job description is not, "I am a promoter of celery,
I market the value and benefits of celery," but rather, "I am an
entrepreneur, looking for entrepreneurs like myself."

And so we run smack into the grand paradox of this business:

> *It's all about the product. And, it's not about the
> product.*

Every successful networker I know not only loves but is
veritably passionate about his or her product. *But we don't market
our product.* Stores market products; catalogs market products;
network marketing leaders don't market products. Here is what
we market:

> *The opportunity to make a tremendous difference,
> in your own life and the lives of those you love and
> thousands of others, through an extraordinary busi-
> ness and lifestyle phenomenon whose value is unchored
> in this particular extraordinary product.*

Making that shift, coming into a place where you feel utterly
comfortable and congruent telling people about your opportunity without having nagging self-doubts about whether or not
you're short-changing your product or turning people off with
your presentation, is a matter of personal evolution.

It is a shift that every successful network marketing leader
has made.

The weirdly wonderful thing about network marketing is

that sometimes celery roots *can* transform into carrots. Sometimes people who came in for the product *do* develop a love for the business.

Still, scattering celery seeds is not the most effective way to grow carrots. What is? Planting carrot seeds.

The Great Balancing Act
How Not to Fall Off Your Horse
April '96

Because of an odd series of circumstances involving a birth defect of my feet, I didn't learn to ride a bicycle until I was in my teens. Because I was already fairly well along in years by that point, I have a distinct memory of how intriguing it was to encounter the sensation of bodily balance, struggling to keep my right-and-left equilibrium while straddling a pair of one-inch-wide rubber wheels.

I was reminded of this sensation recently while reading some C.S. Lewis, where I found a wonderful quote from Martin Luther:

> *Humanity is like a drunkard who, having fallen off his horse on the left side, clambers back on and pitches off on the right.*

Network marketing, being quite human, is like that. We're constantly striving to keep our balance, watching for the tendency to lean too heavily to the one side or the other. The one side or the other of what?

Of the Great Balancing Act.

For example.

Part of your job description as my sponsor is to believe in me—sometimes more than I believe in myself. To be the still point for my turning world, the deciding vote in the contest of self-confidence versus self-doubt. At the same time, another part of that job description is to call me on my illusions and unfulfilled commitments—to be a ruthlessly professional mirror on the wall and point out when I'm kidding myself that I'm in action, when in truth, I'm just spinning my wheels. To remind me that for all my great intentions, "the proof is in the printout."

Your job, in other words, is to be both my advocate *and* my reality check. Two sides of the network marketing horse.

When you're working with someone new who is promising but not yet producing results, how do you know, as the blunt expression goes, "When to fish and when to cut bait"? It's a matter of sensing the balance.

Here's another piece of the Great Balancing Act: being the leader and steward of your entire group, on the one hand, and on the other, focusing your energy on work with your own personally sponsored people—especially your *brand new* personally sponsored people.

Coach and quarterback: sometimes known as "working deep and working wide."

So how do you decide when to work with someone promising on your eighth level and when to say, "Sorry, I've got to focus on my own first tier people"? Both strategies have merit: it's a matter of sensing the balance.

Another: the delicate balance we often call "work and home." Or you could say, *creating* wealth and *enjoying* it. Getting a life (work) and living that life (play).

And another: we call this the "duplication business." *Show me exactly what to do and how to do it. Give me the recipe!* But we also call this "the greatest personal development course." *Forget the external how-to's—help me discover my internal glitches, "lack programming" and self-limiting scripts, and break throug,. my personal limitations!* So what does it mean when my business is stuck? Is my problem what I'm doing—or who I'm being?

Yet another great opportunity to fall off one side of the horse, clamber back up and then pitch off the other side.

I've seen people get so caught up in technical details—of product specs, selling methodologies or how-to recipes for prospecting—that they end up suffocating their businesses. I've also seen people become so deeply absorbed in the pursuit of personal growth—with its endless seminars, cassette programs and trainings—that their businesses wither and die of neglect.

Humanity: drunk again.

What's the greatest requirement of a successful networker? Balance: the willingness to stay unmarried to one particular point of view. To shift your weight from one side of the horse to the other—without falling off.

Ears: An Amazing Communication Technology
They Make Lousy Answering Devices, But Great Listening Devices
May '96

I recently told a friend about a seminar I'd attended with the legendary coach Carol McCall, entitled, "The Empowerment of Listening." "Oh, excellent," the friend replied, "communication skills! Can't ever get too much of that . . . ."

Not exactly. One thing made quite clear during the course was that listening and "communication skills" are not the same thing. What people often think of as "communication skills" might more accurately be called *expression* skills. When people say, "Oh, he's a great communicator," what they generally mean is that the person is a great *speaker*. But that's only part—and the far smaller part—of the business of communication.

The other aspect of communication technology lies not in my speaking but in my hearing what *you* say.

As part of a ninety-day follow-up program to the course, we all are now paired with listening partners: five days a week we have a call wherein one asks the other a series of questions about how today went. The questioner then simply listens—no advice, suggestions or commentary, other than "Anything else?"

No, "Uh-huh" . . . no, "Yeah, I know whatcha mean."

Just listening.

It has been a shock to find how unusual (and wonderful) it feels simply to *be heard*. I have begun to notice how often I am driven, in my listening to others, by the anxious need to "fix" what and who I'm hearing.

When a prospect says, "I could never do this . . . I'm not interested," or a business builder tells me, "I'm stuck and don't know what to do," I can hear that from a context which says, "Now, how am I gonna correct this person's viewpoint or clear up his confusion?" Or I can hear it purely from the context, "Okay . . . now did I hear this correctly?"

In the first case, my focus is not on what the person's saying, but on what I'm going to say back. I give his words my own spin, to see how I can adjust his point of view or solve his dilemma. Problem is, I'm using my ears to speak. Ears weren't made for that. In the second case, I'm using my ears to listen—and trusting that when it's my turn to respond, I'll simply do that.

Ninety-nine percent of what looks like listening in the world is not listening, it's just waiting at a stoplight with the mind's engine running until the light turns green and we can go again.

When you listen, put it in neutral; even better, shut off the engine. Assume for a moment that you in fact *don't know* the best answer or solution to offer when your person finishes his or her tale of woe. And don't burn up any gasoline, either, in worrying about the fact that you're the upline, you're supposed to have an answer, and you don't, and how is that going to look? Just turn off the engine and listen. You don't have to come up with the solution.

However, if you listen carefully and fully and have a conversation about what's really going on for that other person, the chances are that together, you will come up with a solution, or at least a good next step. In any case, simply the fact that she got heard puts you both way ahead.

Something else, too: chances are also very good that the person you're listening to has *nobody else* in her life who listens to her the way you're doing.

There is a local dry cleaner where I take my shirts. I go in, drop them off and get a solid five-minute earful from the lady behind the counter. I've noticed how my listening to her has shifted over the past few months.

At first, I found her funny, colorful and engaging.

A few weeks in, I started to look for ways I might help her address her various and sundry complaints (which were many). Maybe my products could do something for her. Maybe my good humor or my sympathy could. Maybe a thread of thought or aspect of outlook. After another month, I grew weary of hearing her problems; she clearly had no interest in anything I had to say back. After yet another month, I started to find her distinctly annoying. "Annoying" soon turned to "infuriating," and I came to dread the place. I would grow angry just walking in the door.

One day I stopped just before entering her store and asked myself: why was I angry?

My answer startled me. I wasn't *listening* to her. I was listening to my own thoughts about how frustrated my efforts to have an impact on her had been.

That time, when I walked into the place, I stopped using my ears to *answer* her and instead used them simply to *hear* her. What I heard was a person who had possibly never been listened to before in her entire life.

And listen to this:

I found her funny, colorful and engaging.

The Power of Not Resisting
When the Conversation Goes Icy,
Turn in the Direction of the Skid
June '96

It was twenty-five years ago, the summer of '71, and at the ripe old age of 17 I was finally learning how to ride a bicycle.

At birth my feet were deformed, club-footed, bent so that my toes at rest touched my heels. Some ingenious doctors found a way to correct the problem without surgery, but it took several years of repeated applications of heavy plaster casts, each a bit straighter than the last. Eventually my feet arrived at normal, but I was now a few years behind in crawling, walking . . . and bike-riding.

Of course, I could've learned then—but my friends already knew how, and I was too embarrassed to let them see me start. So I let it pass.

Now, at 17, I'd decided it was time.

Since I went through the bike-learning process as a sentient adult (more or less), I still recall a distinct awareness of the process. When you feel yourself falling to the right, what do you do? You turn the wheel *in the same direction*, stopping the fall. Right? Right. But my greenhorn instinct screamed, "No, you idiot!—the other way! Turn the other way! You're falling *right*—turn *left*! Cut it hard!"

So I would. And end up on my butt.

Communicating with human beings works exactly the same way. When your dialogue with a prospect starts to feel like it's about to lose its balance and fall, instinct tells you, "Turn the other way, idiot! Cut it hard!"

"Gee, your product seems kinda expensive—" "Ha! Expensive, you say? Why, not at all! Darn *cheap*, I'd say, worth every penny and more—hey, have you considered how much you spend each month on junk food, aspirin and bad movies?"

Crash.

"So, is this one of those pyramid things—?" "Are you out of your mind?! No way! Absolutely not! It's totally legal! You think I'd be doing it if it were illegal?!"

Smack, right on your butt.

Not long after learning to ride a bike, I learned to drive a car, and I there encountered the identical concept: when finding yourself on an icy road and going into a skid, turn in . . . what direction? *The direction of the skid.* Seems counterintuitive, but any driver who's done winters in New England knows it's the gospel truth.

What does "turn in the direction of the skid" look like in communicating with humans? Something like this:

"So you're saying, X dollars seems like a lot to spend? [Pause, let them say, *Yeah, it does.*] Yeah, I know what you mean. It's a serious chunk of change. I had to think twice the first time I tried them out, too. In fact, these are the top of the line in their field, and I doubt you'll find any that cost *more* than ours. Let me ask you this: what kind of results would you need to see to justify the price?"

My friend Richard Brooke calls it, "Embellishing the Objection." It's a matter of going in the same direction the other person is leaning—not struggling to force them to lean back the other way. It is exemplified in one of John Fogg's favorite questions: "Can you say more about that . . . ?"

It's a matter of *being* with the person—not jousting or dueling with them. Of trusting your products, your opportunity, the facts and yourself enough to not have to push. It shows the other person (and yourself) that you're not afraid of questions.

It's a feeling of balance . . . on your bicycle built for two.

When I first started to ride a bike, it felt awkward and strange, like I'd never get the hang of it. Of course, I did. Anyone can.

And you already know what is the most amazing thing about learning how to handle yourself on a bike. Once you've learned how, it becomes second nature—and you never, ever forget.

Curiosity
Take the Road Less Traveled:
Genuinely Ask Questions
July '96

I'm in love with how this business works. However, I'm more fascinated with how it *doesn't*—with where and how people get stuck, when and why they hit the wall and stop.

And where do people get stopped? The crux of the matter is in making calls. People get stopped by the process of talking to others.

Lately, a lot of people have been telling me, "Oh, the tape system—that hasn't worked for me." ("The tape system" means sending out from twenty-five to one hundred audiocassettes as a prospecting initiative, to be followed up with a phone call to each recipient.)

When somebody says this, I've found that nine times out of ten, *they're not making the calls.* And they're not doing so because in their experience (or, more often, in their imagination), making those calls is uncomfortable.

There are lots of reasons why these calls can feel uncomfortable, but they all boil down to the same truth: when I am feeling uncomfortable on a call, *I am thinking about myself.*

How to change course?

I could attempt to step into *enthusiasm*—for my product, for my company, for network marketing itself. These are all good, but this can feel artificial, and in any case, doesn't necessarily promote *relatedness*. The single most effective way I've found to step away from the thinking-about-how-I'm-doing discomfort is to access my *curiosity*.

Everyone is innately curious. It's hardwired: comes with being human. But we don't all access that faculty with the same ease. It takes practice. At first, it may take consciously pushing yourself to be curious.

When someone says, "Gee, that sounds expensive," or "I've tried those miracle products, they don't work," most people tend to respond with information. Tell, show, expound . . . it's a natural reaction.

The problem is, even if I'm good at talking (which most people firmly believe they are not), the focus is still on me, me, me. Even if I flip to an other-focused agenda—wanting to find out what *their* "compelling why" is, looking to see how the product could benefit *them*—it ironically is still my agenda: how can I further my agenda by asking about them? It's still more of *me*.

To paraphrase George Benson: "We tried to talk it over, but my thoughts got in the way."

They key is to let go of the thoughts in your mind by evoking your own curiosity: by putting *questions* in your mind. What's going on with that person? What do they mean by what they just said?

Ask.

Take the other fork in the road. Instead of evoking knowledge and information, let your thoughts and agenda be replaced by curiosity. That's the skill of follow-up calls: connecting with the person *without* your thoughts getting in the way.

And the most direct road I know of to reach that place is curiosity.

In the Wind Tunnel
Pick Up the Phone, Dial That Number—
It's Time to See If This Baby Will Fly
September '96

When I was a kid, my older brother and I built a go-cart. It was truly cool: huge plywood fins, eight feet long, lots of style. We nailed down the motor, started it up—and right in front of my shocked seven-year-old eyes, the vibrations of the motor shattered the poor thing to pieces.

It sure *looked* solid. It's just that it wasn't.

Let's say you've built an aircraft in your garage. Hmm . . . *looks* strong. Whack the wings with a sledge—nothing. *This thing is rock solid.* Will it fly? Only one way to tell, right?

So you take it up. You're up, up and away, over the village square . . . you can see the church steeple way below . . .

Oh, no—one wing just flew off! And there goes the other one!!

Maybe you should have stress-tested this thing in a wind tunnel before taking it up into the wild blue yonder.

You love your products, right? Believe in them wholeheartedly—and your company, too? And, let me guess: you passionately believe in the value of network marketing. When you offer your opportunity to people, you're doing them possibly one of the greatest favors anyone will ever do them in their lives—yes?

That belief structure feel solid? Okay, let's take it up: let's see if this baby can fly.

Dial the phone.

Everything looks good so far . . . and then the person on the other end of the phone says, "That material you sent me? Yeah, I thought it was stupid," or, "Say, are you trying to make money off me?"

Suddenly your palms feel clammy, your stomach starts to tighten, and—*what was that?!* That ripping sound?! *Oh no—both wings just fell off!*

Prospecting stress-tests your beliefs, all right. Fortunately, you're not hundreds of feet in the air, and the fall will not, repeat, will not injure you. (Remember that.) You're experiencing the real value of prospecting.

You're in the wind tunnel, and that is a powerful place to be.

The deepest benefit that you receive from actively prospecting is *not* the actual recruitment of the prospects themselves, although that is certainly a nice fringe benefit, when it occurs. The deepest benefit of the process is that the process itself anchors you firmly in your own convictions.

And here's the remarkable thing: when you are a shining beacon for your products and opportunity, the people who turn out to be your strongest leaders will appear.

It's amazing: they simply show up. Sometimes they'll come because you went looking for them and pursued them energetically and persistently. Sometimes they will approach you when you're not even looking, seeming to appear as if by magic, out of left field. It'll seem to have nothing to do with anything that looks even remotely like a prospecting activity.

Either way, it's the same thing: it happens because you're the right magnet. You're stress-tested.

You've put in your time in the wind tunnel.

One Way or the Other
The Secret to Effective Prospecting
November '96

Something I've noticed lately about the prospecting efforts of people in my network: when I see people floundering, feeling plateaued, unable to get into momentum, I typically find they are using one strategy—and only one strategy—for prospecting. When I see people who clearly *are* in momentum, it generally turns out they are employing at least two different prospecting strategies, and usually three or more.

This is no accident.

This is a strategic key.

If you want to reach escape velocity in your business and achieve that magical quality of momentum—which is what separates hope-it'll-happen networking businesses from it's-happening! networking businesses—design for yourself a plan that employs at least two prospecting strategies, and *preferably three or more*.

Create a menu of different prospecting methodologies, and then choose from your menu, putting together a program that fits you, your resources (time, money, sphere of acquaintances) and your temperament.

Mailing 5,000 postcards or placing national display ads with an 800 number takes cash; it can also serve to winnow the field of prospects, so that you're calling only people who have already "sorted" themselves and are somewhat pre-qualified with serious interest.

Mailing 100 audiotapes or information packs and then calling each one to follow up takes somewhat less cash, a good deal more time and involves a whole lot more of you talking with people who may not be interested.

Going to Chamber of Commerce meetings and other local networking opportunities, making new acquaintances and simply sharing your story and your enthusiasm with people, one on one, takes no cash, as much or as little time as you choose, and a willingness to be bold on a whole different level.

Classified ads, video-a-day programs, web pages, handwritten letters to your holiday list and high school yearbook addresses . . . prospecting methods come in too many shapes and sizes to count. Some will fit you like a glove; others will be a stretch, or even wrench you fully out of your comfort zone. The key is this: *do more than one*.

Of course, this doesn't guarantee success. No matter which approaches you use or in what combination, how effective you are ultimately will come down to your own attitude and beliefs (sometimes called "posture") and the quality of your follow-through. Still, adopting a portfolio of at least two or three prospecting methods almost invariably creates a dramatic increase in results.

Why? Is it simply that you're doing more, or the fact that trying a few different approaches ups the odds that you'll find at least one that works? Perhaps that's part of it—but the real answer is more intriguing and far more powerful: *it creates an entirely different mindset*. A more proactive and entrepreneurial mindset.

When you embark upon a plan that involves a whole range of prospecting approaches, this telegraphs a different message to your own subconscious.

Using just one method says, "Gee, I hope this works."

Using several methods says, "I've got a goal, and I'm going to reach it—and if these three methods don't get the results I want, hey, I'll just move on to the next few methods. Because *one way or the other*, I'm getting there!"

Having a range of methods exercises the brain's entrepreneurial muscles, and those are the same muscles that make your business a success . . . one way or the other.

What People Want
It's Not about the Money . . . or Is It?
December '96

You've heard people in your company on stage, saying, "It's not about The Money." You've also heard them in private conversation at the party afterwards, saying things that strongly suggest it is very much indeed about The Money. They're not speaking with forked tongues: both points are correct.

Even when "It's not about The Money," believe me, *it's about The Money*. And even when it is about The Money—*it's not about The Money*.

"The Money" is shorthand, a code.

Code for what?

For something else.

When you say, for example, "five thousand dollars a month," you are really talking about something entirely different—something *real*. I mean, real in the way that money is not. Money is general and abstract; what you want is specific and concrete. It could be, "My husband leaves his job," or "We move to Maui," or "My kid goes to college," or "We have our retirement totally nailed down." It might be, "We get to spend our time helping starving kids in third-world countries," or "Finally! We're taking off six months to drive cross-country!" It could be any or all of those, and a thousand other things.

It is whatever is real and meaningful—*to you.*

It is remarkable to see how many people get stopped in this business (scene: you're sitting in a gorgeous thirty-foot sailboat in the middle of a beautiful lake when all breeze comes to a sudden and complete halt) because of their uneasy, ambivalent feelings about wanting The Money.

Perhaps the cultural roots of that ambivalence trace back to the famous, oft-misunderstood biblical dictum, "the love of money is the root of all evil." That aphorism, penned by an aging Paul to a young Timothy (who evidently had grown up without much of a father) has been misquoted to death: "*Money* is the root of all evil." *Money: Look out! Evil! Bad juju! Dangerous stuff!*

No: let's set that record straight. It's the *love* of money, says Paul, that gets people into trouble.

(Of course, then there's Mark Twain, who said, "*Lack* of money is the root of all evil." And I have the funny feeling he had his tongue only partly in cheek.)

Why is the love of money dangerous? Because it's a seductively easy way to lose your way.

"Loving The Money" means you've become captivated by the shorthand, forgotten the reality for which it stands. You're staring at the road directions as if they were the destination—as the Buddhists say, you've confused the pointing finger with the moon to which it points.

If you forget about what The Money means *to you*, why it's important *to you*, then sooner or later your business will come to a grinding halt.

That's true for your people, too, by the way—which is why it's your job as a sponsor to know what The Money means to each person you're working with. (If they should start to forget, at least one of you knows and can bring it up again.)

What's more, what people want changes. This is surprisingly easy to forget. All of a sudden, I'm using the same shorthand

("$5,000 per month" ... "financial freedom" ... "reaching Diamond Director," etc.)—only I don't really know what it stands for any more. I'm standing here, knocking on the door to an exclusive club, this big guy pokes his head out and grunts, "Password?" and I'm pretty sure I *know* the password—but am not so sure whether or not this is the door I really meant to enter.

I once heard Hyrum Smith, the cocreator of the Franklin Planner, teach a course in how to use the planner. At one point in the day Hyrum asked us, "Do you know why people do things?" and I'll never forget how profoundly his triumphant answer reverberated, obvious though it looks here on paper:

"They do things because they have *Reasons*."

Hyrum's training, and indeed the whole Franklin idea, was not about efficiency or productivity so much as it was about the crucial importance of remembering your Reasons.

The truth is, achieving financial success in this business takes tremendous persistence and endurance. Is it worth it? Honestly, no ... *Not unless you have good Reasons.*

Your Reasons, and the results of your Reasons—not The Money—are what you need to love.

Increase Your R.Q.
Three Ways to Improve Retention Through Leadership
February '97

We've all heard that the only way you can fail at network marketing is by quitting too soon. For those of us who know this to be true, attrition is one of the biggest frustrations in this business.

How can so many people quit before giving the process a real fighting chance? More to the point: what can we do about it? How can you address attrition locally, within your own organization?

How can you improve your Retention Quotient?

Here are some of the best ways I know of to improve the retention ratio in your organization. They all come down to the same thing: *leadership*.

KNOW YOUR PEOPLE

As a leader, one of your most important roles is helping people in your group feel connected. That means *knowing* them—knowing who they are, being genuinely curious about their lives, asking questions and really listening to the answers.

When it comes to bringing people into your organization, it can sometimes be helpful to think of network marketing as a "numbers game." When it comes to *keeping* them in, that concept is worse than useless, because this aspect of the business is all about each person's uniqueness.

Leaders know what each person they've brought into the business wants to get out of the business, why he or she made the commitment in the first place. This is the only way you can effectively help people get the results they want.

And by the way, chances are the results they want are not the same thing as the results *you* want. Never assume that others' reasons are the same as your reasons.

Most people will not drop out if they start seeing the results they want early on. Whether it's achieving a certain title (because recognition matters) or getting their first significant check (usually in the $300 range, but it's a good idea to find out what "significant" means to them), reaching that first milestone is one of the surest ways for people to feel connected and committed. Unless you understand who they are and what they want, people in your group will be more likely to be attracted by another opportunity or to simply quit in defeat.

And "what they want" is not necessarily limited to money or title. For a lot of people, the sheer fact of getting the kind of committed support a true leader gives is a milestone all in itself. For many, genuine friendship is a palpable reward of the business. The more lifelong friends you make in your business, the longer the life of your business will be.

Of course, your organization eventually grows to the point where you simply cannot know everyone personally. As that happens, maintaining consistent communication with your group becomes more important than ever. Whether through voice mail, newsletters and other mailings, or conference calls, that communication helps people feel they're part of the larger organization, larger team, larger vision.[14]

People often think they can rely on the parent company to

provide that larger sense of connection. As a leader, you can't afford that thinking: *you* provide that connection.

The tools are there—use them.

LEAD BY EXAMPLE

Network marketing is often described as a duplication business. This is true—but not always exactly in the way the theory suggests. Yes, people duplicate the systems and strategies they're *taught* . . . to some degree. To a much more striking degree, they duplicate what their leaders actually *do*.

Is this a good or a bad thing? Hmm . . . makes you stop and think.

As a rule, if you want your downline to be doing it, *you had better be doing it yourself.*

When you sponsor someone new, you are her model for doing the business—that is, not how you say the business should be done, but how you actually do it. For example, she will tend to approach her own prospects in exactly the same way you approached her. However you trained them (or didn't), that's precisely the way she will likely train her new people (or not).

It's not a bad idea to take some time to build a model of exactly the kind of behavior you want to see in your group. In fact, it's essential to the growth of business. Success doesn't come from waiting for someone else to lead the way.

Once you've taken the time to define this model, you have your own marching orders: your behavior is the blueprint for your group.

Network marketing is one place where you simply cannot get away with not "walking your talk." And the beautiful thing about leading by example is that new leaders *will* spring up all over the place. In this business, "leadership" is not some abstract quality or rarified trait. It's not talking from a stage or looking good in a photo shoot. Leadership is action: it's doing the things it takes to build the business.

Do that effectively, and duplication is inevitable. And so is the success that keeps people involved.

CREATE AND UPHOLD THE RIGHT ATTITUDE

There is something powerful about attitude, and there is something scary about it. The powerful thing about attitude is that it can spread like wildfire. This is also the scary thing.

An organization with a solid, entrepreneurial attitude of determination is headed straight for success. On the other hand, an organization of people who complain about their problems and worry that every new obstacle means *we're all in big trouble* is headed straight for nowhere.

There will always be problems. How big they become depends on how you regard and approach them. And yes, how you regard and approach them *will* duplicate—like wildfire.

Leaders focus on solutions. Leaders consistently view circumstances as something that we create, not something we react to.

Leaders are not derailed by challenges, not because they are in denial but simply because they understand that challenges do not mean the sky is falling. Challenges simply mean that we have a pulse and life is unfolding. Challenges are there for us to exercise our ability to mobilize our resources and grow.

As a leader, you are in a position to create the attitude that will prevail in the group. This is both a huge responsibility and an even greater opportunity to keep your organization facing the right direction.

This is more than lip service to a principle: this is truly a make-or-break factor in determining the future of your organization. Your mental and emotional posture is incalculably powerful in shaping the course of the organization.

In fact, the single factor that most strongly determines the long-term health and vitality of your organization is the bearing, mindset and character you bring to the table day after day—especially when faced with challenges. Tools, techniques, training, information . . . these are things people can always get elsewhere. The attitude of their leader is something they will invariably get from you, and that is something irreplaceable.

So there you have it: a three-part yardstick for measuring your R.Q. If people are dropping out of your organization, examine how well you know them, what kind of action you are modeling for them, and what kind of attitude you are providing to shape their business.

The key to retaining your downline is providing the leadership to help people feel connected to you, to the products, to the company, to network marketing itself, and to their own inevitable success and the realization of their dreams.

Residual Leadership
Don't Let George Do It
February '97

George is a leader. He cares, he listens, he is always there with an encouraging word, a provocative insight, a helping hand. With every new challenge, people look to George. George runs the teleconference, handles his people's tougher objections. At his local meetings, people look to George for new inspiration, refresher tips, and always-useful insights brimming with how-to-do-it practicality. That's George, all right . . . always seems to have his ego in check, too, truly leads from the heart, always with a spirit of giving. Oh, he's not perfect, and he's the first to admit it. But he is one heck of a guy, is George—and one heck of a network marketer, too, and he shares his expertise and experience generously. When George speaks, people listen—dozens, hundreds, even thousands of people.

George is a leader of leaders. There's just one thing wrong with this picture: there's a bit too much George in it.

What would happen if George disappeared for a few months? Or longer? (Mom suffers long illness . . . marriage in trouble, needs undivided George attention . . . George is suddenly diagnosed with a mysterious case of acrophobia, agoraphobia and ariphobia—fear of high places, open places, and dry places, especially Phoenix and Salt Lake City . . .)

His top people don't even want to think about it. Because the truth is, if George doesn't do it, it probably wouldn't get done.

The sternest test of leadership might be this: how residual is it? What happens to leadership's results if you take away the leader?

For networkers headed for the top of their plans, a syndrome sometimes occurs that I call "Diamond Plateau." People reach the next-to-the-top achievement title (in my company, it's Diamond, the top being Double Diamond)—and can't quite seem to make it to the top title (whether Double-, Blue, Royal Crown Cola or Crystal Palace Diamond). "I just can't seem to make that last lap. I'm really clear on this goal, but my people just aren't keeping up."

Usually the best strategy at Diamond Plateau is this: let go. Understand that it's not you who's going to create the Crystal Palace Diamondhood, anyway: it's your co-stars who are taking you there.

Let them.

Don't George them.

It's a paradox. When you start building your business, you are the prime mover. It is you who generates all the action. If you don't do it, it doesn't get done. At a certain point, the balance shifts, from full-time starring role to Best Supporting Actor. It's no longer about you. Morgan Freeman in *The Unforgiven*, Sean Connery in *The Untouchables*: breathtaking star quality—in a supporting role.

Getting the job done (the prospecting, enrolling, coaching) is the easy part. The harder part is finding co-stars, helping their star quality emerge, and then, without simply abandoning them, easing back and getting out their way.

Lao Tzu said that when a truly great leader is in charge, the people don't even notice he's there: they think they're doing it all by themselves. Jesus called it "washing the feet" of those you lead.

We call it "residual leadership." A little less George—and a lot more of George's results.

Build to Last
Create a Culture of Commitment
September '98

What are the most important factors in determining whether or not a particular network marketing situation will last for the long haul? What factors determine whether or not this is the right opportunity for you, one where you can safely invest your hopes and dreams along with your time and effort?

There are of course two major factors to look at: 1) product and 2) company, which includes founders, management, history and compensation plan. Making this choice carefully is crucial, because once made, it is essentially fixed in stone: you can't do anything to change product or company. (As with marriage, there's no point saying, "I'll join them because I'm sure that with my help, they can change!")

But there is a third factor, and it is one you can do a great deal to change. In fact, you can *determine* it—and it has everything to do with the health and longevity of your business. That factor is your own organization's *culture*.

The truth is, while the first two factors, product and company, are more visible, and they're what we tend to promote, it's really the third factor that is often the push-comes-to-shove glue that binds an organization together, keeps people going and coheres them to your business when times are tough, either professionally or personally. When your people run into problems, they *may* be kept in the game by loyalty to the product line or to the company, but it's most often loyalty to their *relationships*, to the connections with the people with whom they actually interact, that keeps them committed.

In fact, while a positive personal experience with the products and a firm belief in the company are both powerful ingredients of coherence, neither of these alone will really create a strong culture of commitment, nor will both of them together—because the day-in/day-out process of building and maintaining a network marketing business does not occur in a human vacuum, but in the context of the organization's culture.

The company and product provide only a foundation. Choosing a strong foundation is essential—but only the beginning. No matter how good the products and how artful the company's support, building upon that foundation a business culture that will stand the test of time is a responsibility that rests on the shoulders of the distributors themselves.

In other words, it's *your* job to create it.

What sorts of traits define an organizational culture that will go the distance? Ask any leader in this business and you'll get all sorts of answers: trust, integrity, personality, dedication to training and education, fun, excitement, frequent acknowledgment, support, teamwork . . . While the strongest traits are fairly universal, every culture is unique in its emphasis.

But if it's a long-lasting, durable community of cooperative commerce that you want to build, I think there is one characteristic that stands head and shoulders above the others:

Commitment.

By this I mean specifically *your* commitment. And I'm not speaking of anything especially high-falutin or esoteric. I mean simply that rock-solid, unshakable clarity that *you are not going anywhere*: that whatever else happens, you'll still be here.

Of course, you'd love it if everyone else duplicated your level of commitment, too, and you want to seek to have that happen. But it won't. It's one of those ideals that one strives for but never fully attains. Some will match your commitment with their own; many will not, and that's all right. For the culture to hold, you don't need *everyone* to evince this level of unswerving resilience. You just need to reveal it in *yourself*. There will always be times when your downline falters, when the course feels rocky, and people look to you to hold up a level of unflappable commitment that provides a power source upon which they can draw.

There's a biblical scenario that beautifully illustrates this.

Shortly after leading the Israelites across the Red Sea, Moses leads his people into a battle where their side is badly outnumbered and the odds are not looking so hot. Joshua leads the ground troops, but it is Moses who provides critical aerial support. Standing atop a nearby mountain, he simply holds his hands in the air. The sight of him up there, hands outstretched, keep the people going. In fact, Moses finds that every time he lowers his hands, the tide of battle starts turning back the other way—so he *has* to keep them airborne.

Eventually his arms grow simply too tired to stay up. (After all, Moses is only human. Hey, sometimes the same thing happens to us, too.) He *has* to lower them—yet this is precisely what he *cannot* do.

What to do?

Finally he finds the solution: he has two aides stand at his sides and literally prop his arms up in the air. The arms never go down, and that unvarying show of support wins the battle.[15]

Oftentimes, that's exactly what you need to do. And I'm not speaking about those rare times of true crisis that can crop up occasionally, like when *20/20* runs a piece of horrible press that claims your company is a fraud, or your competitors send a mailing to everyone in your company claiming their product is ten times more powerful at half the price. Those times require leadership, too—but those epic PR calamities are rare. I'm talking here about the everyday crises of confidence that occur all the time. Joe's best prospect decided that "this is just not a good time to start something new," or Joyce ran her first major home meeting, with fifteen guests confirmed, and nobody showed up.

In those moments, for Joe and Joyce, the odds don't look good. They are outnumbered. They need to look up and see your arms outstretched. (Even if you need two aides, like your upline, to help you hold them up.)

Commitment simply means staying power. Staying stubbornly on course and not letting *circumstance* dictate or sway your *stance*.

In the long run, your particular gifts or skills as a teacher, speaker, recruiter, enroller, trainer or manager don't matter. What does is your staying power: your ability to hold onto people's dreams, to be unwilling to be affected by problems. Your people will feel kicked in the teeth. Their best people will quit, their new prospects will fail to keep appointments, the company will suddenly not deliver on a promise or unexpectedly change a policy. *Your* response to those mini-crises will be the *number one factor* that determines your people's ability to ride them out and hang onto their own vision.

My friend Gilles Arbour defines a sponsor this way: "a sponsor's job is to be the steward of other people's dreams." You need to believe in your people—often more than they do themselves.

When people are starting out, no matter how confident or skilled they may be on the surface, the bald fact is that they have *no evidence whatsoever* that this thing is going to work for them. They look to you for that evidence.

You need to be the still point of their bewilderingly turning world. You are the keeper of the flame, the bearer of the torch, the holder of the vision.

Want to know what it takes to be a successful leader in this business? Hold out your arms—and keep them there.

Don't Present!
Be Kind to Your Friends: Give Them an Invitation, Not a Machine-Gun Blast of Words
September '98

In just a moment, I'm going to offer you a precious secret, a secret, in fact, that is worth a fortune. I'm going to offer you the ultimate secret to giving smashingly successful, knock-em-dead presentations when you're starting out in this business.

And here's the really amazing part: this incalculably valuable secret is contained in a *single word*.

But first, let me ask you a question.

Have you ever known anyone who tried his or her hand at network marketing, but didn't make any money at it and quit within a few months or even weeks after he or she started? Sure you have; you've probably known a bunch of people who fit that description. I'm not psychic, but I'll bet I can tell you what happened: *they talked to their friends.*

This is probably the number one reason that people experience early failure in their freshman forays at network marketing: they get signed up, get enthusiastic, get a little knowledge (which as everyone knows, is a dangerous thing)—and then they go talk to their friends.

You might as well *shoot* your friends.

This is the single most common problem I see in people's

failed prospecting and enrolling efforts: they say too much.

Okay, are you still waiting for that secret? The one that holds the key to new distributors making killer, close-em, lock-em-up presentations? Remember, it's a single word. Here it comes . . .

Don't!

The system my network marketing organization is using at the moment starts with a ten- to fifteen-minute phone call. While we don't literally script the call, here's pretty much how it goes:

> *"Hey, Randall, this is John Mann. We met at the . . ."*

And if we're only vaguely connected, I'll remind Randall who I am and how we happen to know each other. (This part is flexible. If Randall is my brother, I probably don't need to remind him how we happen to know each other.) Then, once Randall recalls who I am:

> *"Did I catch you at a good time? . . . I'm working with a new business, it's going really well, and I'm looking right now for one key new associate to work with in this area. I thought of calling you first, because you're such a people-person and you're respected by so many people in the community . . ."*

And here I'll say whatever wonderful qualities, skills or other attributes Randall has that I think would make him a great partner to have in my business (I should point out that it's a good idea to give this a few moments' thought *before* the call)—

—and then I'll get right to the question that is foremost on my mind, the question I want to get to within no more than two or at most three minutes from the beginning of our call:

"Do you have ten minutes?"

Usually, Randall will say something like, "Sure." If he says, "Now is not a good time," then I'll make a date with him for ten minutes on the phone within the next day or so, when he *does* have time—and I'll let him know that I do really mean ten minutes, not twenty-five or forty. Then I'll say:

> *"Hang on a sec, I'm going to connect us to an eight-minute message that tells the whole story from A to Z."*

And I'll three-way Randall into a pre-recorded eight-minute audio presentation.

Here is what makes this approach so effective: I'm not on the phone long at all, and most importantly, I'm not presenting—*I'm only inviting.*

Presenting effectively takes some real skill. Pretty much anyone *can* develop that skill, but for most, it takes some time and good training.

Inviting does not take skill. It's easy. We do it all the time.

That's why this method works.

Now, you may not have an eight-minute pre-recorded audio presentation to bring your prospects to hear, but that's not important: you have *something*. It could be a CD or audiocassette to put into their hands (or in the mail); a live conference call held by your upline (lots of organizations hold daily live recruiting calls for exactly this purpose); a web site to go see, event to come check out, skilled upline to put on the phone. Whatever. Something that tells the story—and that isn't *you*.

The thing I like about a short pre-recorded message (and I'm starting to think five minutes might be better than eight) is that I can three-way the person to that message right then and there: no delay; no need for action on their part, like getting themselves to a meeting; and since I go along with them to hear the message, I'm there with them and can control the process. But it's a highly flexible formula: you can plug in almost any sort of tool. The key is that *you don't make the presentation*: the tool does that job.

There, we've come back to the key—this is the expanded version of that secret I revealed to you earlier. Before, I said it was just one word:

Don't!

But the full-length, unabridged version of this presentation secret is actually four words:

Don't present, just invite.

And here's what I've found: when people report that this process isn't working for them, *in every single case*, it's because they are saying too much.

Today, since I began writing this article, I've gotten two phone calls from people in my organization. One was a brand new distributor who said he was really excited and couldn't wait to start talking to his friends. The second was someone who called to report that a new person in her downline was "really enthusiastic—she's already talked to fifteen of her friends!"

I nearly had a coronary.

No! Don't go talk to your friends! Get thee to a Getting Started Training, ASAP, find out how the process works, and do it right.

In a former career as a nutritional counselor, I had a recurring experience that told me something fascinating about the limits to people's powers of self-observation. I'd tell a client that he might consider cutting down on dairy products, only to hear him assert, "Oh, I hardly ever eat any dairy." Hmm. Then where was all that bronchial mucus coming from? Upon closer questioning, I'd discover the cheese, sour cream, cream for coffee, butter on everything, yogurt for snacks, and assorted cornucopia of various other dairy products that densely populated his daily fare. But because he didn't actually drink *milk* per se, he thought he was telling the literal truth when he declared that he "hardly ever touched dairy."

I find the same thing in network marketing. Here's a conversation with George, whom someone in my group just sponsored this week:

> GEORGE: "I'm not having much success with this invitation call."
>
> ME: "Are you doing it the way we talked about—not presenting about the business, just asking if they have ten minutes and then going with them to the pre-recorded message?"
>
> GEORGE: "Well . . . yeah."

Uh-oh. That "well . . ." is a telltale clue.

> ME: "Give me a for-instance. What did you say on your last call?"
>
> GEORGE: "Well, let's see. I called my friend Kevin, and he wasn't even interested in going to hear the eight-minute message."
>
> ME: "What did you say to him when you first got him on the phone?"

GEORGE: "Let's see . . . I told him I was in a new business, that the products had helped me and my family a whole lot, and I knew he'd be good at this because he was already involved in nutrition, and that this would be a great way to earn an extra thousand dollars a month—or if he wanted to and really applied himself, that he could probably earn as much as ten times that amount, like my sponsor is doing, and . . ."

Stop! You see what happened? George called Kevin and then presented *like crazy*. He probably never used the word "presentation," so he honestly thinks he didn't present—but present he did.

If you're going to call your friends and present to them right off the bat, tell 'em all about your product and opportunity, shoot the whole informational nine yards . . . it would be quicker, easier, kinder and more painless to simply go over to their house and shoot them.

But if you want to provide them with the best possible opportunity to take a serious look at what you're doing and see if there might just possibly be something there for them . . . then *don't present*.

Just invite.

The Cello Lesson
If You Can't Sing It,
There's Nothing There to Play
March '00

Playing the cello since the age of 13 has given me the opportunity to study with quite a few masters of the instrument. The
most fascinating cello lesson I ever had was from a maestro in
Cambridge, Massachusetts. Having heard a great deal about
him, I was apprehensive as I sat down in front of him and took
bow in hand.

He asked, "What are you going to play for me?" I said,
"Haydn, C-Major Concerto." He said simply, "Play," sat back,
closed his eyes, and prepared to drink the sound.

I had learned the entire first movement to perfection, I
thought. I drew a breath and plunged in. But I'd completed only
the first section when he said, "Stop." I looked up.

"That was very nice. Again, please." Again? But I hadn't
even gotten to finish the movement! Okay. I reassembled my
concentration, drew another breath, prepared for a glorious
seven-minute sky dive, and again began the sonorous opening
passages of the great C-Major.

This time he stopped me after just the first eight notes.
"Again, please," he said. I started over. Eight notes. "Stop. Please,
again." Furrowed brow. Beads of sweat. Another breath. Eight

notes—"Stop."

Now I really stopped. I looked at him. He looked at me. He said, "Your cello sounds marvelous. Now I want your cello to disappear. I want to hear *you*. Try it again." Eight notes. "Again." Eight notes. "Again." Eight notes. "Stop."

Then he did something unexpected. "Here, look . . . put your cello down for a moment. Sing it to me."

I protested, "Sing the Haydn Concerto? I don't think I can sing that." (I am a decent cellist. Pavarotti I am not.)

"If you can't sing it," he told me, "then there's nothing there to play. So sing it."

I sang it, over and over. Eight notes, the maestro stopping me each time. After the ninth or tenth try I must have found the conviction in my voice that he was listening for, because he stopped me once more, this time agitated with excitement, and exclaimed, "That's wonderful! Now do that with your cello." I picked up the cello, played those eight notes—and he smiled.

As we enter the year 2000, we're all frantically trying to figure out what kind of impact the Internet is having (and is going to have) on network marketing. "Network marketing in the Internet age" is still more of a question than an answer. Scratch the surface of most companies' confident claims and ambitious campaigns, and you'll find most are still testing, still experimenting, still worrying.

We know this new technology will play a major role in our business. The Internet will remove barriers to entry and productivity and dramatically amplify our capacity to communicate. It is a vastly higher tech—and it will bring forth a vastly higher touch.

We just aren't sure how yet.

Like the audiocassette, the conference call and desktop publishing, the Internet will be used (and has been used) clumsily at first. Like the fly-by-night ads that promise "We will build your downline for you!" the Net holds the allure, the illusion, that new technologies always leave, whispering promises like perfumed veils draped seductively at our front door: *we'll make your life easier*.

But the truth is, they don't, and won't. They don't build your business for you and they won't make your life easier. True, they make the mechanical, technological, fundamentally impersonal functions of your life easier. They give you more room to get down to the business of being human, of communication and relationship. But make your *life* easier? Ha!

The real tasks of this business, the tasks of leadership and relationship, are probably the hardest things we do. That's why machines can't do them.

Web pages will never build your business, no more than audiotapes or teleconferences. They can be marvelous instruments. What builds your business is *you*.

If you can't sing it, then there's nothing there to play.

So sing it.

Leaders Hold a Vision
Your Job Is to Show Others Your Faith
May '00

Master motivator Zig Ziglar recently said, "People with hope take action. Encouragement is the fuel on which that hope runs. That encouragement is what everyone needs."[16]

That's a great job description for a network marketer: you are the fuel on which others' hopes run. You create a context for others' actions by articulating and embodying that hope.

The apostle Paul (at least I think it was him, the scholars still aren't entirely sure) enunciated an intriguing leadership concept: "Faith is the substance of things hoped for, the evidence of things unseen."[17] When people start out in this business, they *hope* it will work. But hope alone is not a force sufficient to keep them in the game long enough to get results.

In Paul's original Greek text, the word we translate as "substance" is *hypostasis*, which literally means "standing under." Look inside the English word "substance" and you'll find the same concept. That's a good definition for faith and for vision, too. Your *stance* is where you stand, your thoughts and ideas, your wants and intentions—and your hopes. Faith is what exists behind or *under* your stance.

Sound esoteric? It's wonderfully practical. The single biggest challenge to any young and growing organization (as with any young and growing person) is the constant current of emotional disorder that swirls around within it. Your fledgling business-builders are surrounded by doubts, fears and disbelief—both others' and their own. Your job as a leader is to *hold the vision* for your people—the company's vision, the industry's vision, your own vision. *Their* own vision. They count on you and rely on you to do this. It is perhaps the biggest job you have.

Virtually everyone who follows you, or who *may* follow you, is to some degree infected by a universal epidemic of low financial self-esteem. People are just *looking* for evidence that "this won't work." Your evident skillfulness at what you do won't help the situation, either: the more impressive your skill at speaking, presenting, or performing the more likely the other person is to say to him- or herself, "That might work for you—but I'll *never* be able to do that!"

Those swirling currents of doubt, fear and skepticism that bathe your people's psyches are what surrounds their stance—literally, their *circum*stance.

One of the most important leadership attributes you can bring to your prospects and to the people in your organization is your clarity about what you're offering. If you are conflicted or discontented, apologetic or defensive, they won't "catch the vision" from you, they'll instead catch *your ambiguity* like the infectious disease that it is.

The people who look to you for leadership don't need you to have all the answers or to be sure to the point of fanaticism. They want you to have the unshakable courage of your convictions. They want to know that you know what you're talking about. They don't necessarily want you to always be in charge, but they do want you to lead the charge.

The moment your vision falters—your substance—is the moment their faith starts to fade too, eroded by the entropy of their circumstance.

Those are the two forces—your substance and others' circumstance—that battle for influence over their *stance*, over what they believe and feel, which determines the decisions they make and the actions they take. This goes for prospects, too. Sponsoring is not an event, it's a process. In the course of that process your confident vision and their context of motivational hydrogen-death play tug-of-war.

Some people look as if they're ready to set the world on fire once they join your business, your organization, your cause. Don't believe it. Everyone, absolutely everyone, needs to be not just signed and enrolled but also re-enrolled, and re-enrolled again.

Circumstance will serve as a continual drag on their confidence in the business; that's why a simple "info pack" or "follow-up kit" from your company won't do the job. People need more than informational content; they need emotional content, personal content, belief content. They need the most important thing you have to offer, which is something they cannot get from anywhere else. They need leadership. They need your unshakable substance. They need your faith.

They need *you*.

You are the evidence of what they can't yet see.

You Are What You Think
Review: Three Success Classics
July '00

AS A MAN THINKETH
By James Allen

As a Man Thinketh is considered by many the flagship in the entire fleet of success literature. Written around the turn of the twentieth century, James Allen's poetically succinct treatise proposes on its first page that "mind is the master weaver, both of the inner garment of character and the outer garment of circumstance."

Read as an armchair self-help book or sourcebook for platitudes, Allen's hundred-year-old prose is distant enough in time and culture to allow for a comfortable holding at arm's length. However, taken to heart, its words are an imposing and stern taskmaster. The following, for example:

"The circumstances which a man encounters with suffering are the result of his own mental inharmony . . . Suffering is always the result of wrong thought in some direction."

Or, "Disease and health, like circumstances, are rooted in thought . . . The people who live in fear of disease are people who get it. Anxiety quickly demoralizes the whole body and lays it open to the entrance of disease; while impure thoughts, even if not physically indulged, will soon shatter the nervous system . . . Change of diet will not help a man who will not change his thoughts."

Ouch! Allen takes Epictetus's famous dictum, "If a man is not happy, it is his own fault," and wields it like a broadsword.

However, facing Allen's thesis head-on in all its implications is a double-edged proposition. On the one hand, it is a highly sobering read: a serious once-through of its fifty-two little pages will effectively strip away any and all accretions of alibi you may have acquired through the compromises of a lifetime, leaving you quite naked with all the truths of your life as created by its architect, that is, you.

At the same time, Allen's guidebook will also effectively equip you to the task of straightening any bent pathways in your life and building upon that exposed foundation whatever edifice of life experience you choose.

As a Man Thinketh could easily be read in a sitting, but I do not recommend it. The preferred course with a book like this would be to absorb a chapter at a time, highlighter in hand; a chapter an evening makes this a one-week project. (When I first read it, I broke the longish second chapter, "The Effect of Thought on Circumstance," into two bite-sized evenings for more careful and thoughtful chewing.)

If you were to choose a single book to have always on your bedside table, from which to take rejuvenating nightly nips before sleeping or daily draughts before rising, *As a Man Thinketh* would get my vote.

THINK AND GROW RICH
By Napoleon Hill

Think and Grow Rich is perhaps the best known of the success books. In its 250-plus pages, Napoleon Hill takes the poetic threads of Allen's philosophy and from them weaves a novel-length tapestry. Where Allen says his book is "suggestive rather than explanatory," Hill's is fully explanatory indeed.

Think and Grow Rich also reads a bit like a mystery novel. Hill begins by describing how, when he was "but a boy," he was casually given "the money-making secret which has made fortunes for hundreds of exceedingly wealthy men"—that this "secret" was "carelessly tossed into my mind" by the steel magnate Andrew Carnegie. What is this "secret"? Hill is intriguingly coy about naming it, which is good story-telling, because it makes us want to know the answer all the more. And it (the "secret"), not Hill nor Carnegie, becomes the protagonist of the story.

Carnegie challenged the young Hill to spend at least two decades studying the lives of the super-successful and articulating this "secret" which they all held in common. Hill took the challenge; the rest of the book traces his discoveries.

Think and Grow Rich is also shot through with delightful anecdotes that illustrate his various theses: from the genesis of the conflict that led to the drafting and signing of the Declaration of Independence, to the "$600 million after-dinner speech" that led to the creation of U.S. Steel, to the creation of the Coca-Cola Company.

One of the most charming (and most pedagogically potent) characteristics of the book is the fact that Hill is, again, quite obtuse about overtly identifying "the secret." Unlike the how-to success manuals churned out these days by the hundreds, which seem never to tire of coming up with clever anagrams, catchy phrases, sequences of aphorisms and other ways to make their "success formulae" stick in your mind—presumably so that you could remember the "secret" later on even if you were barely paying attention when you read it—Hill makes the (correct) assumption that the reader who will actually use his wisdom is willing to work for it.

"The secret to which I refer cannot be had without a price, although that price is far less than its value. It cannot be had at any price by those who are not intentionally searching for it. It cannot be given away, it cannot be purchased for money, for the reason it comes in two parts. One part is already in possession of those who are ready for it."

As mystical as this may sound, Hill's treatment of the central idea is rigorous and thorough. By about the midway point of the entertaining read, you begin to realize that you are following a well-organized progression, starting from such fundamentals as Hill's treatment of the tangibility of thought and the importance of vividly articulating goals ("Thoughts are Things," he says), to "Desire" and "Faith" in the early chapters, to later chapters on the "Master Mind" concept, "The Sixth Sense" and Hill's conception of intuition and spiritual insight.

An autobiographical note:

Years ago, I decided one day that I was tired of being poor, of struggling from dollar to dollar, but knew that I had no knowledge, expertise or background in business. Shortly thereafter, I found myself reading *Think and Grow Rich*. It was a revelation, and I was absolutely thunderstruck by what I read. I vividly recall being captivated by this paragraph:

"Our brains become magnetized with the dominating thoughts which we hold in our minds, and, by means with which no man is familiar, these 'magnets' attract to us the forces, the people, the circumstances of life which harmonize with the nature of our dominating thoughts."

If we'll put ourselves in the necessary frame of mind, Hill said, the appropriate vehicle or mechanism for success will present itself. (This is, in fact, "the secret" around which Hill's entire thesis is artfully wrapped.)

I was intrigued. I believed what I read and followed the author's suggestions. He proved to be right. When I first read that passage, I had never heard of network marketing; within a few months, I was laying the foundation for a network organization that would earn me more than two million dollars over the following decade.

This is a book worth reading—carefully.

THE GREATEST NETWORKER IN THE WORLD
By John Milton Fogg

John Milton Fogg's "network marketing fable," as it was called in its early printings, takes the Allen-Hill theme one valuable step further. Where Allen says that your thoughts form your character and circumstance and Hill details how your thoughts create your financial success, Fogg's story builds upon these ideas to show how one can design one's thoughts to create a successful network marketing business.

Included in distributor kits, sponsoring packs and training programs for years now, Fogg's book has sold more than a million copies in eight languages—and it's not hard to see why. In the course of his instructional tale, the author uses the fictional narrator's struggles to understand the master's lessons as a vehicle for the exposition of dozens of the most crucial success principles in the business. *The Greatest Networker* is not a how-to-do-it manual, such as the Gage, Yarnell or Kalench classics. It is more of a how-to-*be*-it manual and as such, complements those books well.

The real value of *The Greatest Networker* is that where most such books brush lightly, Fogg takes a subject—for example, changing habits of thought, the nature of learning, or how we form beliefs—and unwraps it thoroughly and with penetrating insight. Fogg has studied with some of the best, and it shows.

Like the book's nameless protagonist, Fogg has served as an often anonymous force for others' success in this industry, championing many now-famous success stories. *The Greatest Networker* will give you a glimpse of how he's done that—and how you can, too.

"What Have You Done for Me Lately?"
Keeping Leadership in Perspective
September '00

If we were to elect a patron saint of network marketing from the annals of history, Archimedes would get my vote.

Archimedes, you may recall, is the man who yelled, "Eureka!" when he noticed that he had spilled water out of his tub and all over the bathroom floor, and thereby discovered the principle of forced-matrix spillover.

However, that's not what makes him the patron saint of network marketers; what does so is his discovery of *leverage*.

Now, Archimedes was not the first person to discover leverage, but he was the first person to articulate and clearly demonstrate it as a generalized principle. He did this publicly (and rather dramatically) by hooking up an elaborate series of levers and pulleys, pushing on a single lever—and causing a fleet of battleships to move in the water.

Impressive stuff, this leverage.

Over the drum roll leading to his float-the-boats trick, Archimedes was heard to exclaim, "Give me a place to stand on, and I can move the world." It is my favorite one-sentence ode to networking.

However, sometimes when I hear it as expressed by network marketers, it comes out sounding different. Sometimes it sounds more like this:

"From where I stand, I'd say the world owes me."

You see, while leverage works smoothly and invariably in the worlds of geometry and physics, things are not always so in the all-too-fallible worlds of human thought and feeling. We get confused. Shakespeare wrote, "The course of true love never did run smooth . . ." and had the bard but known the trials and tribulations of modern network marketing, he doubtless would have added, "—and that's also true of sponsoring, by the way."

I was sitting once at dinner with my friend John Fogg when, halfway through the meal, he said in a very when-E.F.-Hutton-speaks voice: "Network marketing: it's the most brilliant business system ever created. It would be perfect, except it has that one, fatal flaw . . ."—everyone lean forward now—". . . it involves people."

When you start seeing the results of having gotten that little tiny "you-tell-three-who-tell-three" snowball rolling—that human snowball that can turn eventually into a happy avalanche of thousands of product consumers—it's hard not to notice that you, by your actions, often by your perseverance in the face of challenging circumstance, were the origin of all that snowballing. That you indeed are the cause of two epic chains of events:

1) Because of you, thousands of people have been introduced to these wonderful products and this wonderful opportunity. In many cases, lives have been changed.

2) Because of you, the people who preceded you in this chain of events (that is, your upline) have been immeasurably enriched in many ways, including financially.

Bathed in the afterglow of these two realizations, it's pretty easy to come to the conclusion that you are, in fact, pretty hot stuff. This readily gives rise to two corollary epiphanies:

1) Your downline owes you—*big time!*

2) What's more, your upline owes you, too—*even bigger time!*

Let me set the record straight: no, they don't.

My friend Art Robbins taught a training session years ago that enumerated a series of twenty-two "laws of success" for network marketers. My favorites were this pair: a) don't depend on your upline; and b) don't depend on your downline. Art's observation is not an existential cry of despair over the futility of the human condition. It is a simple call to common sense: stop expecting your success to come from other people's efforts. Count on yourself. Take responsibility for your own success. Yes, this is the leverage business . . . but let's keep it in perspective.

We love our heroes—and sometimes we resent them, too. Writing in our "Letters to the Editor" column about the injustices that routinely parade themselves across network marketing's awards-ceremony stages, one reader offhandedly comments that the "vast majority [the 'little people'] are really the people who make the biggies big." He states this as though it were a self-evident truth of the business. But is it entirely true?

Sure, a network is a team effort; everyone counts. But if that charismatic, driven, laser-focused individual upline personality had not come onto the scene and led the charge, would all those teeming "vast majority" have spontaneously come together to form a consistently, continuously purchasing network? What does your experience tell you? Mine suggests the answer is, "Nope."

It's easy to resent the leaders (the "biggies"), to view them as having "gotten lucky" or been "in the right place at the right time" . . . to see them as the fortunate ones whose success is purely the measure of the team's effort, not of their own. And it's true, sometimes people in leadership positions forget where they came from and how they got there. Yet it's also easy for the rest of us to forget that without the magnetizing effect of the leadership, the team effort likely would never have coalesced in the first place.

Moral:

If you start noticing yourself walking around and muttering, "I am Archimedes, mighty man of mental muscle, mover of many battleships"—take a sober look in the mirror. So you're an eccentric mathematician who spills his bathwater. Talented, dedicated: yes. Master of the universe: no.

If, on the other hand, you start noticing yourself looking at your upline resentfully, saying, "Aw, he's always bragging about those boats he moved, but I was the guy that tied all those knots in all those pulleys; he never could have done it without me!"—realize that until Archimedes came along, those boats were all just sitting there, dead in the water.

And you have to admit: they actually did move.

Your Words
"We Tried to Talk It Over,
But the Worms Got in the Way"
September '00

Your most powerful, important tool is something far more sophisticated than a telephone, palmtop computer or interactive web site, and is far more complex and mysterious than these as well. It is the one tool that every single network marketer, no matter what one's individual style, will absolutely use and must, to some extent, certainly master.

It is your words.

I love the moment in Steve Martin's masterful Cyrano remake, *Roxanne*, when the Cyrano character is dictating a seduction script to the bumbling Christian, who is secretly wearing a headset. "I'M AFRAID," he whispers into the mike; Christian repeats to Roxanne, "I'm afraid!" "Of what?" Roxanne wonders. Comes the whisper, "—OF WORDS." And Christian triumphantly asserts, "*Worms*, Roxanne! I'm afraid of WORMS!"

Words. They have the power to move, to sway, to convey—and sometimes, to blow up in your face.

THEY KNOW YOU BY YOUR VOICE
First, that carrier of words: the voice. If words are the software of communication, your voice is the hardware, and in this

business, you're going to rely on that throat-and-thorax-based acoustical modem more than any other piece of equipment you'll ever own.

You can "dress for success" all you want, floss that million-dollar smile, get yourself posture perfect. But it's not your face that's going to build your business. Let's face it: more than 90 percent of this business happens by voice, and by voice alone.

The voice is personal; seeing your face is not. Don't believe me? Look at a video presentation on the web. The engineers can mess around with the visuals as much as they want, cutting down from normal video (thirty frames per second) to half-speed or even lower, to those six- and eight-per-second frame speeds that make the image look like Max Headroom under a strobe light. Hey, they can even can the illusion of motion altogether and make it a one-at-a-time "slide show." And here's the amazing thing: it still communicates—*as long as they don't mess with the voice.*

Aha, but alter the fidelity of the audio track even a tiny bit—let a fragmentary pause slip in every few seconds, alter the speed or pitch even slightly, distort it any way at all—and suddenly it's utterly unacceptable.

The way a dog knows his owner by the smell, we humans know one another by our voices.

WHAT STATE ARE YOU CALLING FROM?
Years ago I interviewed a man who'd made a fascinating discovery about music and musicians. Dr. Harvey Diamond, author of *Your Body Doesn't Lie*, is a master of applied kinesiology, commonly known as "muscle testing."

In his study of those influences that strengthen or weaken an individual, he had learned that when you listen to Beethoven, say, your acupuncture meridians demonstrate an awareness of the Viennese master's own physiological condition. In layman's terms, if Ludwig was wrestling with a hangover the day he wrote the sonata you're listening to right now, your body resonates to "wrestling with a hangover" like a struck tuning fork. (That isn't exactly how Diamond explained it, but that's the general idea.)

In other words, your voice does far more than simply communicate your *words*. It transmits your *state*.

When you talk on the phone, stand up, walk around, breathe. If you're crouched into a chair and gradually going supine, your caller feels it. Do you really want your best prospects or brand new distributors going fetal on you as they hear your inspiring words?

There are two pieces of equipment I need to conduct a conference call properly: a good portable phone (headset, of course) and a pair of comfortable shoes—or bare feet. I cannot, will not, never do, conduct a conference call sitting down.

And smile when you say that. In fact, smile when you say anything. Better yet, smile for a minute *before* you start the call. It makes a difference. (Endorphins.)

THINGS I LEARNED IN TELECOM KINDERGARTEN

The art of communication over the phone can be a broad topic of study, but only if you want it to be. The truth is, you don't really need to *master* it to be successful; you just need to get the basics right. And the basics are pretty simple.

Never start a conversation with "Who is this?" It's not polite. Always announce who's calling—that is, you—first.

Always ask, "Is this a good time?" within the first minute. There's nothing worse than spilling all your words into your phone when the hearer is struggling to get in a word edgewise to let you know that this is, in fact, *not* a good time.

Always provide a time limit—and always stick to it. Never say, for example, "Have you got five minutes?" or "This'll just take five minutes," unless you really mean that. Let your hearer know how long you genuinely expect this call to take, and then watch that clock as if your life depended on it.

Never take time extensions for granted. If you are nearing the zero hour and can sense that a) you really need some additional time, and b) the call so far is relaxed enough that it feels like that might be okay, then ask, "Jim, I promised you this would take just twenty minutes, and I can see that our twenty minutes is almost up. I feel like we've got about ten more minutes worth of stuff to cover here—do you have the extra time right now? Or should we make a date to talk again soon?"

Always make the call on time—and if you can't, always acknowledge that you're late. If you said you'd call at 7:30, and you could not retrieve your phone from the neighbor's pit bull until 7:45, then start out, "Jim, it's Amanda. I apologize, I'm fifteen minutes late for our call. Is this still a good time?"

Notice you didn't get into the pit bull story. Don't. It isn't necessary to explain *why* you were late; in fact, it's generally better *not* to. It's not of any value to your listener, it sounds defensive, and it ends up wasting even more of the other person's time, which only exacerbates the offense. Just acknowledge the lateness, apologize briefly, and get right to the purpose for the call.

Use the person's name in conversation—but do so only as often as feels natural.

Sometimes we are coached to use the first name as much as possible. This can sound and feel awkward, bordering on manic. Really: does anyone you know in normal conversation say, "Well, Janice, I know how you feel, Janice. I felt that way too, at first, Janice, but you know, Janice, gosh—Janice—darn it, Janice, here's what I found"? Use the first name like a good seasoning: to bring out the flavor of what you're saying, not to smother it.

When you do use the other person's name, get it right! "Duh," you say? Perhaps, but you might be surprised how often we blow this one. My name is "John"; it is rare for an English-speaking person to goof that one up. But my friend Ana McClellan's name is Ana (rhymes with "Ghana," "Botswana" or "mañana"), not Anna (rhymes with "banana," "Ipana" or "Santana"). Guess how often she gets Annanized (rhymes with "canonized" but doesn't mean the same thing), even by business partners who otherwise know her pretty well? And guess how that makes her feel?

And by the way, it is *your* job to get it right, not the other person's to correct you.

Getting a person's name right conveys respect; getting it wrong conveys carelessness and disrespect.

Not long ago, I spoke with a prospective business partner named Chip. I had a one-hour conversation, in which I sagely used his first name, oh, at least six times. So very friendly. Yet he seemed distant, somehow. When I got off the phone, I glanced at my call sheet. Oops. His name is not "Chip." It is "Skip."

If you're reading this—sorry about that, Skip.

MESSAGE ETIQUETTE

I'm sure you know the basic etiquette of e-mail. Don't use all caps because IT FEELS LIKE YOU'RE SHOUTING. (Hurts my ears just to look at it.) Don't leave a message longer than a screenful, unless you're sure the other person has the time and interest to read it. Spell-check before sending. And please, write in actual sentences, with nouns and verbs and capital letters and periods and everything. Your reader deserves to be addressed in actual English, not in Ransom Note.

This is basic staff, but often ignored. And oh, what a difference it makes in how your message lands in the reader's eyes.

Same with the messages you leave on others' voice mail or answering machines. There are three simple rules here.

First, say why you're calling. Don't simply leave a name and number: give at least a one-sentence or one-phrase summary or reference to what the call is about. When I receive messages that simply say, "Hey, John, this is Jack Slater at 800-123-4567, call me [click]"—I generally don't.

Second, don't repeat yourself. Just carefully leave your message. Don't rush: take your time, speak clearly, and explain why you called. If for some reason we miss one piece of your message, we'll replay it. But don't say things twice; it's annoying and distracting.

Third—and it absolutely baffles me that nineteen out of twenty people still don't get this one right—when you leave your phone number, say the numbers s l-o-w-l-y. Saying it once at ninety miles per hour and then repeating it once or twice (again at 90 mph) is of no help. Give it right the first time. Otherwise, your listener has to replay the entire message, possibly even twice, just to get the damn number.

THE MOST POWERFUL WAY OF SPEAKING:
NOT SPEAKING

Think for a moment of the worst, most obnoxious "salesman" stereotype you can picture. Got him conjured up? Now: what is this guy's most outstanding trait? What's the first adjective that comes to mind?

Was it "fast-talking"? Chances are, it was. Why do such characters talk fast? To get in more words. The more words, the more information, the more selling, right?

Hmm. What's left out of this picture? The other person. You.

Trainers in network marketing often sing the praises of enthusiasm. It's true: enthusiasm is contagious and infectious.

But like other infectious and contagious conditions, it sometimes makes the other person get reeeeal quiet and slowly back away.

Don't force enthusiasm. You may be a naturally outgoing, bubbly person, or a naturally slow-talking, measured, quiet sort of person. Either way, there are two things you need to do to be an effective speaker.

First, be yourself. Start with your own personality as your foundation.

And second, learn to modulate. Change it up. Learn how to get excited and show it; and learn how to be quiet and let the other person talk. To paraphrase Ecclesiastes, Pete Seegar and The Byrds: To every conversation there is a season—a time to enthuse, and a time to refrain from enthusing.

The worst offense of amateur layout artists is clutter. Learn how to use "white space" in your conversations. Don't be afraid of silence. You're allowed to think; there's no urgency to fill every microsecond with noise. Don't be afraid to stop your stream of brilliance and give your listener that most considerate of gifts: the pause.

The pause is perhaps the most powerful part of speech there is.

Every network marketer ought to spend one night, early in training, watching two movies: *Mumford* (1999) and *Being There* (1979). They are both hilarious, and both speak volumes about the power of not speaking volumes.

LEARN TO TALK GOOD (OR AT LEAST, GOODER)
I've heard people actually insist on hanging onto incorrect grammatical structures and refuse to use correct ones because the former "sound normal" and the latter "sound affected."

Sorry, I don't buy it. As long as you're using English to communicate, using it correctly makes you more effective. Build a tiny library of classics on language usage, such as *The Elements of Style*, by Strunk and White, or William Safire's *Fumblerules*. They're a lot of fun, and they will help straighten out the kinks in your language's posture. It might *feel* right to say, "Would you like to talk with Bilbo and I?" but it *ain't* right—and it telegraphs illiteracy to the listener, irregardless of whether or not they realize it consciously.

Pop quiz: did you notice what was wrong with that last "they"? Being plural, it didn't agree with "the listener" (singular). And altogether, now: there is no more "irregardless" than there are unicorns. You have a choice: "regardless" or "irrespective." Puhleeze.

If you have the courage, do the following: record yourself talking on the phone, and then listen to the tape. It's painful, I know, but worth it. You will become a better communicator.

Note your verbal tics—"um," "uh," "y'know," "like," "okay?" and "soanywayze"—and set about systematically to exterminate them. It will take time and consistent effort, but it's no harder than correcting a slouch in your posture, and just as beneficial to your well-being.

ESCHEW OBFUSCATION AND DEEP-SIX THE JARGON

Colloquialism is from the Latin for, "like, how you talk every day, okay?" and it refers to one's ordinary, everyday conversational speech. It's amazing how cute phrases from the latest movie worm their way into our language. Remember, "E-e-e-excellent!" "Excuu-u-use *me!*" and "Duh!"?

People actually, like, *say* these things in serious conversation. Gag me.

A teacher of mine once said, "When you are first dating, your boyfriend's pimples look cute. Once you're married, pimples are just pimples." The same is true of colloquialisms. They turn uncute quicker than you can say "Austin Powers."

The colloquialism "twenty-dollar-word" means what you're doing when you use a word like "colloquialism" when a good two-bit word like "slang" would do just as well. Watch out for these. They tend to communicate the message, "Hey, I think I'm pretty important, don't you?" Twenty-dollar words, like $400 toilet seats, are the hallmark of governmental and bureaucratic excess.

In other words (and I use that phrase with care here), don't say, "You stand to effect a significant long-term cash-flow-positive remuneration situation in our opportunity," when you could just as easily say, "You could make good money here."

Then there's the worst of all verbal vermin, for me: the dreaded *jargon*. These are code words or phrases that a particular "in" group has decided mean something decidedly different or more significant than the rest of the populace knows about. I know of no more effective way to distance and offend your listener, and network marketers do it far too often.

The other night on a conference call, I heard a speaker say he likes to tell people to "Get off their RAS." Well, that's just great—if you know what a "reticular activating system" is and what on earth it has to do with growing your business. To most people, it's gibberish at best, insulting at worst.

When you are talking with someone who is new to network marketing, use plain English: terms such as "downline," "upline," "pay group" or "first level" may communicate nothing but the fact that you're excluding them from your in-group conversation.

The worst offenders are the Werner Erhard language contortions, where verbs get nouned, weird constructions abound, and we're all supposed to *get* that this is somehow profound.

When I have a hearing of that speaking, I get a knowing that I'm about to do a leaving.

Reach for the Stars
A Pull Is Always More Powerful Than a Push
November '00

The other night, I was dozing off while listening to NPR on the radio. I vaguely remember hearing fragments of a news story: "New Frontiers in Space Travel Research."

It seems we're breaking ground in an area of science that may lead to a whole new *modus operandi* in out-of-this-world locomotion. It has to do with a technology that allows a ship to access, isolate and amplify the gravitational pull of distant bodies, such as other stars and even planets, thereby overcoming the Earth's gravitational pull. Instead of repelling a space ship away from the Earth's surface by creating the controlled explosion of rocket fuel combustion (an inherently violent process), this technology allows the ship to escape the Earth's pull by being drawn up and out toward heaven by the stars.

Now *that* is one evocative image.

It's often said that there are two reasons we do things: to avoid pain or to seek pleasure. As network marketers are often taught, these are the two great motivational forces: desire to get away from X or to move toward Y.

(You might think of these as your "ex-"—as in ex-job, ex-boss, or ex-husband—and your "Why" —that is, *why* you want to build a successful networking business. The ex-/Why axis.)

Which would you prefer to evoke in a new or prospective business builder: X, the power of moving *away from*, or Y, the power of moving *toward*?

The first, pain avoidance, is palpably stronger. Or at least it is easier to access, simply because so often it is far more vividly present. Most folks can readily describe their desire to escape present circumstance—the dead-end job, high-pressure lifestyle, heavy debt load, the lack of quality time with family.

But the long-term dreams, the answers to the question, "If money and time were no object, what would you do?" . . . they're not so easy. Most people have long forgotten their dreams. It can take some real time, effort and dialogue to tap those—and even then, they're fragile; it's easy to let go of them again. You can evoke someone's dreams on a Sunday evening teleconference; come Monday morning, *boom!*, they're awash in the present they'd love to avoid—and the dreams are suddenly far, far away . . .

As far away as the stars. And that is exactly my point.

There are two ways to escape the gravitational pull of present-day reality. One is the controlled-explosion repulsion of rocket fuel: tapping into how much your prospect hates the grind of his days-for-dollars life. As Randy Gage's famous prospecting tape says, "Escape the Rat Race." The other is the pull of the distant stars.

The rocket fuel of our discontent is dramatic, it is powerful, and it is very present. The downside? It doesn't last. Worse, as soon as some negative associated with the new business comes along—products were shipped late, the company didn't deliver on a promise, a favored prospect quit—that negative produces its own rocket fuel, propelling your new guy *away* from the business. Building your business on the allure of pain-avoidance is sandcastling on a foundation of negativity.

It's a business built on *pushing*.

I'd rather pull.

Take an ordinary window fan. (This demo is cheaper and easier than space travel.) How far can you push a column of air with a fan? Not far: within a few yards, the column of air starts to double back in a mushroom shape. Now, put that same fan in a window blowing out: you can pull a column of air from a single open window clear on the other side of the house, even hundreds of feet away.

To put this another way: how far can you push a rope?

When you push people, they don't go far because they push back (like the column of air) or collapse upon themselves (like the rope). But motivate them by attraction instead of repulsion, and you can pull them vast distances—further than they ever dreamed they could go.

Mark Twain demonstrated this pulling power in his story of Tom Sawyer drawing all those kids into doing his fence-whitewashing chores for him. Tom would never have been able to get his friends to do his work by pushing on them. Instead, he pulled.

I've often heard network marketers say, "I'm moving product, but I haven't really been pushing the business." Their words paint a picture I wouldn't be interested in, either. When you "push" the business, what you typically get in return is pushback: resistance, rebuttal, resentment.

I don't *want* them to "push" the business.

I want them to *pull* the business.

Don't tell people what they ought to do; that's pushing. Ask them questions and listen to the answers: that's pulling. Don't set goals *for* them; that's being a "boss." Support them in setting their own goals, and then hold them accountable—not to you, to themselves. That's being an entrepreneur's coach.

Okay, I need to confess something here. That radio broadcast about space travel? I didn't exactly hear it *as* I was dozing off; I heard it *after* I'd dozed off. That is . . . I dreamed it. I actually have no idea whether or not scientists have ever thought about accessing the gravitational pull of the stars as a means of powering interstellar transport.

If they haven't, I think they should—don't you?

The Myth of the "Ordinary Person"

If "Anyone Can Succeed in This Business," Then Why Doesn't Everyone?

January '01

Network marketing is shot through with contradictions.

"Always be there for your downline; you are responsible for their success—and don't do anything for your downline that they can do for themselves." Got that?

"It's all about leadership . . . and the best part is, it takes no special skills, anyone can succeed!" Okay, I think.

"Be the best you can be, strive to be exceptional—and make sure everything you do is totally duplicable." Say what?!

As contradictory as it all sounds, this is not evidence of a fatal flaw. In fact, anything of lasting value is founded squarely on paradox. That's how life works. Network marketing is a celebration of the exceptional lurking in and revealed through the ordinary . . . for example, Dexter Yager.

The man is a legend of positively Paul-Bunyanesque proportions. You don't get any bigger.[18]

I have never met Dexter Yager; before we did a story on him for this issue, I really knew very little about the man. But I had heard . . . .

Of course, I knew that he has one of the biggest distributor organizations in the world—perhaps *the* biggest. I had heard that he pioneered the basic elements of what today is reverently called "the system" and forms the foundation of network marketing methodologies throughout the profession, from the biggest "boot camp" to the tiniest startup distributor manual. ("Doing a Yager," in some circles, is shorthand for "creating your own comprehensive system and group culture, independent of the company.")

These are all true.

I had also heard that he was basically an unremarkable, ordinary guy who just happened to get lucky enough to be in the right place at the right time.

That last is *not* true.

It never is.

In this business, you'll hear the "Oh, he just got lucky" story turn up with all the annoying regularity of a flat tire's thump-thump-thump. Both tire and story carry about equal weight.

In the course of doing our piece on Dexter Yager, I learned quite a bit about this "unremarkable" guy who fooled all his doctors and recovered from a devastatingly hopeless stroke through sheer determination and will—after first offering his wife a divorce (declined) because he didn't want to be a burden to her.

Ordinary guy. Uh-huh, right.

Are there ordinary aspects to Dexter? Of course. And don't let that fool you for a moment.

The myth is that in this business, ordinary people accomplish extraordinary dreams. Not true. What happens in this business is this: *People who up until now have held themselves as ordinary and have presented themselves that way to the world stop holding themselves that way.* What happens is that "ordinary" people step up to become extraordinary people.

Your dreams cannot become extraordinary without the

whole of you making that same shift. Your dreams are not something that exist independent of you; they are an extension of you. Your dreams are the expression of who you are today, minus the limitations (real or imagined) of your current reality.

Dexter began his interview with us by saying, modestly, that he was an ordinary guy with extraordinary dreams. I say, Dexter Yager was always an extraordinary man. When he discovered network marketing, he stopped masquerading as an ordinary one.

And Dexter's not the only one. I've watched thousands of caterpillar-ordinary people step through the chrysalis of this business model and unfurl hitherto-hidden wings of extraordinary quality and breathtaking ability.

Seeing that happen is the single thing I love most about this business.

True Leadership
Tell Me What to Do—So I Won't Have to Do It
March '01

Among orchestral musicians, there is a favorite story about Fritz Reiner, the brilliant maestro and stern taskmaster of the Chicago Symphony.

Reiner was famous for his tiny, hyper-controlled conducting movements (more or less the opposite of the grand-sweep-gesture Leonard Bernstein school). One day, as a joke, a double bass player brought in a pair of binoculars to rehearsal. As Reiner began conducting, the bass player raised the binoculars and peered through them at the maestro. Without missing a beat (literally), Reiner continued conducting with his left hand while with his right, he scribbled a hasty note and held it up so the bass player could read it.

It said, "You're fired."

That's one leadership style. My father has a different one.

For fourteen years, my father conducted one of the country's most famous amateur Bach choirs, in Bethlehem, Pennsylvania. For some seasons I played in the orchestra. My father's voice is so soft it's often hard to hear in normal conversation, and on a crowded rehearsal stage, practically impossible. However, I have noticed that not a single musician ever misses a word. Why? Because they are so quiet, a dropped pin would sound like cymbals clashing in the *1812 Overture*. Why so quiet? Because they are craning to hear his every word.

I've seen the most cynical, don't-tell-me New York union musician turn into putty when my father makes a suggestion to start this passage with an up-bow, or to take that passage sotto voce so we can clearly hear the tenors. People turn themselves inside out to follow him, and they would follow him anywhere. There are two reasons for this: he is superb at what he does—and he treats them with respect.

That is another leadership style.

Reiner was brilliant with the Chicago Symphony. He would, I submit, have been a lousy network marketer. Why? It's about leadership—and leadership style.

It's like the difference pushing and pulling. How far can you push a column of air into a room with an ordinary window fan? Not far: within a few feet it starts doubling back on itself. But reverse the fan's position so that it is blowing out and you can pull that same column of air from a single open window clear on the other side of the house, even hundreds of feet away.

There is leadership that pushes. And there is leadership that pulls.

How far can one push people? And how far can one pull them? (The question makes me think of Tom Sawyer leading his friends to whitewash the fence. Twain knew about pulling.)

Why is leadership so crucial in network marketing? Because of the nature of the beast. Professionals expect to be told what to do. They expect to show up, do a job (whether or not they "feel like it") and get paid. That describes the Chicago Symphony. It does not describe the Bethlehem Bach Choir. And it does not describe us.

We are amateurs. We inherently don't expect to answer to any authority. We even tout this as a many-splendoured benefit of the business: "Be your own boss, choose your own hours, choose where and how and with whom you work."

We also crave the holy grail of the "duplicable system." Yet there's a funny thing about a duplicable system: it only duplicates when people do what they're told.

A fundamental contradiction: we are professional amateurs. We want a system that tells us what to do, except that we don't want to be told what to do—and pride ourselves on the fact that even when we *are* told what to do, we don't *have* to do it.

What does it take to make this work? Leadership.

We are having a crisis in leadership. You see it everywhere: in politics, in business, in education, everywhere. This isn't news; Richard Brooke, for one, has been saying it eloquently for years. And, adds Brooke, whatever it is you may think your company is selling and you are offering to others—a product, a service, an opportunity, a lifestyle, an income—the greatest gift your business has to offer the world is *leadership*.

I agree with Richard.

What our world needs most these days is leadership: not just the glitz, gloss and gives-good-press media veneer that so often passes for leadership in the public eye (and yes, we have our version of that kind of leadership in this business, too), but true leadership.

When true leadership speaks—even when in a voice as soft as my father's—people listen, because they trust. That kind of leadership, we'll follow anywhere.

First, Do No Harm
And Kiss the Three-Foot Shuffle Goodbye
May '01

The Three-Foot Rule: If anyone near me has three feet, I should step on one . . .

No, that's not right.

The Three-Foot Rule: If anyone comes within a meter, well, I'd like to meet 'er . . .

Nope, wrong again.

The Three-Foot Rule: The first two are for turning and walking away after I've put the third in my mouth . . . Um, wait. *Three feet is exactly half of how many feet you wish I were under whenever I come near . . .* Dang! *Three feet are what it takes to run as fast as you wish you could in the other direction when I start talking about my business opportunity . . .*

Why oh why can't I get this right? Hmm. I know why: I have no love for the "Three-Foot Rule."

Could you tell?

Now, it really (no kidding this time) goes like this: *Whenever anyone comes within three feet, tell her about the business.*

What is it I dislike about this rule? Simply this: what if she doesn't want to hear about my business? Doesn't she have a choice? What if the anxious, excited, driven new network marketer doesn't have the discernment to know when to apply this rule and when not to, and thus verbally beats up on every-one within earshot, irregardless? And ends up doing as much violence to other people's sense of privacy—and to their view of network marketing—as the word "irregardless" does to the English language?

I say, deep-six the Three-Foot Rule—and replace it with the network marketer's Hippocratic Oath:

First, do no harm.

A multiple-choice question: When on the phone or in a face-to-face encounter with a prospect, your number one priority for the conversation should be:

a) Get her to try your product;
b) Get her to take a look at your opportunity;
c) Get her to share with you her core values, her "compel-ling why."

The answer? It's a trick question. The answer (at least, my answer) is:

d) None of the above.

In my book, your first priority in any encounter like this should be:

Make sure to leave this person with a better impression of network marketing itself than when the conversation began.

That way, irrespective of what your prospect chooses to do, you've made the world a safer place for networkers. And that's a productive outcome, regardless.

It's something like the goal of conscious agriculture: *Leave the soil in better shape than you found it.* Hey, future generations will want to farm this soil, too.

Part of attaining to maturity in network marketing is coming to grips with the realization that not everyone is a prospect, no matter how close to you they may be in feet, inches or common interests. The truth: not everyone wants to be part of your business.

Now, don't get me wrong: the world around you is just brimming with potential partnerships, with friendships bursting to be found. The truth of the "cold market" is that the moment you touch it, it begins to warm.

My friend Ana McClellan can prospect anyone, anywhere, anytime. I marvel at how she can spark a conversation in virtually any situation. She makes the Three-Foot Rule come to life, and in her hands, it works. Why? Because for her, *it is authentic.* She is genuinely interested in these people. For her, it is not a "rule," three-foot or otherwise. It is simply how and who she is.

Carol McCall makes a great point about listening: when it becomes a technique, it's no longer listening. It's the same thing with "establishing rapport." Establishing rapport is great—when that's really what you're doing. But if what you're really doing is carefully "dialoguing and relationshipping" with a person, all the while noticing what a fine job you are doing of dialoguing and relationshipping . . . you're not making friends, you're "doing the business." You are not saying, "Who is this person?"—you are saying, "Ah, what a clever networker am I!"

And the other person knows it.

When making friends becomes the self-conscious technique of *friendship-making*, it's really no different from hitting on someone at a singles bar. That's not enrolling; it's *cruising.*

And sure, you might sell a product, even enroll a distributor—but will you still respect her in the morning?

Secrets of a Great Presentation
How to Make Your Presentation Sing and Dance, and Laugh and Cry . . . and Tell the Truth
June '01

A good presentation will do four things. A *great* presentation will do those four things, plus a fifth. A good presentation will sing and dance; it will laugh and cry. A *great* presentation will sing and dance, laugh and cry—and tell the truth powerfully.

HOW DOES A PRESENTATION SING?
Through variation. A dull speaker speaks with the same pitch (high vs. low), same volume (loud vs. soft) and same pace (fast vs. slow) throughout. An engaging speaker plays with all three of these knobs.

Your audience is drawn into your stories, vignettes and messages by the ebb and flow, the *movement* of your speaking. A good movie will do the same: some scenes are long and leisurely; then, as we move nearer to a key point of the story, the emotional intensity picks up—and so does the pace.

The greatest storytellers make their greatest impressions not in what they say, but in the silence—that magnificent pause before a punch line. Think of Johnny Carson, Jack Benny, Bob Newhart, Jon Stewart. Think of George Burns: the funniest thing he ever "said" was the look that greeted whatever inanely

goofy situation Gracie had just presented. The sharpest word-smith is an even sharper pausesmith.

HOW DOES A PRESENTATION DANCE?

I'm not speaking here of the rhythm of your words, but the rhythm of your *images*.

Imagine if John F. Kennedy had said simply, "You should ask, what can you do for your country?" Or if Neil Armstrong had commented, "Well, that's one giant leap for mankind." Would we remember either phrase? I doubt it. Because neither image is paired with its contrast, its counterpointing partner. Neither image dances.

Now, listen:

"Ask not what your country can do for you—ask what you can do for your country."

"That's one small step for a man—one giant leap for mankind."

That's how a presentation dances.

The song "Amazing Grace" is one of my favorites because, among other reasons, it dances. "I once was lost, but now I'm found; was blind, but now I see." The salesman's classic "feel, felt, found" formulation doesn't get any more poetically expressed than this!

Which brings up a good point: one reason that feel, felt, found ("I know how you feel Bob; I felt the same way, first time I heard about this—but you know, here's what I found . . .") is so tried and true is that it has *rhythm*. It dances.

HOW DOES A PRESENTATION LAUGH AND CRY?

You know that people are motivated by two things: the desire to secure pleasure, and the desire to avoid pain. It's like the classic icon for the dramatic arts: the laughing mask, representing comedy, and the crying mask, representing tragedy. "Amazing

Grace" types of stories also evoke both of these dimensions: "I once was broke, but now I'm financially secure; was enslaved, but now I'm a self-employed entrepreneur . . ." (No, it doesn't have quite the majestic simplicity of the original lyrics, but it illustrates the principle.)

A good presentation will offer a before-and-after story, and also weave in a little poignant imagery to more vividly evoke in the audience those twinned feelings of pain and joy.

"My little girl looked up at me and said, 'Mommy, how come you're always at work and I never see you except weekends?' "

The key is to find a gesture, a moment that captures the pathos of the situation and gives it a human face. To say, "I decided I didn't have enough time for my family," is abstract and dull. It conveys your point, but there is no laugh or cry in it. But if you were to say instead, "And in that moment, it hit me—'Laura, you're watching your own daughter grow up on video tape!' "—you've made the same point, but you've made it vivid and *real*.

HOW DOES A GREAT PRESENTATION TELL THE TRUTH POWERFULLY?

Now, I do not mean that merely good presentations are not truthful. But in a *great* presentation, the speaker discovers and shares with the audience a powerful truth—a truth that is discovered in the moment, uniquely and for the first time.

My father attended a very traditional, conservative university as a young man in pre-WWII Germany. He recalls one of his instructors looking up from his podium and announcing, "At this point in the syllabus, I am accustomed to telling the following joke . . ."

That is my favorite example of precisely what does *not* make a great presentation. A *great* presentation is new. It has never been presented before—and will never be presented again. It is

blessed with the sacrament of genuine, in-the-moment *discovery*.

Can a great presentation include certain elements—specific stories, vignettes or images—that you have told before? Of course. It's not as if these poignant and powerful elements of storytelling are used up after only one telling. But if you approach your presentation with the sense that it is routine, you eliminate the possibility of greatness, and thus cheat yourself as well as your audience.

Growing up as a performing musician, I am comfortable on stage. Still, I always prepare for every talk, no matter how brief the time, how elementary or familiar the topic. I have a goal of never giving exactly the same presentation twice—because I want to keep alive the possibility of conveying some powerful and newly grasped truth each and every time I take an audience's time and attention.

No matter how well you know your material, no matter how many times you have presented on this particular topic, no matter how easily you could go onto automatic pilot, here's what I urge you to do before each talk: stop for a moment, adopt an attitude of taking absolutely nothing for granted, and ask yourself:

What is the single most valuable thing I could possibly convey to these people?

Telling the Truth
In Search of the Credible and Believable
September '01

"Dad, when we can afford it, can we hire a misogynist?"

The request was reasonable enough; my son's seven-year-old shoulders were aching for a good massage. Heck, if he didn't have the right word at his disposal, why, some other word snatched from the environment would do just as well. Here's the thing, though: when a seven-year-old bends his vocabulary to his will, it's cute. When adults do the same thing, it's somehow no longer cute.

"When I was a child, I spake as a child," says the apostle Paul sheepishly (at least, this is how I read it), ". . . but now it's time to put away childish things."

I'm with Paul on that one.

Sometimes I think our industry has already gone through its childhood and awkward adolescent years and is finally entering adulthood—a new chapter, one of greater responsibility and maturity. Then I hear more AWESOME!!-speak . . . and have second thoughts.

"John, it's the most unbelievable opportunity! UNBELIEVABLE! I'm telling you, it's absolutely incredible!"

Absolutely incredible. Okay . . . as opposed to, what, *relatively* incredible?

Oh, how I hope my grandchildren see the day when there is not a single network marketer using the words "unbelievable" or "incredible" in presentations. Does it never occur to us that both words literally mean, "You ought not to believe what I am telling you"? This surely cannot be the speaker's intention. When you tell your friends about your "unbelievable opportunity," why are you then surprised when they don't believe it? Isn't that what you just told them not to do?

Oh, c'mon, you're splitting hairs. That's just the way people talk!

Perhaps. But I think there's more to it.

I think the language of grandiose gesture and sweeping superlative betrays a profound ambivalence. I think we have a fascinating love-hate relationship with our own business, or perhaps that's more accurately described as a *belief-disbelief* relationship. I suspect that underneath the exclamation points, many networkers are privately insecure about whether or not this business really works. More specifically, about whether or not it is really going to work *for them.*

Have you ever heard a network marketer bemoan our bad reputation "out there in the world"? It's practically canon—but is it true? From what I can see, most of the "outside world" honestly has very little opinion about network marketing. In fact, most of the "outside world" is barely *aware* of network marketing. There is plenty enough poisoned opinion to go around, though, right *in here*—among network marketers.

No wonder Mark Yarnell once quipped that this is the only business he knows where, when we are under attack, we bring our stage coaches 'round in a circle—and shoot inwards.

If I had a nickel for every time I've heard a network marketer say that his or her company did it right, "not like all those other companies," why, I'd probably have enough nickels to earn that $300 that we always say would prevent the majority of U.S. bankruptcies, but which we for some strange reason never want to acknowledge is what *our* people are actually earning.

Hmm.

One company has routinely boasted as one of its distinctions that it has created more millionaires than any other company. Another has lately been touting its goal of creating 100 millionaires in the next so many years. Now, there's nothing wrong with millionaires . . . but is that really a responsible way to represent our business? I know everyone *wants* to be a millionaire, or at least, so ABC tells us. Truth is, though, millionaires is not what we do best. What we do best is thousandaires and hundredaires.

Sure, our top earners are worth millions. But it's our medium earners who are the true success stories of our profession: hundreds of thousands of people who have been able to carve out a decent way of life, working at home, for themselves, with dignity, pride and a sense of contribution. Frank Keefer puts it beautifully: "I have helped dozens of people cut the chains of economic bondage."[19]

Jay Sargeant explains it this way: "This business rises and falls based on how well it serves the part-timers. At our company, we intentionally don't use slippery or unethical words like 'easy' or 'quick.' There is no such thing as *easy*. We emphasize words and concepts like *focus, work ethic* and *professionalism*."[19]

Hallelujah, amen. Let's put away childish things.

The word "hype" derives from the word *hyperbole*: unreasonable exaggeration. If we believe in the value of this business, let's make a pact: let's stop speaking fluent Hyperbolese and give authenticity a shot.

You know: tell the truth.

Who knows? It's so crazy, it just might work.

Love at First Sight
Forget the Legend of the "Reluctant Heavy Hitter"
November '01

In just a moment, I'd like to bring Bob Roberts up to the stage . . . but before I do, let me say a few words about how Bob first got into this business. Now, it's no secret that Bob and his amazing group are responsible for well over two-thirds of my entire organization. Over the years, you can bet that a lot of people have come up to me and said, "Man, were you ever lucky the day you signed up Robbie Roberts!" But the truth is, Bob was one hardwood character—now Bob, note that I didn't say 'hard-headed'! [obliging laughter from the audience] But seriously, it took a few months of sawing through that tree trunk before we was ready to yell "Timber!" and watch Bobbie fall. Truth is, first time I told Bob about what I was doing, he looked at me like I was just a few squirrels short of a nuthouse. First words out of his mouth was, "What is this, one-a them pyramids?! You crazy?! Wouldn't catch me daid near one-a them rah-rah meetings!" Well, I don't know if you'd say those words was prophetic—or pathetic! [more scattered laughter]—but here he is, ladies and gemmen, my biggest leg and best buddy Bob Roberts, gonna rah-rah you all—and he sure don't look daid to me! [laughter swelling into applause] . . .

Like that story? It's fiction. And I mean, *it's fiction*. It's a variation of the story we love to tell, the story of how the best people in this business are those who first said, "No way!" Those who started out as our biggest rejection stories. Those, in other words, who are here only because of our own persistence in the face of their insistent and categoric refusal to look at what we were offering.

We might even say, our heroic persistence.

"Bob (or Claire, or Jim, or Debbie) was totally negative the first time he/she heard about network marketing . . . but I was doggone persistent—followed up like a doggone a bone, you might say [audience chuckles on cue]—and eventually, Bob-Claire-Jim-Debbie had to take a look just to get rid of me [disarmingly self-deprecating, toothy grin] . . . and the rest, well, the rest is history . . ."

Note the active ingredient in this story-recipe: "because I was doggone persistent." In other words, this is an instructional tale. The reason I am telling it from the stage is that I want all five thousand of you in the audience to be doggone persistent, too. In fact, I want you to *hound* that already-successful-person prospect who tries to run the other way when he or she hears you coming, and I want you to do so in the hopes that you will triumph over the odds—and reel in a truly big dog, I mean big fish.

This is the reasoning behind the oft-told tale of the Reluctant Heavy Hitter. It is a fable complete with Aesop moral:

> *You, too, can land a heavy hitter—if, that is, you are willing to chase them to China.*

And this, alas, is a message with some truly awful consequences.

Now, I'm not saying it never happens. Sure it does, sometimes. But not often. Most of the truly successful people I know in network marketing, first time they heard about the opportunity, had some version of the same response I did:

"Really? Wow. Sounds fascinating. Tell me more."

The concept that in those days was usually called MLM was first explained to me in 1986 by a friend named Bill Tims, a brilliant and talented fellow I'd known from macrobiotic circles. Bill was in Wachters, the venerable marine algae (seaweed) company. With Bill on one end of a long distance call (he was in Arkansas) and me on the other (in New York), there were no visuals to aid the presentation: just words. But I saw the picture immediately—and it was a true case of love at first sight.

That is a story I tell often. Why? Because it, too, is an instructional tale: "I want you to look for people who *get* it. People who fall in love with the idea. Who can't *wait* to get started."

Kim Klaver has put this beautifully: "Your mission is to find those people for whom this is the right thing to be doing—now."

The truth is, I don't *want* you chasing people to China.

I don't want you to chase people at all.

If you have to drag them *into* the business, you'll need to drag them *through* the business—week after week, month after month. If you have to break your neck selling them into the business, you'll have to keep breaking your neck keeping them in the business.

> Q: *How do I convince this guy to join my business?*
> A: *You don't.*

This is not a business of "convincing." The very idea that it takes pestering, arm-twisting and the thick-skulled persistence of Job's dog to enroll "a good one" sets up a set of expectations that does not serve you or the profession well. It teaches all who would listen (and if you remember the power of duplication, you know that there are tens or even hundreds of thousands listening) that people who say they are not interested ought to be pursued, that those who balk and resist are really saying, "Prospect me! Prospect me!" It teaches you to spend your time chasing people who say, "No."

A one-word definition for this strategy: *harassment*.

Can you think of a better way to assure failure—and to guarantee a lowering of our reputation in the process?

Finding the right partners for your business does take persistence. When you find them, you'll recognize them. Chances are, they'll recognize you, too, and see your business for what it is. Maybe even fall in love.

Bright Beams on the Highway
Will the Internet Leave Us for Roadkill?
June '02

It's an inspiring vision: over the past several years as we stepped into a new decade, century and millennium, network marketing has planted its feet firmly out on the highway of free enterprise, standing still, head tall, eyes fixed unblinkingly into the brightness ahead . . .

Oh, shoot. I just realized what I am describing: a deer frozen in the headlights.

Overdramatized? Perhaps a bit, but that's been the feel of it—waiting, gazing, waiting, gazing . . . Gazing at what? At that set of blinding headlights boring down on our business.

In a word, the Internet.

Look out, look out, it's coming right at us, burning up the fiber-optic pavement, accelerating from zero to 100 in less than a decade, the Internet, look out, the Internet, get off the road! Few would actually say it out loud, but many wondered: "Is this thing gonna kill us?"

Some have said, *Yes—we're dead. Network marketing,* they said, *is based on the idea of removing the middleman, connecting consumer to manufacturer—through the distributor. But the Internet will do that now. Distributors, who needs 'em! The only way to survive: mutate!* And lo, the "portfolio approach," a concept as ideologically seductive as communism and just as ruinously impractical—was suddenly resurrected. Hey, why work one old-fashioned company when with a great Internet-driven system, you could work a dozen affiliate programs!

(The portfolio-of-affiliate-programs concept does provide fascinating perspective on one's view of this business. How logical it is depends on your metaphor. "Don't put all your eggs in one basket" may be excellent advice if you're considering stock investments, perhaps less excellent if what you're considering is marriage.)

Once our eyes adjusted to the glare, the truth stood in plainer view: technology can drive recruiting, but recruiting is like flirting—it goes only so far, and then you either get serious, or don't. Individual relationships are what drive this business. Technology can support those relationships, but can neither create them nor render them obsolete.

Internet aside, a more interesting question intrigues me: if the Internet is the headlights, what's the car? After all, it's not headlights that strike and kill deer, it's the machine behind them. What has been rushing toward us on the highway is the eight-cylinder, 300-horsepower engine of full-bore American commerce.

In a word (okay, two), "mainstream acceptance." Far from making us obsolete, the onrush of the Internet is symptomatic of American business heading straight for us. You've heard the expression, "Be careful what you wish for." Well, here comes what we wished for. The question is, are you ready?

Gossip

Review: Gossip—Ten Pathways to Eliminate It
from Your Life and Transform Your Soul,
by Lori Palatnik and Bob Burg

December '02

"The authors, quite sincere and dedicated . . . tell us how to expunge gossip from our lives in order to live in a 'gossip free world, or at least a gossip-free environment.' The authors refer to many biblical laws regarding speech and tell how these laws relate to us today. Reading such, we may be chastened and led down the path to redemption. If not, those who 'speak evil' will develop skin lesions similar to leprosy, according to the Good Book. Yikes! Well, although I have the occasional itch, I hope I'm not en route to leprosy. I try to behave reasonably, in print and out. But maybe I better put in a call to my dermatologist."

There you have it: if this lady says authors Palatnik and Burg are worth the read, you want to sit up and take notice: the passage above is excerpted from a review in the *New York Post*, August 4, 2002, by Liz Smith, the "First Lady of Gossip."

Burg (*Winning Without Intimidation* and *Endless Referrals*) and coauthor Palatnik (a noted author, educator and speaker on Judaism and host of the Toronto television show *The Jewish Journal*) draw on the rich heritage of Jewish storytelling, combined with modern-day vignettes and a liberal seasoning of quotations from famous personalities of all stripes, to create a little something that is both charming and compelling.

Why are we reviewing a book on gossip in a magazine devoted to networking? Well ... the answer is in the question, isn't it? We are the word-of-mouth business, the person-to-person, friends-telling-friends, power-of-the-tongue industry.

In a word, we talk.

Boy, do we talk. And in so doing, we change the world. At least, we certainly *believe* we are doing so, and who is to say our descendants will not look back in 100 years and agree? By the power of our personal testimony over the backyard fences of the coffee shop, telephone and Internet, we spread the word, and we do it more effectively than the priciest Super Bowl ad or most bloated direct mail campaign.

And sad to say, we are also really good at spreading that *other* type of word. You know the word I mean. Hint: it's the one that Burg and Palatnik used to title their book.

"You're with *which* company? Really? You know what I heard about their comp plan ... product line ... president ... ?"

In my seventeen years in this industry, I have seen more lives positively transformed, more people set free of various sorts of shackles and indignities, and more overall ingenuity, productivity and positive *esprit de corps* applied here than in any other venue. And to be truthful, also more instances of ... yes, gossip.

If there is a Bible within arm's reach, grab it and check out what James has to say about the power of the human tongue (James 3:1 ff.): "Look at ships: although they are huge, driven by fierce winds, they can be turned by this teeny tiny rudder in whatever direction the pilot chooses. That's the power of the tongue . . . ." The man ought to know: he was involved in some pretty powerful networking circles and saw both sides of the word-of-mouth coin. In fact, he ended up being hurled off the temple wall and stoned to death because of stuff people said about him in their first-century version of the telephone game.

Obi Wan told Luke that the power of The Force could be used for great good, or for great evil. Since we are the Jedi Knights of this particular Force, it's a lesson we urgently need to know. Palatnik and Burg make a great Yoda.

No Fair! . . . or Is It?

The Physics of Compensation

April '03

No fair! If you're a parent, you've heard this strident mantra, doubtless many times. Grown-ups say it, too, or think it anyway. *No fair!* is the universal human code for, "I don't understand: why did things work out like this?!"

For example: *Isn't it unfair how much our society pays rock stars, sports stars and movie stars, while the unsung heroes and heroines of our world, the ordinary people, the school teachers and beat cops and farmers and firemen, are so grossly underpaid? When you think about it, it's really downright criminal, isn't it?*

Or is it?

Compensation is like achievement: until you understand its governing laws, it seems . . . well, unfair. Most of us grew up with this often-unspoken, three-step rule for how to get things in life:

First, aspire to a worthy goal. Then, work hard. Meanwhile, be a good person.

The key to getting more of what you want, says this paradigm, is simply to pump up the volume: don't just want something, want it *real bad*. Don't just work towards it, work *real hard*. And while you're doing all this, don't just be good, try *really hard* to be a *really good* person.

It makes so much sense. Except for one thing: there is absolutely no evidence that it works.

Nonetheless, in stalwart, don't-confuse-me-with-the-facts-ma'am manner, we keep following the formula anyway, because by gosh, it *ought* to work.

But people don't get what they want, says the Law of Achievement: they get what they *expect*. The first time I heard this (it was Richard Brooke who had articulated it), I was electrified. Illumination! Here at last, something that had always seemed fundamentally unfair now made lucid, perfect sense. The world was *not* a capricious place: there actually was an orderly, consistent principle that could be understood and exercised. Einstein declared, "God does not play dice." Evidently, neither does success.

Nor money. Bob Proctor talks about the "Law of Moral Compensation": *The amount of money you earn will always be in exact ratio to the need for what you do.* Here is another way I have heard this expressed:

> *The size of your income will directly reflect the number of people on whose lives you have an impact.*

Money is not a measure of your goodness or worthiness; it is a measure of your *impact*. It's pure physics. Rock stars and sports stars and movie stars make such huge amounts of money not because society has a skewed values system, nor due to some inherently corrupt loading of the economic dice, but as a result of the simple fact that *they have an impact on so many people's lives*.

That's the power of network marketing: through leverage, you can have huge impact. The bigger the impact, the bigger the income.

And here's the best part: the impact lasts long after you build the network. Residual impact equals residual income.

Can You Say the B Word?
Watch What You Say Today—
It's Where Tomorrow Comes From
May '03

A dear friend used to call me periodically to tell me that she was ready, now—really, really ready—to build her business. One problem: she could not bring herself to actually use the word "business" in her prospecting conversations. She asked, "Is it okay if I use the word 'enterprise' instead?"

Of course it was okay, and I told her so. Still, I couldn't entirely dismiss my doubts as to whether or not she was really, really ready to jump in, with gusto and momentum, and build her ... you know, her "B." It reminded me of a scene in Steve Martin's wonderful film *All of Me.* Martin is mourning his advancing age (occasioned by the advent of his thirty-eighth birthday) and says to his girlfriend, "I've been thinking, and you know, maybe we should get ... you know, the M word."

And she says: "Darling, if you can't *say* the M word, I don't think you're ready to *do* the M word."

You can't help thinking, the lady has a point.

I don't believe it's possible to overstate how powerful an impact your words have. On others, too, of course, but that's not what I mean. I'm referring to the impact your words have on *you.*

I worked with another distributor for months to help her excise references to death from her working vocabulary. When she was overtired, she'd say, "Oh gosh, I'm brain-dead." Looking forward to a conversation with a friend, she'd say, "I'm dying to talk with her"; looking back at it, she'd be "tickled to death." She eventually changed these to, "living to talk with them," and "tickled to life." Instead of declaiming her brain-death, she'll say simply, "I need some rest." And you know, I think she just might live longer for it.

When people tell you they're going to "try to get organized," they are making a subtle declaration that not only are they presently not organized, but in fact, the attempt to become so runs counter to the status quo and is therefore more than likely to fail. Yoda was right: do, or do not, there is no "try."

Here's another I often hear: "I'm talking to people, but I'm not really pushing the business yet." But we don't want you to "push" anything! We're not pushers. If anything, we're pullers; we want to talk *with* people, not lecture *at* them.

When people ask you what you do, what do you say? Do you get all squirrelly, feel an evasive look come over your face, and mumble, "Uhh . . . actually, I'm involved in an enterprise where we help people leverage themselves to take advantage of indirect referral-distribution trends and online-affiliate click-through residual potentials, to support an overall accrual of their financial freedom quotient . . ."? And then do the people back slowly away with funny looks on their faces?

As a network marketer, it's critical that you can state, clearly and unapologetically, what it is you do for a living.

In fact, here's an image I like to use to drive this point home for new distributors: if someone awoke you from a stone-cold sleep at 3:00 A.M. by shining a flashlight in your face and shouting, "What do you do for a living?!" could you sit bolt upright and give a clear, immediate and unhesitating reply? Until you can truthfully answer "Yes," you're not fully in the business.

A little dramatic, I grant . . . but you can't help thinking, Steve Martin's girlfriend had a point.

Darling, if you can't *say* the B word, are you really ready to *do* the B word?

Giving Up Your Right to Be Right

What It Takes to Play on a Team

June '03

I am driving north on Route 81, somewhere between Virginia and Massachusetts, when I realize that all my attention is riveted onto a single sentence.

> *"The obsessive need to be right is an expression of the fear of death."*

I pull over, stop the car's audiocassette player, rewind and listen again. And again. I am enthralled. I am listening to the voice of Eckhart Tolle reading the text of his astonishing book, *The Power of Now*. Has this man just identified the single most compelling cause of conflict—from friendly spats to global warfare—in the history of civilization?

> *The obsessive need to be right . . .*

I believe that giving up my need to be right—even my *right* to be right—may well have been the single most important discovery of my adult life.

No, that's actually not quite right.

The giving up is not itself the discovery. That's a decision, a choice, albeit not one necessarily made all at once. (Like most life-changing decisions, it's one that you make, only to make again and again.) The discovery—the one that inspired making that blue-ribbon, gold-medal, number-one, single-most-in-history distinction—is the *freedom* that flows from exercising that choice.

A proposition: you will participate in and serve a team only to the degree that you give up the right to be right. A corollary: the person most driven by the need to be right is ultimately the one most likely to destroy the team. Another: the person most free of that need is where the heart of the team most resides. And a team in which *all* the members significantly give up that need? There may be no force more powerful.

Legendary screenwriter William Goldman (*The Princess Bride, All the President's Men*) tells a story about being on the set with Clint Eastwood. Goldman was flabbergasted to see the Hollywood icon standing in line at the commissary along with the rest of the crew, patiently waiting for his turn at the makeshift lunch counter. Not drawling, "Feelin' hungry today—punk?" Just waiting his turn.

Eastwood? The Man with No Name? Dirty Harry? *Standing in line?!* Yep. Even in silverscreendom, the Land of the Giant Egos, you can find people of Eastwood's stature who have not forgotten the truths of humility and teamsmanship: the willingness to be no better than the guy next to you.

Next time you're at a company event, look around. Are the top pin levels—the Clint Eastwoods of that world—waiting in the food line with the rest of the crew, or keeping off to themselves, hobnobbing with the "power players"?

What makes a team work? Is it humility, perspective? Is it as simple as giving up the right to be right? I think so.

But, as Dennis Miller's trademark sign-off goes, that's just my opinion . . . I could be wrong.

Loyalties Beget Royalties
But Only Over Time
July '03

Something funny about this word, *loyalty*. Add it to a lineup of your favorite positive traits and it sort of sticks out. What is it, exactly? Did we not brush its hair? Do its socks not match? *Integrity, honesty, flexibility, commitment, open-mindedness, courage, perseverance* . . . Yes, yes. Of course. Noble things, all. But what's that one over there, lurking listlessly in the corner, the wallflower that nobody's asking to dance?

Bob Proctor put it this way: "For most people, loyalty requires a respectable amount of thought to define, or even just to consider with any level of care." There's something a little elusive about it.

And that's fascinating—because loyalty is *the* human behavior that most clearly drives this business of network marketing. We build a network of repeat consumers, people who keep buying and using our product or service, over and over *even in the face of competition* (loyalty).

For this, we earn a residual income.

"Residual"—the residue, what's left over from the initial combustion of the enrollment—was originally called "royalties," tracing its roots back to the rents collected by the wealthiest and most powerful landowners . . . the royalty.

Repeat customers, *over time*, create residual income. Loyalties, *over time*, beget royalties. And there it is: that quality that has made loyalty an increasingly and strangely challenging concept in these post-modern times: *over time*.

No matter how generous, noble, honest, affable, enthusiastic, flexible, personable or charismatic you may be, no matter what other wonderful traits you may exhibit when I meet you and start to get to know you, how can I actually tell anything about your level of loyalty? I can't. Because there's only one way to tell: over time.

By definition, loyalty is something you cannot judge, detect or perceive *right now*.

And that's tough, because we live in an increasingly right-now world.

"We'll build your downline for you!" "Get in while it's in pre-launch, it's going through the roof!" *Right now, right now, right now, fast, fast, fast.* I stand in front of my microwave and mutter impatient incantations—*Is it ready yet?!*

It's not that fast is bad. It's human nature to want to experience momentum; seeing results quickly is a great (and time-tested) way to allay fears and bolster faith. But note two things about speed and networking:

One: every time the networking idea is abused, that abuse is associated with *speed* (front-end-loading, "get rich quick," gotta-get-in-now, crash-n-burn, sign-em-and-leave-em).

And two: the very essence of our business model—residuals from repeat consumers, a community of long-term, faithful consumers—while it may be ignited at first by the fires of passion and enthusiasm, puts out heat throughout the long night only by virtue of the slow-burning and steady warmth of loyalty.

Loyalties beget royalties—and that happens, always and only, over time.

It's Not What You Say
The Gift of Not Talking
August '03

My nineteen-year-old daughter has stopped talking: she's taken a self-imposed vow of silence. It's not a religious thing; more, I think, an identity-seeking, life-figuring-out thing. She said (on e-mail, this is) that she's getting some "interesting" reactions from people.

I told her, I think it's a fabulous idea.

The legendary architect and futurist Buckminster Fuller hit a deep crisis in his twenties. Having just gone broke and lost his infant daughter (to influenza, I think it was), he felt his life was a shambles. Standing on the verge of suicide—literally, about to jump into a wintry Lake Michigan—he stopped to think. His life was a mess, he reasoned, because he had spent his years thus far listening to what other people told him.

In that moment, Bucky decided to close his mouth and not open it again until he was sure that the words he spoke really came *from him*.

For the next two years, he uttered not a single word. (His wife, Anne, must have been a saint; somehow, she managed through it all.) When he did, what came out was arguably hard to recognize as "normal English," but the passion and conviction were unmistakably, unequivocally, unambiguously his and nobody else's. It was only decades later that people came to recognize that the words also contained genius.

My point: you tap into your greatest power, authenticity and value when you are not speaking. It's not that what you say isn't important. That's just not where your power lies.

The most common way new distributors shoot themselves in the foot is by *saying too much* when they talk about the business. Why do people say too much? Because they don't yet really trust what they're talking about. True conviction is best conveyed not through more words but through fewer; it dwells *behind* the words.

The most important words that will ever pass between you and your team are spoken by them—not by you. When you ask someone what she wants from the business, the purpose is not simply for you to know the answer: it is *for her to say it out loud*—to clearly articulate her own vision with her own tongue, without the safety of vagueness and generalities, without ambivalence or ambiguity. It's not enough for you to know that she wants to escape from her job, to have time freedom to spend with her family and her own pursuits, to earn enough residual income to send her kids to college, build a bigger house and become a major contributor to her local halfway house—you need to *hear her describe all that*, out loud, in clear and vivid terms.

While you're doing nothing but listening.

We're often counseled to write down our goals—but ironically, written goals are among the least powerful of declarations. When you write a goal down on paper, it's just you telling you. It becomes far more real when *you tell me*. You'll only tell me if you trust me. You'll only trust me as a result of who you've decided I am—not what you've heard me say.

What you have most to offer others, you have to offer least of all through your words; in greater part, through what you do; but in greatest part, through who you *are*.

People Do What People Do
But If They Would Only Read the Manual . . .
September '03

In 1994, I wrote an editorial in *Upline* about an experience I'd had doing a training on live video-conference at a Kinko's. It was an amazing experience . . . I was flabbergasted and enthusiastic . . . I could see the future unfolding before my very eyes. I closed by breathlessly predicting that within a year, we'd all be using live video-conferencing as a staple of our training methodologies.

I was wrong. Never happened.

Pop quiz: what do all the following have in common?

> *The paperless office. Video phones. The demise of book stores. The worldwide takeover by communism. Genuine election reform.*

Answer: they are all vivid and perfectly rational predictions—none of which have come true, because they all overlooked one critical scientific principle:

> *People do what people do.*

I recently consulted to a startup networking company that in its first few months was swamped with customer service problems. Being an Internet-based company, they had planned to handle all customer service and distributor service issues via an e-mail response system. Logical enough, one might think . . . and one would be wrong.

As the stream of customer service issues swelled to flood tide, they continued in their stalwart insistence: 95 percent of the problems people were having would be avoided if people would simply read the manual, extensive online help files and regular e-mail newsletters.

Excellent. Except for one problem: that pesky word, "if."

Because in the real world, people won't read the manual, nor the online help files, and they either won't read or won't understand the newsletters—no, not even if you pay them.

Then they told their distributors: only prospect people who are tech-savvy enough not to have these technical challenges—a strategy worthy of King Canute. (Legend says this early English king had his throne placed on the shore and commanded the tides to abate. History adds a note that he actually did so to demonstrate the limitations of kings.)

The next step was to castigate the distributor leadership: if the leaders would only teach their networks properly, they said, people wouldn't be having these issues with the technology.

Hmm.

Perhaps not. But how many people do you know who ever learned to program their VCRs? If your business depended on people's VCRs being properly programmed, which would you put your energies into: redesigning the people—or the VCRs?

What these well-intentioned but misdirected strategies fail to grasp is a principle of human nature that I recently heard summed up beautifully by a friend, Craig Case: "If you make something idiot-proof, the world will build a better idiot."

People do what people do: smart education starts there.

All for One and One for All
Or Is It "Every Man for Himself!"?
October '03

"The network marketing community." Is that an oxymoron? Shouldn't be, doesn't have to be. But . . . (sigh) in most ways, times and places, has been.

Network marketing is a strikingly *American* phenomenon (albeit a globally exported one), and there is something inherently inimical to community in the makeup of the American myth. The American hero draws his (and I do mean "his") identity from the fact of not getting along with others. The misfit, the underdog, the one-man show. Clint Eastwood's Man with No Name. Superman: nobody even knows who he really is!

In our iconography, when we do raise "community" to hero status, it's usually by evoking its more insidious qualities. Da Family. The Firm. The Stepford Wives. The Matrix. Get thee behind me, blind and choking conformity, lest thee become murderously megalithic . . .

This is, after all, how we got here: one man with a few ships and a vision . . . which worked out to include the systematic elimination of the somewhere between ten and one hundred million indigenous people already living here in a strikingly well worked out socioecosystem . . . oops. We are, in a historically very real sense, *constitutionally* anti-community.

Besides, isn't community . . . well, boring? After all, the community-minded guy is usually the one who gets killed by the end of the first reel.

It's much more exciting to be Dirty Harry.

Ever notice how network marketers love to describe our opportunity in terms of how we don't do things the way everybody else does? In opportunity meeting jargon, "corporate world" is a phrase roughly equivalent to "police state." We are, as Helen Reddy sings so sweetly (and insidiously) to her child (or is it to her lover?), "You and me against the world."

It is extraordinary how often we each define our own companies as being *different from those other companies,* how consistently we breed a culture based on the proposition that network marketers are petty, scurrilous characters—except for us. *We're not like the rest of that sorry bunch, y'see.*

It's a pretty weird way to go about building credibility for the profession.

I consulted to a startup group a few years ago who wanted to base its company philosophy on the concept of a "river of hate" flowing between American consumers and our perfidious industry. Their plan: define this new company as the sole network marketing company swimming heroically against that toxic tide. (I'm not making this up.)

The CEO of another company I consulted to over a decade ago put it this way: "We're not like all the other MLM companies: we care about more than just money." Can you imagine house-shopping and having your realtor tell you, "This here is the house you want—'cause this neighborhood is awful and all these other houses here are pieces of junk that are about to fall apart . . ."?

There are plenty of people in the network marketing world who are devoted to the call of transcending this do-it-yourself, me-against-the-world mythology and helping to forge a true ethos of community within our profession. I wish there were more of them.

There is a famous remark of Gandhi's, who upon being asked his opinion of Western civilization, suggested he thought it would be a marvelous idea.

"The network marketing community . . ."

What a marvelous idea.

The Anonymous Gift
When You Give, What Happens to the Power?
December '03

It was 1974; I was assistant principal cello in the Fort Wayne Philharmonic Orchestra in Fort Wayne, Indiana, where it gets plenty cold in the winter.

Every Friday, I would walk to the bank nearby (no car), cash my paycheck, walk home and stash the money away in my tiny apartment. (I was saving for a new instrument, and in my conspiratorially suspicious youth, I didn't trust banks.) I don't remember how much I earned in those days. Not that much, but I spent a lot less. That fall I bought a gorgeous new cello, paid cash. (I mean *cash*: we're talking a few grand—quite a few—in rolled-up twenties, much to the bug-eyed shock of the violin-maker as I took delivery of the instrument.) Even so, by deep winter I'd socked away some change.

Then I heard about my neighbors.

I want to say their names were David and Lisa, though that's probably not right. I remember she was pretty and too thin. They both looked young enough to be hopeful, broke enough to know the taste of hopelessness. We never had a conversation, at least not that I recall. Somehow, I heard that "David" had lost his job, that they couldn't make rent and would have to vacate the next day.

That night, I silently slipped over to their building and slid an envelope into their mailbox. It contained a thick sheaf of twenties with a note saying only that this was from a neighbor who wished them well.

They stayed . . . at least as long as I did, which was till summer. They never knew where their rent that month came from.

I told no one. I knew instinctively, intuitively, that I couldn't. Why not? Had no idea—I just couldn't. For the next thirty years I maintained so strong a sense of privacy over the event that my own memory soon lost their names and other particulars of their history, retaining only the faint outline you've just read. This is the first time I've mentioned it to a soul.

Now I think I know why.

Primitive tribes the world over believe that if you take a photograph of another, you have power over that person. If David and Lisa had known who I was, would that have given me power over them? If so, I didn't want it.

Now I realize, there are two ways to give. One is to give something of value to others (money, knowledge, comfort, perspective, time, attention, care . . .), but to retain—or even, by the giving, to *increase*—your power over them. You get to look generous, but still have the upper hand.

The other way is to give something of value away—just give it away, holding onto nothing. To give away the power, too.

Which is more common?

And which, the more satisfying?

The Sky's *Not* the Limit
Dare to Step Out of Your Horizontal Plane
January '04

This evening, a cold December dusk overlaid with a chill of crystalline clarity, I am taking a walk near my home, wrapped tightly in my winter coat and the petty concerns of the day. Halfway around the block I am stopped in my tracks by the oddest feeling.

Am I being watched?

I gaze around at the postcard-perfect horizon views—gorgeous purple frieze of Blue Ridge Mountains, dying pastel explosions of the slow Virginia sunset. Then I look up.

It's the sky . . . just the sky. That gray-black December sky.

We peer at each other, the sky and I. A handful of seconds tick past. *That sky—it's so big!*

All at once, the sky feels not like a transparent nothingness, but an opaque somethingness. No, more: an *everythingness*. I am aware of myself perched on the rim of my little terrestrial orb, my head brushing up against the bottom edge of the sky's ponderous enormity.

I experience a sudden shift in perspective—an M.C. Escher moment, two facing profiles resolving into a water goblet—and I wonder how I could possibly have missed it: the sky is not something I'm looking "up into." I'm not walking *underneath* it but swimming *through* it, breathing it, submerged, immersed in something infinite. All I need do is lift my chin a bit and I'm breathing it in directly.

When I observe your life, you may appear to me as something happening "out there," one more far-off constellation in the endless scenery of the humanly possible, your accomplishments and experiences distantly visible, but not really tangible. Perhaps, when you look at me, you see the same thing. And both of us, when we gaze upon the brilliance of stations and accomplishments we admire, may well feel we're looking off into astronomic distances.

But the vast expanse of human possibility is not "out there" at all. We're not standing earthbound, gazing up at it—we're immersed in it, flying through it. All we need do is lift our chins a bit and we're breathing it in directly.

In the pursuit of our ambitions, we often look first into the horizontal plane to see what exists today, and then ask, "Given that, where can I reasonably expect to be a year from now?" By that strategy, an infant could learn to crawl a bit more gracefully, yes—but to walk? To run?

To soar?

Incremental gain—making your life the same as today, just a few inches more so—is not what many of us want. We want breakthrough accomplishment. That bolder strategy starts in lifting your line of sight out of the horizontal plane, looking square out into the sky of possibilities, and asking, "Where to?"

All you need do is lift your chin a bit and you're breathing it in directly.

Do you want your 2004 to be more than just a slightly enhanced upgrade of 2003? There's no good reason it can't.

That sky—it's so big!

Network Marketing at the Oscars®

Four Films Every Network Marketer Ought to See
February '04

Every year in (usually) March, the Academy of Motion Pictures Arts and Sciences holds the annual Academy Awards® . . . the Oscars®. This year, it's our turn: here are four feature films from the last few years (okay, the last twelve) that every networker ought to see. Each has something powerful to say—for better and, in some cases, for worse—about the human condition and, at least obliquely, our noble profession.

BEST LEADING CHARACTER
Door to Door (2002), written by William H. Macy (also starring) and Steven Schachter, directed by Steven Schachter

William H. Macy won an Emmy® for his achingly delicate portrayal of Bill Porter, the now-famous Watkins top salesman with cerebral palsy. An amazing story, beautifully done, and while it's all about the world of a door-to-door salesman, it convincingly shows that your real business is not what you sell but who you are. *Door to Door* won a raft of awards (including six Emmys) and was nominated for many more (including six *more* Emmys!).

BEST SALES NIGHTMARE
Boiler Room (2000), written and directed by Ben Younger

Other side of the spectrum: an object lesson in how the slick, fast-lane guys operate. Giovanni Ribisi runs with the wrong crowd and gets wrapped up in a high-stakes off-Wall-Street "boiler-room" operation that teeters on (and topples off) the edge of illegality. Ben Affleck's frightening "Are you man enough for this business?" rap reminds me chillingly of real-life talks I've heard in person, given by throw-em-up-against-the-wall-and-see-who-sticks network marketers I've known. One self-styled "heavy hitter" excitedly told me that he was modeling a recruiting meeting script—I kid you not—directly on this very Affleck scene. Spooky.

BEST TALKING
Glengarry Glen Ross (1992), written by David Mamet, directed by James Foley

What an astonishing film. In its original form as a stage play, this script won a Pulitzer Prize, no mean thing. David Mamet spent time in his youth as a salesman and has down cold the classic patter of the shuck-'n'-jive, cold-calling salesman. Some of the finest acting anywhere, ever, and what a cast: Al Pacino, Jack Lemmon, Ed Harris and Alan Arkin all work for a sleazy real estate operation, with Kevin Spacey as their sulking, much-abused sales manager. Alex Baldwin (in a scene Mamet wrote specifically for him for the film version) puts in a chilling appearance as the hot dog from the downtown office who humiliates them all with his "pep talk."

BEST LISTENING
Mumford (1999), written and directed by Lawrence Kasdan

This one has nothing to do with network marketing *per se*, but it is the most deliciously spot-on film I've ever seen about *listening*. Remember the famous study about the psychologist on the airplane? (Everyone finds him fascinating because he listens like nobody has ever listened to them before.) The eponymous protagonist of *Mumford* is just like that. As it turns out, he really is interesting . . . but that's ancillary to the story point. Even after you find out the details of his bizarre past, it's still the fact that *he listens to people* that carries him in the end.

A READER RESPONDS

The movie *Glengarry Glen Ross* offers no redeeming qualities. Salesmen are negatively presented as the sleaziest manifestation of the human condition. It is amazing to me why anyone who honors the profession of selling would give this production the time of day.

Effort should be made to recognize and commend movies that present a positive commentary and can be emulated by aspiring networkers. Rather than suggesting that *Glengarry Glen Ross* is worthy of a "Networking Oscar," it should be condemned for the trash it is and given the No Hope Award.

I found this movie so demeaning to salespeople that after thirty minutes of watching this travesty, my wife and I returned to the box office and demanded that our money be refunded.

— A Reader

Amazing that two people can watch the same thing and yet see two such different things! Where you see a travesty of no redeeming qualities, I see a masterpiece with portraits of such tragic poignancy they make me fairly weep.

You point out that Mamet portrays salesmen negatively, as the sleaziest manifestation of the human condition. On this you and I heartily agree: Mamet's Pulitzer-Prize-winning play is a cautionary tale, like Wall Street, *or* Death of a Salesman, *or for that matter,* Hamlet. *We don't marvel at Gordon Gekko or Willy Loman or*

Hamlet because we aspire to be like them, but because they show us with extraordinary power some of the pitfalls in the human condition. Such is some of humanity's greatest art, that it leaves us murmuring, "There, but by the grace of God, go I . . ."—and now with a deeper insight into exactly what that "there" looks like.

Glengarry Glen Ross *lies at the other end of the spectrum from* Door to Door, *and I included both for that reason. Here, with two films, you have an A to Z encyclopedia of sales: all those noblest of human qualities we aspire to have, and those meanest which we aspire not to have.*

Door to Door *is the drama of someone struggling to rise above his flaws (in this case, his physical handicap)—and to a great extent, succeeding.* Glengarry Glen Ross *is the drama of men struggling to rise above their flaws (in this case, their own emotional handicaps, fear and greed and loss of moral compass)—and to a great extent, failing. I've known people whose lives have fit both descriptions. At different times, mine has fit both. Honestly, hasn't yours? ("There, but by the grace of God . . . ")*

— *JDM*

Be Careful What You Fish For
When You Wield Your Power, Wield Wisely
May '04

I read about a couple who had a remarkable experience with goals.

One day, while this man was on the job, he made the acquaintance of a mentor who told him something amazing about the power of having clear goals. The man could have anything he wanted in life: all he needed to do was clearly articulate it.

The man instinctively knew this wise mentor was telling the truth, but as he thought deeply about what he had heard, he came to a sobering realization: he could not in that moment think of any goals to articulate.

That night, he excitedly told his wife what he had learned. And while he wasn't able to articulate a dream, she was—and did. She described to him the kind of home she longed for them to live in, exactly what it would look like, feel like, taste like, smell like .... She encouraged her husband to share this vision, and to keep talking with his new mentor. In less time than one would think possible, the vision she had painted for him that night became a reality: they were living in the very home she had described to him!

But this is not where the story ends.

The woman instinctively understood the importance of stretching beyond one's comfort zone; she knew that if we only dare to dream really big, virtually anything is possible.

As her dreams grew in scope and daring, she continued describing them to her husband in vivid detail. He continued to dialogue with his mentor, and over the course of time (again, less time than one would think possible), one by one, the dreams this bold, entrepreneurial woman had envisioned all became reality. Their wealth grew prodigious; soon they were living a lifestyle unimaginable to most.

It was truly a remarkable course of events . . .

Until one day, alas, it all came to an end. The husband's mentor (who was, it so happened, a magic flounder) grew weary of the fisherman's wife and her unceasing demands and stopped granting her wishes—and the hapless couple in this most cautionary of Grimm's Fairy Tales, "The Fisherman's Wife," found themselves living once again in the same wretched hovel where they'd started . . . just a few days earlier.

There is a bit of Fisherman and Fisherfrau in each of us: the part that knows how to be content, to truly live in the moment; and the part that perpetually aspires to have more. Each side has its limitations, and each potentially serves to balance the other.

Mr. and Mrs. Fisher of the fairy tale did not have a particularly harmonious relationship, nor were they able to embrace each other's aspects in a productive way: their conflict did not end well. Perhaps within our own natures, we can achieve a more graceful balance—and happier outcomes.

We each have the power of the Flounder in our hands. Let's use it well—and wisely.

Why Not?
Lessons from My Mom on
Staying Young Forever
July '04

I am 6 years old and I've just asked my mom to help me make a list of piano compositions I have learned to play so far. I've come up with three, maybe four, all of the two- and three-note variety. (Mozart, I am not.) She glances at the list and comments, "Away in a Manger." I look at her with genuine astonishment. *Away in a Manger?!* That's pretty advanced stuff . . . I can't play that!

She says, "Sure you can."

We sit down at the keyboard; thirty minutes later, she's right: I can. I feel exuberant. Come to think of it, everything I've been able to accomplish in my life I attribute to youthful exuberance. Not mine: hers.

Fast forward seven years.

I am 13 and my mom is planning a school trip to Greece with me and about a dozen classmates. We're going to perform Aeschylus' *Prometheus Bound*. She says, we ought to have music for the choruses. She asks if I wouldn't mind writing it. Just like that. Like she was asking if I wouldn't mind doing the dishes.

But . . . I'm no composer! I'm 13! I can't set Aeschylus to concert-quality music!

She says, "Sure you can."

A few months later we are performing the music in the ancient stone amphitheater at Epidaurus—the same spot, incredibly, where the play had its premiere a few thousand years ago. A few years after that I'm at a reception at the Waldorf Astoria in New York . . . because I've won the international BMI Awards for Student Composers.

My mom was right again.

About the same time as the BMI ceremony, I'm doing something a little radical: I'm about to drop out of high school in order to start our own school with some friends. We've been talking. We're all going to schools we hate, and one day we think, wouldn't it be cool to start our own school, where we could actually learn something? *But we're only kids.* We can't really start our own high school . . . can we? And you already know what my mom has to say about that.

"Sure you can."

We meet. We dream, talk, plan, take action. A year later we're an independent alternative high school that goes on to send its graduates to places like Yale and Harvard.

The bumble bee, Mary Kay used to say, flies because it doesn't realize that it can't.

When I was young, adults would ask, "What do you want to be when you grow up?" I never knew how to answer them. I still don't. Maybe I never grew up. But why "be" one thing? My mom had a different approach. She simply said, "You can do whatever you set out to do." For five decades, I've been putting her belief to the test. If I were a high-wire performer with my mom's philosophy as my only net, I'd still feel pretty safe.

They say children will drive you crazy asking the question, "Why?" But we know we've truly taught them well when we hear them ask this one: *Why not?*

And if you think you can't, my mom has three words for you: *Sure you can.*

The Best Plan
On the Folly of Selling Your Comp Plan
September '04

You've gotta join this program, you've just gotta. Why? It's the plan, man—we've got the plan. I mean, you've seen a lot of plans, but you've never seen anything like this: we have the best, most revolutionary, most amazing compensation plan, a plan that'll really make you the big money . . .

Please.

Stop.

Time and time again, I've had people fervently pitch me on the exceptional, extraordinary, amazing benefits of their plan—the reasons this plan, as distinct from all other plans, will go where no other plans have gone before.

It's nonsense. I promise: every time, it is nonsense. "Yeah, but . . ."

—No. I'm sorry: no exceptions. There is no plan that will "really make you the big money," for the simple reason that a compensation plan does not earn you money. That's not its purpose.

Here's what earns you money: people purchasing products. Volume. Period. (I include services in the term "products.") A lot of people purchasing products repeatedly, regularly, over a long period, generates incomes. That's it.

What a compensation plan does is sort out how that income is distributed. It's a sorting system, like the mailroom in the corporate basement—no more glorious, dramatic or exciting than that.

A niggling point? Semantics? Not at all: it's a crucial point. When you trumpet the virtues of your plan as a top selling point, you actually hurt your case, because you're confusing substance with incidentals—and on some level, even if not consciously, your prospect knows it. Selling a strong, qualified prospect on your comp plan is like selling a hungry person on the nutritional value of the package the food is wrapped in.

In fact, you do have a great compensation plan: the multi-level marketing concept, aka network marketing. *That's* the plan whose value is worth selling.

Does this mean your company's particular plan doesn't matter? Not at all. There are still good plans and bad plans, strong ones and weak, depending on how fair they are, how balanced they are, and how well they execute the multilevel concept without creating roadblocks or bottlenecks. A good comp plan is as Lao Tzu described a good government: it doesn't get in the way.

So please, stop telling me with breathless wonder about your plan's amazing coded-bonus, matching-bonus, car-bonus and bonus-bonus. I simply don't care, because in the final analysis (actually, even in the preliminary analysis), it doesn't matter that much. All you're convincing me is that you haven't yet figured out where your opportunity's real strengths lie.

Have you got good products? Will people buy them and use them? A lot of people—over and over? And are there people of substance, experience and integrity running the operation, people who demonstrably know what they're doing?

Good.

That's a great comp plan.

Envisioning
That Tricky Business of Making Things Real
November '04

I just attended my friend Luke Melia's wedding and came away moved by something he did. Smack dab in the middle of the ceremony, Luke read to us from a document that read like a diary entry—written some fifty years in the future. He spoke about his life with his wife, Jeanhee, the richness and fullness of their half-century of living, learning and growing together. It was vivid and deeply moving.

Why? Because it was *real*.

The most critical skill of the successful networker is envisioning, the ability to create a vivid picture of something that hasn't factually happened yet, and to make it so vivid that it feels real.

Envisioning is vastly different from "goal-setting," which deals in the logical. (Fix a concrete point in the future, and then deduce the concrete steps that will take you there.) What I'm talking about has nothing whatsoever to do with logic. Nor does envisioning happen simply by creating a picture in your mind. If your dreams and aspirations are happening in your mind only, that's not envisioning, that's wishful thinking. It's like saying, "I'll give it a try"—which, as Yoda pointed out, will not lift a spaceship out of the mud, or accomplish anything else, either.

Envisioning means making something up out of thin air—and *making it real*. By definition, you can't do that within the confines of your own skull. It needs to become sensory. Writing it—good. Making pictures of it—better. Speaking it—best.

My friend Scott Ohlgren calls this "future journaling," and it's the most powerful training exercise I've ever seen—when read out loud, as Luke did at his wedding. The "100-name prospect list" is another example. The value of this famous exercise is not in the names themselves, it's in the *process of envisioning* that you necessarily engage in as you face the blank page.

When I began my first serious networking business, I made a wall chart of a twenty-leader organization *before I had any idea* whose names would actually end up going in those twenty boxes. The chart, for me, was reality. Sure, it didn't pay real money until the boxes were filled in with actual people. But it was real *first*; the specific people followed.

Growing a network is more agricultural than industrial. You plant, and only later on reap a harvest. There's no on-off switch; it takes seasons, not moments.

"Momentum" is thrilling, but it comes only from the patient waiting and powerful seed-planting of those willing to gaze out over an expanse of nothing-yet and call it already-something.

That's what Luke did that so moved me. And that's what you do when you build a network organization. You build it first; then people come along to inhabit it.

That's envisioning.

The Art of Presentation
Ask Yourself the Right Questions
January '05

". . . So please give a great big welcome to Bill Jenkins!"

[*Applause. Bill Jenkins shambles amiably to the stage, peers out at the audience as the applause recedes and trickles out.*]

"Hel—hello?"

[*Looks around, taps his lapel mike.*]

"Am I on? Can you hear me? Good. Okay . . . wow, what a great-looking group! Seriously, have you guys looked at yourselves? Hey, I can't tell you how excited I am to be here tonight. Before I go any further, I just want to thank Jim Bilkins for putting this together—everyone, give Jim a hand!"

And just like that, before he's even really gotten started, poor Bill's presentation is over. From here on, nobody in the room is going to hear a single word he says. Why not? Because you only get one chance to make a first impression. Bill wasted that chance blathering on about himself.

Every time you open your mouth to speak, you are responding to a question in your mind. Here are the questions Bill's opening is responding to: "How do I look? What should I say? How'm I doing? Am I still nervous? Will they like me?"

I don't mean to pick on Bill. His heart is in the right place, and he does have something of value he genuinely wants to share with this group. But asking himself the wrong questions has led to this pseudo-folksy, gosh-I'm-excited, break-the-ice opening riff that is how 99 percent of all speakers open their talks.

And the percentage of *great* presenters who start their talks this way?

Zero.

Why? Because they're polished, skilled, have nerves of steel? Nope. It's because truly great speakers know how to take their focus completely off themselves.

When a great presenter faces her audience, she asks herself questions like, "What do these people want most? Who *are* these folks? What are they searching for? Why are they here? *And what is the single most valuable thing I could possibly convey to them?*"

You might think this all doesn't really matter, because the truth is, as network marketers, we rarely present from the stage. Our presentations happen on the phone, through e-mail, over coffee at Barnes & Noble. But here's the thing: the art of presentation works in all these arenas, too.

Of course you want to have a grasp of your informational key points: product, company, opportunity, benefits, vignettes and anecdotes . . . but relax. You will not be graded on how well you've mastered delivery of this information. What you will be graded on is the quality of the interaction. Bring yourself to the conversation with these questions: "Who is this person? What does she want? What is she searching for? What is the single most valuable thing I could possibly offer her?"

Because the truth is, your "audience" is not here to hear about you. They are here to hear about *them*.

You can help shed light on that fascinating topic.

That is the art of presentation.

Lies, Damn Lies and Statistics
How Important Are Your Words in Your Overall Communication?
(Hint: It's Way More Than 7 Percent)
May '05

I have a sobering fact for you; are you ready? Here it is: of the statistics network marketers cite in support of their businesses, a recent study showed, *more than 87 percent* are not based on solid research.

Shocking, isn't it? But guess what? I just made that up.

Did you know that . . . there have been more millionaires made through network marketing than in any other profession?

. . . that 93 percent of your communication is based on nonverbal cues and tone of voice, with your actual words conveying only 7 percent of the message?

. . . that according to a study done by Hartford Insurance, at retirement, 96 percent are either dead, dead broke or just getting by, and only four are financially successful?

. . . that according to a Harvard study, only 3 percent of people ever write down their goals—and at retirement age, those 3 percent are worth more than the other 97 percent?

Each of these deserves its own article; we'll do what we can in one paragraph each.

"More millionaires in network marketing . . ." Maybe some

day, Virginia. For now, most millionaires got that way by being frugal, working hard, saving consistently and investing in real estate.

"Your words make up only 7 percent . . ." If that were true, I guess it really wouldn't matter that much what we actually said, or whether or not our words told the truth. But it's not—and it does. This widely quoted "research" is a tortured distortion of genuine findings by UCLA social psychologist Albert Mehrabian in his book *Silent Messages* (1971), who was describing how conflicting or "mixed" messages are interpreted between two people who know each other. Not public speakers in front of a group.

How did we ever fall for this one? Our words convey *less than one-fourteenth* of our meaning?! Has our collective esteem for the power and majesty of language truly sunk that low?

What about the Hartford study? Doesn't exist.

The Harvard (Stanford, Yale, etc.) study? Nope, sorry.

However, there actually *was* a "landmark Harvard study" on people in their retirement years, and you can read about it in the book *Aging Well*, by George Valliant, recently released in paperback. Of "goals" or "goal-setting," Valliant evidently has little to say: neither term rates a single entry in the book's index. However, among the major longevity factors Valliant *did* observe were these gems: the role of play and creative activity; the benefits of forming new friendships and social networks; and the importance of intellectual curiosity and lifelong learning.

"Intellectual curiosity." Hmm. Would that include the habit of checking to see whether the things you've heard are actually true or are simply urban legends?

What you say duplicates. You have a responsibility to speak the truth—not just with your body language and tone of voice, but with your words, too. Remember: "intellectual curiosity and lifelong learning" *have* been proven to help you live longer.

P.S. Who said, "There are three kinds of lies: lies, damn lies, and statistics"? Mark Twain, right?

Yes . . . but he was quoting Benjamin Disraeli.

The Days
Good Night and Good Morning
July '05

How does your day end? Do you succumb to gravity and crash into the mattress, feeling defeated? Nod off to the chatter of the television? Or spend a moment looking back over the panorama of your day and pronounce it, like God on the sixth day, "Very good"?

Some nights, I hate the idea of going to bed, resist it like a hyperactive 8-year-old, because I feel there's still so much to do. I'm not satisfied with what I got done during the day, don't want the opportunity to end. Other days, I welcome the rest and look forward eagerly to sleeping, and when I feel myself hit the sheets, actually let out a big *Ahhhhh* of satisfaction, as if I had eaten all my dinner and as a reward have now been served a delicious dessert.

That latter is how I *like* my days to end. It is also how I want my *life* to end.

And you? How do you want your life to end?

"Eeuuwww, that's too macabre—I don't want to think about it."

But hang on. They're not so different: how you end your days, and how you end *this* day. It occurs to me that what your entire life amounts to is simply the sum of whatever your individual days amount to. As the Virginia Woolf character says in the magnificent film, *The Hours*: "Always to look life in the face and know it for what it is . . . always the years between us; always the love; always the hours."

Our lives really do come down to this: how we spend each day. *Always the days; always the hours.*

I once asked a friend, Scott Ohlgren, if he knew what, when the time came, would be his preferred cause of death. He answered with a single word: "Use." I love that. Another friend, Gianni Ortiz, once shared with me her preferred exit strategy: "To be taken by a sniper's bullet while in an asana at a yoga retreat." Now *that's* a classy way to go.

What are the hours like for you? How does your day end? How does it flow? Is it brimming over with joy, with excitement, with fulfillment? Have you seen through the illusion of "someday" and made the decision to live a life of vigor, élan and passion right now, *today*, and not just "someday"?

Too often, we have turned Rene Descartes's famous dictum, "I think, therefore I am," into the modern achievement-obsessed, "I do, therefore I am." We too easily confuse our accomplishments with our selves, as if productivity were the sole measure and evidence of our worth.

Funny thing, too, about Descartes: *The Power of Now*'s Eckhart Tolle says he got it precisely wrong—that it's only when we're thinking that past and future come into existence and we lose touch with present reality. According to Tolle, the truth is closer to this: *I think, therefore I am not—but when I stop thinking, I am.*

As I write these words, it is exactly ten years since my mom put aside her toys, donned her PJs and crawled into bed for the final goodnight.

When I was little, she once told me, I had a peculiar way of preparing for bed. I would brush my teeth, say goodnight, then slip into my room and change back into my day clothes, carefully make my bed, and lie down to sleep on top of the covers. Observing this one night, my mom inquired, what was my purpose? According to her, my answer came without hesitation:

"That's so when I wake up in the morning, I'll be ready to get up and play right away, without any distractions."

I like to think that's how she felt when she closed her eyes for the last time.

I like to think that's how I'll feel the last time I close mine.

The Core within the Core
Five Levels of Learning
September '05

Network marketing is certainly a teaching business, but it is even more a learning business, and the learning is something like the way Aslan the lion describes the world in C.S. Lewis's *The Last Battle*: each successive world of learning is larger on the inside than it is on the outside.

1) THE PRODUCT

First thing you learn about (usually) is the product or service and company, what people often refer to as The Story. Every company has its Story. It might be about the founders, the exotic ingredient, the breakthrough science or unique function . . . whatever it is, it is the magnetic core of your business and it generates a field of charisma, mystique and uniqueness.

There is lots to learn here—salient points about the marketplace, timing and commercial context. But sooner or later, you discover there is a core within this core:

2) THE BUSINESS

Sooner or later you learn the Product Paradox: while your business is all about the product, it's really not about the product. Yes, people are drawn to your product like iron filings to a magnet—but those who will build the business with you are ultimately drawn by time freedom, lifestyle freedom, long-term security, the rewards of the accomplishment. Your product may heal their joints, their skin or their digestion; your business offering can heal their family schedules, retirement plans, maybe even their dreams.

There's lots more to learn here: the compensation plan, economic stats on society and home-based business, and more. But the more you learn about the business, if you're paying attention, the more you realize there's something else inside that's even more essential:

3) THE PROCESS

The majority of distributors never really penetrate this far—beyond the numbers and concepts, to the dynamics of how it actually *works*. How to conduct yourself on a three-way call; why it pays to extol the strengths and other finer qualities of your upline *and* your downline; how to allot your time and attention within a growing organization where it will do the most good; how to discern the value and keep your bearings when you hear different coaches and mentors offer conflicting advice.

This is the stuff of how the business *really* works—from the inside. You will not find this information in a manual or on a web site, and you cannot learn it from CDs or DVDs. This is where genuine hands-on apprenticeship takes over. And here, the more you learn, the more you discover there is to learn, because here you enter the world of

4) THE PEOPLE

Get deep into the nitty gritty of enrolling, training, partnering and teaming, and you start to grasp the true inner workings of the business. Now you're listening not because you learned you're supposed to, but because you want to know. Learning how to draw and hold boundaries (like a parent!), to support someone without making him codependent (like a spouse!), or how to tell the truth with compassion when you see someone making excuses (like a best friend!).

This is where you genuinely learn network marketing.

And as you do, you start to sense that there's something else even more basic that's driving the results you're getting and the situations you keep bumping into. You discover that underneath your dealings with people, what you're really dealing with is

5) YOURSELF

Soon you discover something startling: that objection you keep getting? The excuse you keep hearing? The conflict that keeps cropping up in your organization? That difficulty with the way your upline is treating you? They're echoes of your own state of mind. That downline member who drives you crazy, the one who really pushes your buttons? The real issue may be the buttons themselves, not the finger that happens to be doing the pushing.

It's been said that you cannot grow your income any larger than you grow yourself. The most powerful curriculum for a networker is one the Delphic oracle taught three millennia ago: *gnôthi sauton*—Know Thyself.

The Greatest Contribution
Sometimes It's Simpler Than We Think
November '05

Two decades ago, soon after starting my first network marketing organization, I met an ambitious young man named Larry. Larry came to work at my health center and live in my home as a sort of apprentice. Skeptical at first of my "weird MLM sideline," he gradually saw the potential; soon he cautiously enrolled. Caution gave way to enthusiasm, then to a whirlwind of activity. Larry took off.

At the time he was just twenty-three; when we soared to the top of our compensation plan together, he was the youngest person in the company to attain that top rank. I had other leaders, too, but Larry's youthful energy and dedication grew an organization that went on to become well more than 50 percent of my entire network. The company thrived, our organizations thrived, our lives thrived.

But our friendship did not.

Early on, something went wrong; our relationship went off the rails. We both had our opinions of where (and why) it went sour. But whatever its elemental ingredients, the stew that simmered on the low burner of unspoken resentments made for one poisonous potation. Occasionally it boiled over in vitriolic phone calls; more typically it bubbled beneath the surface, seeping out into rancorous conversations held behind each other's backs. Civil in person, professional in public, we worked together as colleagues. And that was that.

Ten years later, I decided enough was enough. I called him on the phone, left a message: I was sorry for the years of slights and offenses, I was grateful for all he'd done. I was proud of him. And as far I was concerned, the hatchet was not only buried, it was moldered into dust.

He called back, and we talked.

I *would* say that phone call initiated a slow healing process that gradually, over time, led to a deep and lasting friendship . . . except that there was in fact nothing at all gradual about it.

It was *instantaneous*.

From that day on, we became the fast friends we'd never let ourselves be before. All at once, we allowed ourselves to make a genuine *contribution* to each other. We had already contributed hundreds of thousands of dollars to each other's lives. From this time on, we contributed immeasurably more, I to his life and he to mine.

A few years later, I was pulled out of sleep early one Tuesday morning by a phone call from a dear and mutual friend. Did I know? Larry was dead. A freak accident. So young.

I missed him then, badly; I still miss him now. But I don't regret the ten years we spent locked in bitter antagonism—because the few years that followed well more than made up for it.

The greatest contribution we have to make is the giving of ourselves. There's so much we have to give each other. What stops us? Nothing worth holding onto.

An Opportunity to Communicate

Don't Shoot It Down with Facts, Figures and Filibusters

January '06

What we got here is failure to communicate . . . .

When Frank Pierson wrote this line for the 1967 film *Cool Hand Luke*, he was concerned that it would be dropped in rehearsal and never make it to the screen. He feared the director would think, "It sounds too educated, too highbrow—a prison guard would never say something like that." So Pierson concocted an entire "back story" about how, despite his humble background, the prison guard had pursued a program of adult education.

He needn't have worried.

Nobody ever asked about the back story. The director not only left the line in, he loved it. So did the audience, and so have audiences ever since. In fact, the American Film Institute voted these eight words as the eleventh most memorable movie quote of all time.

What made the line so compelling?

I asked Dr. John Gray, author of *Men Are from Mars, Women Are from Venus*, and he said, "That was the beginning of this whole era of communication and the realization that all problems basically come down to communication."

I agree—and I think there's more, too. The guard's line didn't just *speak*, it threw down a gauntlet. It represented the chasm between two men and the worlds they stood for, between oppressive authority and an irrepressibly rebellious free spirit. In the film, the last time the line is spoken, it is Luke's final act—the moment he utters the words he is shot dead. What both Luke and the guard know (and the rest of us know, too) is that there is a great deal more at stake here than whether or not two people understand each other's words.

And so there is in your business. There are dreams at stake—yours, and those of the people you approach.

When John Naisbitt coined the phrase "high tech high touch" in 1984 (in the instant best-seller *Megatrends*), it was to point out that the more sophisticated our technologies, the more profound the consumer's need for the human touch. But Naisbitt's trend has another implication for your business: *the better the tools you have to make your presentations for you, the more you are freed to focus on the human aspect of the interaction.*

The critical skill in your business is not your capacity to reel off facts, figures and filibusters about your product or your company. It is your capacity to be *authentic*—to make a connection, share your excitement and passion and elicit theirs. Your job is to connect and invite, not to present.

The idea that "getting good at network marketing" means learning how to be skilled at making a presentation is still the number one misconception about this business, and it's still shooting down dreams by the thousands.

What we got here is an *opportunity* to communicate.

A Million Little Dollars

Truth Matters—and It's Compelling Enough on Its Own Merits

March '06

This man does not look happy. I am watching author James Frey on *The Oprah Winfrey Show* being publicly flayed for lying in his best-selling "memoir," *A Million Little Pieces*.

A quick recap of events, in case you missed them: Frey's gritty account of his nightmarish odyssey through drug addiction and recovery shot to the top of the best-seller charts last fall and became an Oprah's Book Club selection.

(In my home, we like to follow Oprah's Book Club: the lady has good taste, and she may have single-handedly done more for the noble cause of American literacy than generations of *Sesame Street*. She got me to finally read *East of Eden*, one of the most electrifying reads I've ever had.)

This January, it was revealed that Frey actually fictionalized major elements of the book. Oprah defended him at first, claiming the spirit of the book was genuine, but when it became clear just how fast and loose with the facts Frey had played, Oprah brought him and his publisher Nan Talese onto her show, roughed them up pretty good, and apologized to her millions of viewers.

Her emphatic two-word summary: "Truth matters."

Indeed.

In a recent editorial ("Lies, Damn Lies and Statistics," *Networking Times*, May/June '05), I poked a pin in several popular hot-air bubbles, including the frequently cited "Harvard study" that says only 3 percent of us write down our goals, and that those 3 percent have a greater net worth at retirement than the other 97 percent combined. (No such study exists.)

One reader, a public speaker himself, took issue with my position. "Do you believe," he wrote, "that writing down your goals helps? I sure do. Bottom line for me: the origin of the statements is not important at all. They tell a powerful story that we as writers and speakers can use over and over. Let's say for a moment that they are bogus; what harm has been done? Have you ever made up a story in your speaking to drive home a truth?"

To which I reply: No, sir, I do not "make up stories to drive home truths," and I hope you don't either. Telling fables of the tortoise-and-the-hare variety is one thing. But when I talk about my company's history or the growth of my network organization—or cite a Harvard study—I had damn well better be telling the truth.

My correspondent doesn't want me to "throw out the baby with the bathwater." I think he's in danger of leaving the baby in a polluted tub.

By all means, let's rescue the little dude, clean him off, wrap him tight and warm . . . but isn't the first step to *remove* him from the tainted water?

If Frey had called his book a novel (as did *Memoirs of a Geisha* author Arthur Golden), well, that would have been, as the expression goes, quite another story.

Frey is a talented writer, and it's a shame he didn't write the story the way it really happened. I suspect it would have been compelling enough on its own merits.

And by the way, the same is true for your business and everything you might say about it, whether on a three-way phone call or from an auditorium stage.

People typically "embellish" the truth—or outright lie about it—out of insecurity, the sense that the actual facts are somehow not good enough. But if you don't think the actual facts about your business are compelling enough, then you're in the wrong business.

The truth about network marketing is compelling indeed. When you stretch, embellish or distort it, my correspondent asks, "What harm has been done?"

But I'll bet he wouldn't want to say that live on *Oprah*.

A READER RESPONDS

The so-called "Harvard study" mentioned in your article has been around and quoted by thousands of multilevel marketers for at least twenty years. Do you know how this came about? Even if this was not a Harvard study, is there any truth to the figures quoted, and do you know how they originated?

— A Reader

There actually is a "landmark Harvard study," which I mentioned in the earlier editorial ("Lies, Damn Lies and Statistics," May '05). The researcher, George Valliant, had some fascinating things to say about aging—but nothing about goal-setting.

Perhaps there was an actual study about goal-setting, but if so, I have not been able to find it nor any factual reference to it. I posed the question to the National Speakers Association and heard back from several dozen of their members: nobody else had ever been able to come up with one, either. If there really were such a study, wouldn't someone know the actual reference?

So, your questions: Is there any truth here? And how did this all happen?

Ironically, I think there absolutely is *some truth to the idea, or else the myth of the study would not have carried such weight for so long. People who articulate goals* are *more likely to succeed. Careful observation of our fellow humans tells us that, frankly, most people have no clear goals—at least, no major, ambitious life goals. How many do? Three percent, one out of thirty? Could be. Are they more likely to succeed in a major way? No doubt. While I can find no evidence that this has ever been measured, I can certainly believe that it's generally true.*

I've heard that when Brian Tracy was told that nobody had ever done an actual study like this, he said, "Well, they damn well should." He's probably right—but until someone does, continuing to cite a "study" that never existed only hurts the credibility of the truth being told.

— JDM

When We Will Arrive
Network Marketers *Market*—
But Don't Yet Know How to *Network*
May '06

What's the biggest objection you hear, the biggest reason people you know shy away from becoming involved in your business? Here's the one I hear most:

"Oh, that's the thing where people use their friends."

But that's not true! People only think that because they don't understand network marketing! We're not in the convincing business, we're in the information-sharing business! We don't abuse our friendships, we only sort people, because we're looking for people who are looking! . . .

All good points. But if that's all true, then why do network marketers always laugh when the speaker at the front of the room says, "By the time I heard about this opportunity, I was a member of the NFL—No Friends Left!"

I heard this quip just the other day. I've been hearing it for over twenty years. I notice that it never fails to elicit an embarrassed grin of recognition and a sympathetic chuckle from the seasoned network marketers in its audience. Why is this? Could it be that people have this "that's the thing where people use their friends" objection, not because "they just don't get it," but because *they do?*

I don't think anything has done more to poison the well for network marketing than the odious concept of the "Three-Foot Rule" (i.e., "Anyone who comes within three feet is a prospect"). Early in my networking career, I was taught, "How do you know if you've got a prospect? If he can fog a mirror!" That is direct selling at its most crass, offensive and injurious.

The central problem with the Three-Foot Rule is that is starts with the axiom, "Everyone is a prospect." This mindset, seeing everyone as a potential partner, puts you *on the prowl* and you start to give off a predatory scent, which people can readily detect. Not unlike the stereotypic bar-cruiser who sees every female human between the ages of eighteen and eighty as a candidate for his bed until proven otherwise (and perhaps, in his single-focused view, even *after* proven otherwise), the Three-Foot-Rule network marketer gives off the musk of 24/7, anywhere-anytime mating season. Frequently tinged with the scent of desperation. A decidedly unpleasant aromatic mix.

No wonder people run the other way.

You may have heard the expression, taught in network marketing circles as a way to boost confidence and enhance psychological posture: "If you knew what I know about this business, *nothing* would stop you from getting involved." This may build confidence and posture, but if so, it is likely to be false confidence and a posture of arrogance—because it is simply not true.

There are lots of people in your world who would *not* get involved in your business—no, not even if they *did* know all about it.

Why not? Lots of reasons—and yes, *valid* reasons. Some are genuinely not interested in being involved because they are already quite fulfilled in what they're doing and could not even begin to think of taking on the kind of huge added commitment that this business requires. (And make no mistake about it, "ten hours a week, part-time" or not, building a successful network marketing business does indeed require a huge added commitment.)

This "nothing would stop you from getting involved" idea is just another expression of the "everyone is a prospect" bromide. It's that peculiar mix of arrogance and naïveté that too often distinguishes the way we train ourselves.

And this is precisely what perpetuates the three-foot rule that the rest of the world has about *us*: "If you suspect they are in network marketing and about to prospect you, keep them at a distance of at least three foot."

The truth is, everyone is a *not* prospect. Here, though, is an accurate statement: "Everyone *might* be a prospect."

This is not a semantic difference.

Let's say that in the course of a week, you have contact with 100 people. How many of them are genuine prospects for your business?

You may have been taught, "Well, ask yourself, who would be interested in more income? More financial security? Better health and well-being . . . and the opportunity to make a difference in people's lives? Heck, who *doesn't* fit that description?!"

But this is like saying, "Who doesn't need some love?" Yes, it is easy to argue that a little lovin' is something everyone needs. But not everyone wants the kind of lovin' you have in mind, and not everyone wants it right now, and (let's be honest here) not *everyone* wants it from you.

Out of these 100 people, how many are really prospects? Hard to say, could be sixty. Could be sixteen. Let's say there are a dozen people within that 100 who, given a bit of clear, simple information about what it is you're actually offering, might have a genuine interest—that is, enough of an interest that they would like to look into it a bit further.

A dozen out of 100: that's about one out of eight. Not bad. But how do you know *which* dozen? The answer, of course, is that you don't. You can't. And the only way you will find out is to get to know them a little. Build a bit of a bridge between you, a pathway of trust, common interests and mutual likes.

There is a word for this.

Networking.

I recently spoke with Scott Allen (*The Virtual Handshake*) and Thomas Power (*Networking for Life*), two of the world's top experts on online networking, and they both confirmed this shocking but accurate observation: *network marketers do not know how to network.*

So far, Allen and Power seemed to suggest, we know how to do exactly half our job description. We market. We don't network. In fact, we are still so woefully immature at the "networking" half of the equation that in the world's thriving, vibrant professional online networking organizations (such as ryze.com and ecademy.com), network marketing activity is *banned*, much like spamming or pornography.

Let me repeat that: *much like spamming or pornography.*

Now *that* made me sit up and take notice. When the world's top networking experts hold our profession in the same light as the spam and skin trades, is there something here we need to look at?

For years, networking guru Bob Burg has been pointing out what it means to genuinely network: *connect people with each other in a way that helps everyone benefit.* Here's how Thomas Power defines it: "To give away connections." As Dr. Ivan Misner, who some have called the most accomplished networker in the world, famously puts it: "Givers gain."

See the distinction? Not get: give. Not sell: inform. Not

prospect: serve. Not "sort"—network!

Here's what Scott Allen had to say: "The top network marketers know that the Three-Foot Rule is not what you do. If there is a Three-Foot Rule, it's this: *anyone within three feet is worth getting to know a little better.*"

That's maturity. And when we have it and show it in our profession, not just here and there but as the norm . . . well, just imagine!

Network marketing will have arrived.

The Strength of Weak Ties
You Have the Most Influence on
People You Know . . . Vaguely
July '06

Where will you find your strongest leaders? The answer may sur-prise you: among those people you already know . . . sort of.

Prospects come from three domains: 1) your inner circle or "warm market"; 2) the world at large, or "cold market"; or 3) the fuzzy area in between.

This last includes all those people you *vaguely* know: not exactly friends, but not exactly strangers, either. The teller at your bank; your kids' friends' moms; a distant classmate from college years ago. People whose faces you know, if not their names. Friends of friends of friends.

We don't have a term for this not-warm-but-not-cold-either realm, and that's too bad. Because that's where the overwhelming majority of successful network-building partners come from.

What about friends and family? It happens, but rather more rarely. Complete strangers, from an ad or lead generation system, or people one simply meets on the street, on a plane, on a train? (Imagine *Strangers on a Train* if Hitchcock had been a network marketer: "I know . . . I'll prospect *your* warm list, and you pros-pect *mine*! Criss-cross!") Again, it happens. But 90 percent or more of the successful network marketers I've ever seen have been people whose sponsors knew them, *but only vaguely*, before they joined the network.

Malcolm Gladwell, a staff writer for *The New Yorker*, confirms this observation in his best-selling book about influence, *The Tipping Point*.

Gladwell describes a classic 1974 study in which sociologist Mark Granovetter looked at several hundred professional and technical workers from Newton, Massachusetts to find out how they found their current jobs. More than half learned about their positions through personal contacts. This was no big surprise—but the next part was: of those who used a personal contact to find a job, only 16 percent saw that contact "often" (i.e., close friends), and *more than 55 percent saw that contact only "occasionally."*

According to Granovetter, you are far less likely to learn about a new opportunity through a close friend because your friends occupy the same world you do. You are far more likely to learn about something new from someone you know only vaguely. He calls it, "the strength of weak ties," and concludes that those with whom you share only weak ties represent far more social power than your close friends.

Look at it from the other direction: with what people do you hold the power of weak ties? On whom do you have the most influence? Your siblings? Ha! They were there when you were wetting the bed. (You approach your older brother with, "Do you keep your financial options open?" and he grunts, "Yeah, why, Squirt, you starting a company that sells waterproof pajamas?") From complete strangers? Maybe, in time . . . but you'll have to earn it from scratch.

But acquaintances? That's where you already have power: the power of weak ties. Your *fuzzy* market.

Your greatest power lies with the people you barely know. It's quite a paradox—one you can use to build an empire.

A Walk on the Moon
It's Not about the Big Check Any More—
It's about the *Little* One
September '06

Over the last decade there has been a fundamental shift in the way we look at our business, and increasingly, how we present it to others. We're seeing the business less as a source of disposable income and more as an asset. "MLM success" used to buy a big house and a Rolls. Now it buys retirement.

This is not a slight shift: it is radical and fundamental, because it strikes to the core of how we perceive our identity, and in the process, we have matured to the point of honoring more realistic expectations.

In the 1960s, the JFK White House radically shifted our national identity by focusing us on a new goal: putting a man on the moon. Early MLM was like that—a financial Apollo program. I once attended an event where the woman at the front of the room told the audience, "Why am I here? To get filthy, stinkin' rich." Everyone nodded and grinned. Oh boy.

Did she ever in fact get filthy, stinkin' rich? Of course not. Most never did. But that didn't matter. Most Americans never walked on the moon, either—but a *few* did, and the achievement defined all of us. When Neil Armstrong trod the moon's surface, we all walked it with him. And when Dexter Yager or

Jeff Roberti walked across the stage with a million-dollar check, it validated the dream. *That's one big check for a Diamond—one giant check for Diamondkind.*

But no more. Today the goal has changed.

The snapshot moment that defined our entrance into the world of mainstream business press was the famous February 1992 issue of *Success* that featured Richard Brooke on the cover with the headline, "We create millionaires!" By the late nineties, John Fogg was saying, "Enough about millionaires—let's talk about creating thousandaires."

Back then, Tom ("Big Al") Schreiter wrote a little piece about a guy in his group who applied his measly $300 monthly check to prepaying the mortgage on his house and ended up leveraging it into a sizable asset. The article was brilliant—and it made people squirm. In those days, *nobody* told stories about $300 checks. A "little" check was an embarrassment. Then Randolph Byrd wrote "The $300 Solution," pointing out that while people might be drawn to the business by the dream of big money, what keeps them here is the reality of *little* money.

As both Robert Kiyosaki and David Bach have now pointed out, joining a network marketing company is a brilliant career move—but not because of the big money. Because of the *little* money and what you can do with it. A few hundred or few thousand dollars in monthly residual, sensibly leveraged, could buy you a glorious retirement.

And for hundreds of thousands of us, that is a very big dream indeed.

Ignore the Memo: Fly Anyway
All the Reasons You Can't Succeed
Aren't Worth a Teaspoon of Honey
November '06

I was seventeen and dissatisfied. So were my friends. We were dissatisfied with the schools where we currently punched our time clocks five days a week. We wanted to create a better way, a way where we took the pursuit of our education into our own hands. We imagined a school with absolutely no requirements or mandates, where each student designed his or her own course of study. A place where we learned *what we wanted, when we wanted, how we wanted.*

Does this sound at all familiar?

We didn't know it, but we were thinking like network marketers. We wanted to be a volunteer army, not a lockstep formation of grudging corporate conscripts.

We were educational entrepreneurs.

Among our motley crew, I was the one blessed with unusually forward-thinking parents—parents who believed in me and us and our vision enough to let me leave my mind-numbing career at our local public high school and spend the rest of the school year spearheading the project.

Q: How do a scattershot band of disaffected high school sophomores and juniors start their own high school?

A: They don't.

There was of course *no way* we could possibly accomplish this task. It was impossible. Happily, we did not know this. Much like the bumblebee—you know, that bug that flies because it never got the memo explaining that it can't—we didn't *know* it was impossible. So we did it.

The next year our school opened, and it operated successfully for a solid decade. We had absolutely no accreditation from any private or state body, but we were accredited by our own results. We successfully placed our graduates at such places as Yale, Harvard and various state colleges. The environment we had imagined, that place where students voluntarily pursued their own education, worked.

Here is one reason it worked: early on, we realized we needed someone who could do things we couldn't, like fund-raise, secure a location and help us find teachers. We declared an opening for director (great position, starting salary of zero), and began interviewing. Through our parents and other adults we knew, we found some extraordinary candidates. We eventually chose a wonderful man named Julian F. Thompson, who had a strong background in education and grasped what we were up to.

It's a good formula: decide what you want, commit yourself for at least a year to building the foundation, and then go sponsor people who have what you lack.

And if you happen to get that memo? The one that says bees can't fly, kids can't build schools, and you can't be a major financial success and leader of thousands?

Ignore it. Fly anyway.

The Light and the Bushel
A Time for Discretion, a Time to Let It Shine
January '07

In this issue, Dr. Ivan Misner offers a valuable piece of professional etiquette: when you are part of a formal networking group like BNI, it's better manners to present yourself as a representative of your product—not your opportunity. This is good to know. Careful, though: outside the BNI meeting, that same advice does not necessarily apply.

Last issue Scott Allen contributed an excellent article that was golden in every respect—except one. His "point #5" (out of six) was: it's better to be recruited as a customer of the product than as a candidate for the business. I disagree.

Scott says, "The strongest way to build a downline is to bring people in as customers first. Once they grow to love the product, they'll be drawn to become distributors."[20]

Alas, this seldom happens. Indeed, my experience is quite the opposite.

If you try to build a growing, duplicating network by being a product evangelist, hoping you will "back-door" enthusiastic consumers into discovering their latent interest in building a business . . . well, you'll probably have to wait a long, long time. In more than two decades of building network marketing organizations, I've found it is exactly those people who follow this approach who get stuck in first gear.

"I'm getting people onto the product, but I can't seem to find any business builders; nobody's duplicating . . ." Of course not. If you go around planting celery seeds, it's not reasonable to think you'll grow carrots. If what you want is carrots, plant carrot seeds. If what you want is people with an interest in growing a business, that's who you need to go looking for.

I appreciate both Ivan's and Scott's point of view: they are appropriate to their context, which is the world of formal business networking and what has come to be known as "social networking." In that context, perhaps it is good manners to focus on your product. Outside of that specific setting, it's not the strongest strategy for building your business.

Customers don't duplicate. Most happy consumers of the product stay happy consumers of the product. They don't spontaneously combust into growing networks. Growing a large, thriving network is hard work and takes focused intention.

If I had been recruited twenty years ago purely as a product user, I probably never would have joined. I got involved for the same reason as the overwhelming majority of successful networkers I've ever known: because I saw an amazing income opportunity. Because I fell in love with the multilevel concept. No nutritional product, no matter how exceptional or life-changing, would have gotten my attention the way this brilliant business model did.

You never need to feel apologetic about this opportunity, or that it's more "legitimate" to promote the product first and mention the opportunity only as a whispered footnote. The business itself is your most valuable product.

Don't hide it under a bushel.

Staring at Blank Paper
The Future, Like Beauty, Is in the Eye of the Beholder
March '07

"By the time you read this story, the quirky cult company . . . will end its wild ride as an independent enterprise." (*Fortune*, Feb. 19, 1996.) "Whether they stand alone or are acquired, [the company] as we know it is cooked. It's so classic. It's so sad." (*The New York Times*, Jan. 25, 1996.) ". . . A chaotic mess without a strategic vision and certainly no future." (*Time*, Feb. 5, 1996.) "The idea that they're going to . . . hit a big home run . . . is delusional." (*The Financial Times*, July 11, 1997.)

Who was this doomed company that all these experts were writing about? It was Apple Computer.

Of course, the experts were wrong, and just *how* wrong can be spelled out in four letters: i-P-o-d. And now look: in a few months, this "delusional" company with "certainly no future" will launch the iPhone, very possibly changing the rules of the mammoth cell phone market in the process.

If you had been Apple in 1997, how tempted would you have been to throw in the towel? And if *The New York Times* were to write that your network marketing business was "cooked . . . so sad," would you keep going?

We ask prospects all sorts of questions: *What's your dream, how soon do you need to earn X dollars, what are your strengths, who do you know?* The other day I heard my partner Ana McClellan ask someone a question I found especially captivating: *What's your capacity for disappointment?*

I have a benchmark: when someone enrolls in my organization, I don't consider her business in serious momentum until she has withstood her first crushing disappointment in the business.

My point: the future, like beauty, is in the eye of the beholder.

The hardest thing about this business is that we are all entrepreneurs: businesspeople who determine our own future. The upside: you get to set your own hours, work when you want, how you want and with whom you want; you are your own boss. The flip side: it's all up to you. *All* of it.

Here is one of my favorite quotes on writing (attributed to the late Jeff MacNeilly, cartoonist-author of *Shoe*): "Writing is easy. All you have to do is stare at a blank piece of paper until beads of blood start to form on your forehead."

Network marketing is a little like that—only harder. You don't build it with words, which, after all, will to some extent bend to your will, but with people, who won't.

Most entrepreneurial businesses are motor boats, with you as the engine. As long as you have fuel, you can putt-putt-putt anywhere in the lake. But this business is a sailboat. There is no motor: you're the sail. And the wind? Other people. You must have or develop the capacity to be profoundly disappointed when they change direction and still maintain your faith in your future.

If you don't, you could end up stuck in a dead calm for months.

If you do, you can sail around the world.

Cutting a New Path
The Alternatives Are Looking Better All the Time
March '07

> I shall be telling this with a sigh
> Somewhere ages and ages hence:
> Two paths diverged in the wood, and I—
> I took the one less traveled by,
> And that has made all the difference.
> — Robert Frost, *Mountain Interval*, 1920

When I was seventeen, I began a brief career in "alternative" education. Some friends and I were dissatisfied with the schools where we punched our time clocks, and wanted to see if we could create a better way. A way where we took the pursuit of our education into our own hands. We imagined a school where there were absolutely no requirements—no mandates, no externally imposed strictures—and where each student designed his or her own course of study. In other words, where we learned *what we wanted, when we wanted, how we wanted.*

Does this sound familiar?

We didn't know it back then, but we were thinking like network marketers.

We were educational entrepreneurs.

A few years later, I began another career, this time in "alternative" health. We called it *macrobiotics*, but what it boiled down to was a bunch of people who looked at the then-current model of health care (which was really *illness* care) and wanted to create a better way. A way where we took the pursuit of our *health* into our own hands.

We were nutritional and physiological entrepreneurs.

A few years after that, I put my foot on another career path, this time one in "alternative" business. We called it *network marketing*, but what it boiled down to was a bunch of people who looked at the then-current model of livelihood and wanted to create a better way. A way where we took the pursuit of our *financial future* into our own hands.

We were occupational entrepreneurs.

I seem to keep finding myself on these "alternative" paths. Except something is happening now: we're gradually losing the quotation marks around the word *alternative*. In fact, son of a gun, I think we're even starting to flirt seriously with losing the term altogether.

I put the term *alternative* in quotes because that's how people often mean it: like something that is not quite real, not entirely respectable, certainly not proven and probably not efficacious. We say it in that seemingly open-minded yet patronizing way, making air quotes with our fingers.

At least, that's how it used to be. But now look.

Education? Everyone knows the old system is a dinosaur. The federal government tried fixing it with a plan optimistically named No Child Left Behind, and whoops! A whole generation is getting Left Behind. Suddenly (finally) the alternatives are starting to look pretty good, after all.

Health care? Paul Zane Pilzer is telling us that what we used to called *macrobiotics* is suddenly a $400 billion industry—and fast on its way to a trillion—called *wellness*. Ladies and gentlemen, the alternative, all grown up: speaking in full sentences, wearing long pants and everything.

And network marketing? Just watch:

Born in the sixties; learned how to ride a bike, played stickball and scraped its knees in the seventies; went through that awkward growth spurt as a talented but tantrumy teenager in the eighties (anyone who has teenagers knows what I mean, and so does anyone who watched network marketing during that decade); got its drivers license, started a family and started holding down a real job in the nineties. In the nineties I used to hear this a lot: "Network marketing has come of age," and it was true, in the sense that any eager young adult barely out of four-year college can be said to be *of age*. In the nineties we certainly became more *professional*. And true to type, professionals started showing up: doctors, lawyers, engineers, bankers . . . "serious" people.

And now, in the aughts, or whatever this decade is called? Now we've finally entered into that age when you've made enough mistakes, embarrassed yourself enough times and mounted enough earnest efforts at responsible adult life to begin to have some perspective. Not perfect, not even wise, but at least approaching something resembling maturity, or the beginnings of it.

Network marketing: finally coming of age—or let's say it conservatively: *starting* to. Give you some examples.

Used to be, we talked mostly about the merry-go-round golden-ring style of success, the fractional percentage of people with both the exceptionally good timing and the right skill set or personality profile to hit an opportunity just right and catapult to the top. "Success" in those days was mostly shown off in terms of those elite few with yachts, personal jet planes and ridiculous fortunes. Robin Leach (*Lifestyles of the Rich and Famous*) was just hitting stride in the late eighties, and that gaudy style resonated with gawky young teenaged Em-Ell-Em. Success might happen to only a few, but hey, the rest of us could dream, right?

Today we do more than dream. The way we describe success in the network marketing of 2006 has been shaped by *The Millionaire Next Door*, David Bach's Latte Factor® and hundreds of thousands of serious networkers soberly pursuing a reasonable goal of replacement income and financial stability.

Goodbye *get rich quick*, hello *get smart now*.

Meanwhile, as we've matured, the world around us has changed. The corporate model of financial security has crumbled away. Two generations ago, going to work for a company was "security," working for yourself from your home was "risky." Today it's gone clear the other way around.

In 2004 the Small Business Administration told President Bush that small business accounts for more than half the nation's economic output and employs more than half the country's non-governmental employees—and that more than half of those small businesses are *home-based* businesses.[21]

Warren Buffett, the "oracle of Omaha" and famed billionaire stock market expert, turned heads on Wall Street in 2002 when he bought a network marketing company. Actually, he doesn't own one direct selling company—he owns *three*. (And has been quoted, speaking about that 2002 network marketing acquisition, as saying, "It's the best investment I've ever made.")[22]

Network marketing today is a $100 billion concern worldwide, with some $30 billion of that in the United States. [As of 2014, that's $167 bilion.] Right now, as you read these words, there are about 70,000 people around the world who are not network marketers—and by this same time tomorrow, will be.

The DSA's Neil Offen projects that over the next ten years, more than 200 million people worldwide will join our business.[23] Paul Zane Pilzer projects that over those same ten years, a significant portion of new millionaires will be created within network marketing.[24]

And it goes beyond statistics and demographics. Ten years ago, most people you'd talk to about network marketing either knew nothing about it, or knew someone who'd had a negative experience. Today, most people you'll talk to about network marketing know of someone who's had a positive experience. We're less apologetic and more sensible. We have a track record, and we're getting much, much better at what we do.

But don't take just my word for it. Here are some comments from a few people I've interviewed recently for stories in *Networking Times*, when I asked what were their views of where our business stands in the world:

U.S. SENATOR ORRIN HATCH (R-Utah) is one of our leading friends on Capitol Hill and was the prime mover behind the Dietary Supplement Health Education Act (DSHEA) of '93. Here's what Senator Hatch had to say about our profession:

"The companies that have developed this marketing approach with truly high-quality products are doing a lot of good in the world. . . . [Network marketing] is a critically important way of helping people to use high-quality products . . . it's also a way to give people an opportunity to sell those products and earn a good living from it. I see it playing a very important role in the twenty-first century."[25]

JIM TURNER, author of *The Chemical Feast*, cofounded Swankin & Turner, a D.C.-based consumer advocacy law firm, in 1973; he also serves as chairman of the board of Citizens for Health, a major consumer-advocacy lobbying group, has gone to battle many times with the FDA and FTC and is intimately familiar with the network marketing trade. Here's what Jim told me:

"Network marketing is in the vanguard of a major consumer movement in which consumers and producers are merging and becoming the same thing. In a very interesting way, the multi-level marketing companies are the first generation of what Alvin Toffler calls 'prosumers.' . . . I'd say you could have perhaps 150 million households successfully involved in network marketing, at least part-time. . . . You could easily become a major part of a majority of the households in America."[26]

FRANK MAGUIRE worked with JFK in the White House, helped Fred Smith start FedEx and helped Colonel Sanders run KFC. His first job fresh out of college was head of programming for ABC, where he gave Ted Koppel and Charles Osgood their first jobs at major networks. Frank, in other words, has been around the block. Here's his homily to network marketing, which came right at the end of our interview:

"I think [network marketing] is potentially the greatest economic opportunity that has ever existed. Network marketing is turning off the spotlight of working for a corporation and turning on the floodlight of the greatness that we all have within us. I love what you're doing in network marketing because you're creating an opportunity to affect the self-esteem of many, many people. You're giving people hope and providing a launching pad for people to discover their own greatness. You *are* the future."[27]

With world-class leaders like Hatch, Turner and Maguire saying things about us like that, can we really continue calling this mode of business *alternative*? Our model works; we've proven it, over and over. In fact, it's working a lot better than many of the other, more traditional modes of earning a living.

Come to think of it, the next time a strong prospect tells you he or she isn't really interested in taking a look at building long-term residual income and financial security with your business model, you might just say:

"You're not? Okay, no problem. But I'm curious: if you don't mind my asking . . .

"What's your alternative?"

Trust
Food for the Soul
May '07

I was contacted a few days ago by someone I'd known in my network marketing organization many years ago. Was I still in the business? she wanted to know. She was interested in getting back into it. We went back and forth a few times on email, and then I wrote to her: "People have so many different reasons for wanting to do this, and I don't want to make assumptions: What is it you're looking for in a network marketing venture? What's most important to you?"

And she wrote back: "First, loyalty and trust." Fascinating.

She is keenly interested in a quality product, she went on to say, and first-rate training. And she has clear financial goals, which she told me about—six sentences later. But the most important factor for her came in those first four words: "First, loyalty and trust."

We often think of trust as a condition for doing business, a quality we need to have and instill in order to build a strong network, which in turn will lead to the results we seek to gain from that business. That is, a means to an end. But for my friend, trust isn't simply a means to an end—it *is* an end. It's not just a feature: it's a *benefit*.

And so it is, I suspect, for most all of us in this business—

because trust is food for the soul. Without it, we starve.

We're surrounded today by ample evidence of suspicion and mistrust, division and danger. (We line up at the metal detectors, doffing our shoes to prove we're not out to bomb anyone—and that's just our junior high schools!) Yet these are but the inevitable zigs and zags, the traumatic course-correction growing pains, in humanity's overall onward march of ever-increasing trust.

For example: Can you imagine trusting a complete stranger to hurl a one-ton metal missile at you at hurricane speeds, promising to do his best to miss you by, oh, a least a foot or two? Insane! Nobody is *that* trusting. Yet we do it every day on our highways. Or what about giving a complete stranger the keys to a vault where you keep all your money? "Are you crazy?!" Not crazy, just trusting: we do that too with every online purchase.

Living in a cave requires no trust. Do-it-yourself is a trustless path. But doing anything that involves collaboration means giving up a piece of ourselves: putting our lives, or at least a piece of our lives, into the hands of others. The history of the advance of civilization is the story of making impossible things possible through increasing our capacity to trust.

And it not only makes us more advanced, it makes us more human, too.

Be Their Beacon
On a Clear Day, You Can See Forever
July '07

Are you feeling a little stuck? Growth in your network not where you'd like it to be? Perhaps this hasn't happened to you, but for most people, there comes a point in this business, typically around the 5K to 15K volume range, where one starts to feel like the gears are jammed. You're proud of your title . . . but you'd really like to hit the next one. And the income isn't yet where you want it to be, either.

"It wasn't *that* hard to get to this point," you think. "So why can't I seem to move on and get past this barrier?"

Why? Because getting this far was up to *you*—and getting farther is up to *others*. And for some reason, those others you've enrolled just aren't doing what you've done.

An author friend recently told me about the pioneering work of the late Dr. Elliott Jacques. According to Jacques, we are each born with a distinct, fixed capacity for complex thinking—what he termed *cognitive complexity*—which is revealed by how far into the future a person can project. Most people, said the research, can envision up to two or three months ahead, beyond which the horizon of their imagination dims and fades. A smaller group falls out at one year, a still smaller group at two, then five . . . and only a tiny minority have the inborn capacity to picture a decade or more into the future.

We have a term for that tiny minority: *leaders*.

One reason your people don't do what you do is that they cannot see what you see. Which presents a challenge. This business is not designed for immediate gratification. Like a good savings plan, it is an in-it-for-the-long-haul proposition.

This is one big reason short cuts are so attractive. Big buy-ins and front-loads. Australian two-ups, coded bonuses and razzle-dazzle pay-plan gimmicks. Stacking, "fool-proof" formulae and we-build-it-for-you systems. They all appeal to people struggling to find a short cut. But there aren't any short cuts.

Actually, there are—they just don't *look* like short cuts. They look like doing it the long way. But when you look back, five, ten years later, and see that what *you* built is still standing, while what your short-cutting friends built has collapsed (perhaps two or three times over), and they're having to do it all over yet again ...

As my friend Dan Burrus says, "Are you willing to slow down so you can go faster?"

The rewards ahead are stunning. But who can see that far down the road? You can. And while others may not see the destination as clearly as you do, they can see *you*. And seeing your belief, your firm grasp of where this is leading, is sometimes enough.

Be their beacon.

A Revolutionary Idea: Ask
Let's Leave Slash-and-Burn Behind
September '07

My friend Gilles Arbour tells a story about his early days in network marketing. After explaining his opportunity to a prospect, the man said, "You mean, like Amway?" No, Gilles hastened to assure the man—that is, yes, it was the same general idea, but no, in this way and that way and these other ways, it was really nothing like Amway. "That's too bad," said the guy. "I *like* Amway."

The point: *don't assume you know what the other person thinks*. Because you don't; not, at least, unless you ask.

That was the thing about classical advertising, what Seth Godin calls "interruption marketing": it never asked us what we thought. In fact, it *told* us what we thought.

Classical advertising started out by telling us what they had. A pretty straightforward message: "We have Coke, and it's delicious." Sometimes it even got a little bold, and told us what we ought to do about that. "Buy it today! Don't delay!" Then, in the middle of the twentieth century, it went to school on psychology and realized it could do a great deal more: it could tell us *what we wanted*.

Until our televisions told us to, most of us we had not really thought about ring around the collar, the germs that can *cause* bad breath, or the heartbreak that is psoriasis. We did not realize how profoundly and desperately we wanted—nay, *needed*—to rid our lives of these scourges, until the idiot box (as my mom called it) told us so.

Mass media: mass hysteria.

The web is actually a type of mass media, too, only it behaves in a personal way. It doesn't *tell* us what we want—it *asks*.

Ironic: for too many years, network marketers have been a personal medium that behaved in a mass-market way. In my first year in the business, I was actually told, "How do you know if you've got a prospect? If he's got a pulse!" Then there was the networking legend who would walk into a crowded elevator, wait until the door closed, then face the group and say, "You probably wonder why I invited you all here!"—and pitch his opportunity.

That was slash-and-burn prospecting, and it hurt the human soil as much as its agricultural counterpart wrecks good loam.

Marketing is finally growing up: now that we've externalized our nervous system and stretched it around the planet over fiberoptic cable, we finally have the capacity to market far and wide through human conversation. That is, to treat consumers like people.

This should be, and can be, our moment in the sun. Let's make sure we grow up along with it, and leave the slash-and-burn, mass-attack methods back in the twentieth century where they belong.

A revolutionary approach to marketing: Ask me what I want.

A Wealth of Possibilities
That Childlike Sense of the Big Wide World
November '07

". . . So what we're seeing is that for the first time in our history, humanity is on the verge of becoming an extraordinary evolutionary success."

The man on the stage with the gnome-like body, fuzzy bald head and huge fishbowl eyes held me in absolute thrall. He had just explained the concept of "synergy," as exemplified by the tensile strength of chrome-nickel-steel, and somehow related this to why life on this little planet in the year 1967 was bursting with potential, and I had somehow (though I couldn't have told you how) understood his point.

The man was Buckminster Fuller, I was 12 years old, and I didn't think I'd ever heard anything so captivating in my life.

". . . So let me explain who *you* are," he went on, now a good ninety minutes into his dizzyingly non-stop soliloquy about the universe and everything in it. "I'm holding a rope here"—and Bucky needed no props: when he held out his two hands, everyone in the auditorium *saw* that rope. That was one of his gifts: he could concretely *see* things that were there in thought only. And here was another of his gifts: when he saw them, you saw them, too.

This rope, he explained, was stitched together from several

smaller lengths—cotton, nylon and silk. He tied a slip knot in one end, let the other end droop to the floor, and then passed his slip knot down through the length of the rope that wasn't really there but that we could all see, top to bottom.

"Was the knot cotton, or nylon, or silk?" he asked us. "It was all of them and none of them," he answered for us, "it was the pattern. And you—you are not your cells and tissues, those are last week's breakfast, they're your cotton, nylon and silk, but you, *you* are the knot. You are a pattern—a unique, magnificent, extraordinary pattern, and because you are here the world will never be the same . . ."

When I slipped my cotton, nylon and silk self under the sheets for sleep that night, I knew I'd seen something important. I'd had my first close encounter of the Bucky kind, and it left me changed. Like a piano chord striking sympathetic vibration in a tuning fork, it awakened in me a bone-deep conviction that the universe is a place of boundless potential.

It was that same conviction that vibrated all over again when I first learned about the principle behind the network marketing business model.

Bucky had the biggest appetite of anyone I've ever known. It wasn't an appetite for things, for experiences, or even for knowledge that struck me (although he had all those in ample supply). It was his appetite for possibilities. He saw the universe as the most amazing playground, brimming over with things to be discovered and accomplished, to captivate and delight. And when he saw that, we saw it, too.

To this day, I can still see that rope in his hands.

Without a Net
Living Poised Between Frailty and Resilience
December '07

It was cold and icy, the day before Thanksgiving, and I was pumping gas into my car, or trying to anyway. After a few tries, the gizmo still wasn't working. I was annoyed. I turned to step over the hose and head into the station to get an attendant.

Suddenly I heard an eerie sound: it sounded just like the *thwack!* of a baseball and bat making contact. But it was neither bat nor ball, it was the sound of a human head slamming into concrete. *My* head. I'd tripped on the hose and was now face-down in blood.

It's so easy to forget, but this is exactly how life operates. One second you're standing upright, absorbed in a petty annoyance, and a split second later you're lying prone on the pavement, bleeding profusely and marveling at how utterly and instantaneously your reality has changed.

People have asked me, "What lessons did you learn from having your head cracked open on a filling station pavement?" I had to think about that.

Lesson #1: Concrete is hard. Also, be careful how you step over things. These are two parts of the same lesson, and it's a good one to learn.

Lesson #2: That stitching thing they do at hospitals? That's amazing. I'd never been awake for stitches before. It makes me immensely grateful that we have hospitals, antiseptics, and doctors. (Ana successfully removed five of my six stitches at home. The sixth was coy, and I eventually ended up having the local doc coax it out.)

Lesson #3: Life is shockingly fragile—and astonishingly resilient. I was flabbergasted to find myself so suddenly, unexpectedly and irrevocably at the center of an emergency room event. And equally flabbergasted, just hours later, at how little damage had occurred, and how quickly recovery came on the heels of trauma.

No concussion. No swelling. No pain medication at any point, not even a Tylenol, not then nor in the days that followed. A horrific ugly yellow-purple shiner by day 4, but that soon vanished. And now, three weeks later? You wouldn't even know it had happened. The scar now lurks half-hidden behind my left eyebrow. At the hospital that night, the triage nurse looked in my pupil with a flashlight and said, "Do you feel confused?" I replied, "No more than usual." So far that's holding true.

How human beings are built to mend—it's astonishing.

Then again, we have a friend who has a cousin, a fellow my own age, who fell the other day, slipped on the ice and went down on his head. *Wham*: Bat, baseball, trauma—and no recovery. Two days later, he was gone.

It is both terrifying and marvelous to contemplate how it is we actually live each day: suspended in thin air, without a net, between the two poles of frailty and resilience. We know frailty will ultimately win out and declare our mortality. So while we're here, we throw ourselves into creating works, connections and footprints that will stay on past our departure, declaring our resilience.

Putting People Together
Use the Force that Creates Constellations
March '08

While you sleep, a mysterious force is at work in your home. You find traces of its sabotage everywhere. Favorite dishes, left socks and crucial papers are suddenly gone. Tools slip out of their proper places. Dust bunnies repopulate. The evidence of your tidily organized mind miraculously unravels, as if someone had found the single thread that holds together the knitted fabric of your life and, when your back was turned, silently given it a good yank.

The mysterious intruder is the force of *entropy*: the tendency of all systems to unwind and come apart. Newton's grim Second Law of Thermodynamics.

Buckminster Fuller thought a good deal about entropy. Perhaps this came from his early years, when he worked as the guy who fixed machines when they broke down. Perhaps it was the imprint of tragedy: as a young man, he nearly committed suicide after his infant daughter died of influenza. What could be more bitter evidence of entropy than the death of the innocent young?

Bucky postulated an opposing and complementary force, which he dubbed *syntropy*: a force that, rather than toppling the fruits of creativity and pulling things apart, winds things together into higher levels of order.

Bucky held syntropy as the prime function of the human being. He loved to point out that the word "consider" comes from the Latin, meaning "to put stars together" (from the same root as *sidereal*). To *constellate*. He saw our role in the universe as being *considerers*, the representatives of syntropy on earth.

You can see the forces of entropy and syntropy at work in your business. In your volunteer army, your herd of cats, the tendency towards dissolution is always lurking close at hand. Distraction; disappointment; attrition; loss of faith and lack of follow-through. Network marketers feel entropy breathing down our necks.

In your business, what represents the force of syntropy? A dream. A compelling "why." Clear goals. Powerful intentions. Inspiration. A great story. Clear communication. Genuine caring. *You.*

Left to its own, any organization of people has an entropic drift. It's up to you to supply the syntropy.

The Networker Doth
Protest Too Much
Belief Is One Thing; Simple Knowing
Is Quite Another
May '08

"You can trust me, honest."
"I don't want to influence your opinion, I just want you to hear me out."
"I am not a crook."

What do all three statements have in common? None are entirely convincing. For example, if the speaker is genuinely trustworthy, would he need to tell us that?

What about this one:

"This opportunity is incredible! We are going to the moon on this one—I'm telling you, there's never been a comp plan like this, *ever!*"

I'm not convinced. In fact, the very effort to convince me contains within it the seeds of its own undoing. The word *convince* derives from the Latin *vincere*, meaning *to conquer*. To convince means "to overcome in argument." It is said, "A man convinced against his will is of the same opinion still." And really, is there any other way to be convinced than against your will?

Those who assert their cause with the greatest zeal often

insult or injure those they seek to convert, and even do damage to the cause itself. It's the core problem of emphatic assertions: they follow Newton's laws of motion. Every push invokes its counterpush: zealous declamation creates equal and opposite resistance.

And not only outwardly. As author Arjuna Ardagh points out, every belief we assert *within ourselves* comes with its equal and opposite counterbelief, springing full-grown like Athena from the forehead of Zeus. The assertion "I'm a good person!" can exist only with its sly fraternal twin, *Am I really a bad person?*

"The lady doth protest too much, methinks," says Queen Gertrude in *Hamlet*. In Shakespeare's time, "protest" did not mean *to deny* or *object*: it meant *to assert*, as in "He protested his innocence," or, "I do protest with all Vigour the Goode and Comely Virtues of our Companie's Hybrid Comp Planne." The queen's dry observation is that the lady was making an emphatic assertion—and the queen was not convinced.

That's what happens when you "protest (assert) too much." You push the other person in doubting what you're saying. Oops.

What to do? Abandon all enthusiasm, keep one's passions and convictions to oneself? Not at all. There are two classes of declaration. There is the forceful assertion, and then there is the simple statement of fact that springs from the quiet stillness of authenticity. The first is borne of the realm of *beliefs*; the second, from the realm of simple *knowing*. As the popular Gandhi-attributed epigraph goes, "You must *be* the change you wish to see in the world."

If you're trying to convince others, the chances are excellent that it's not something you genuinely to be true, but only something of which you have yourself.

Don't seek to convince people of the need to change. *Be* the change.

Our Favorite Whats
The Simple Experiences
That Make It All Worthwhile
July '08

The other day I was out taking a walk with our dog, Ben. It was the sort of luxuriantly sensory, lavishly fecund spring days that makes you say, "Oh, right—*this* is why we live in New England!" The kind of day where the oxygen pours out of the trees around you, so palpable you could eat it with a spoon: air by Häagen-Dasz. Ben was going nuts, smelling every blade of grass, his body quivering as it tried to absorb the mob of scents crowding in on his little nose. And I was feeling pretty much the same way.

I heard myself mutter, "*This* is why I'm here."

What exactly did I mean by that? That my life purpose is to take the dog for a walk?

We walked on, Ben wildly sniffing the dirt, and I pondering the meaning of life. (Each doing what he loves best.) What made this spring-day moment so noteworthy was that it felt so *alive*. It was like those flowers we always tell ourselves not to forget to stop to smell. There's the loftiness of one's life purpose, the thing mission statements and vision are all about. And then there are the flowers. (Or, if you're Ben, the dirt.) For twenty years, I've been writing about the importance of knowing your compelling *why*. It occurs to me that it's just as important to know your compelling *what*.

Here are just a few of my favorite whats:

Putting the finishing touches on a book I've been working on for months. Gazing, intimidated, at the blank page that signifies the start of the next one.

Discovering a breathtaking author I've never read before. (This month it's Tony Horwitz; last month it was David McCullough.)

Time with my sweetheart, lying on our backs, talking and talking, about anything and everything.

Brahms and more Brahms.

And in networking? What is the best "air by Häagen-Dasz" moment one experiences in this business?

I was on the phone once with Brian Biro, who was interviewing the top leaders in our company to create a leadership profile. He asked what were my goals in the business. I didn't have an answer. I'd had certain financial goals, but I'd already reached those. As I thought about it, a picture popped into mind: a birdcage door opening, its occupant bursting out into the open air and fluttering up and away into the sky.

Seeing people enter this business, I told Brian, caged in the various ways life can imprison, and then find their way to the point where the cage door opens ... watching them enter the open air and fly high—*that's* my what.

It also makes an excellent why.

Shhhhh
The Art of Quiet
September '08

I remember my eighteenth birthday. I was young and in love, and the road ahead was positively shimmering with possibilities. I was unstoppable, and nothing was impossible.

Then post-teen life began unfolding. Strivings, successes, failures, catastrophes. Fortunes rose and fell, marriages and friendships blossomed and crumbled. Some public triumphs, some personal tragedies, more roadblocks and dead ends and cul-de-sacs than I'd ever dream the universe could supply.

This summer, I turned 54. (That's *three times* 18.) I am young and in love; the road ahead positively shimmers with possibilities, and nothing seems impossible. It's good to be back.

This year I celebrated my birthday by spending twenty-four hours not writing anything.

For a writer, spending time not writing is precious, in the same way that cleaning out your closets helps grow your wardrobe and having earthworms in your garden helps the soil bring forth plants. It's the aeration that comes from introducing emptiness.

Empty space is one of the greatest lessons the passing years reveal. It is the core secret of all creative endeavor, the one that most readily divides wannabes from masters. The value of white space in page layout, of silence in music, of understatement in rhetoric. Of knowing when the greatest eloquence lies in not saying anything at all. I think of Jack Benny and Johnny Carson, of Peter Falk as Lieutenant Columbo, of the peculiar genius of Steven Wright: all masters of the pause.

In traditional churches, mosques and synagogues there are these vast empty spaces above our heads—extra space, someone once said, "to leave room for God." In the same way, the conscious pause in action leaves room for inspiration, and the silence of listening makes room for another person.

The networking business, perhaps more than any other mode of commerce, lives and breathes by the creation and nurturance of vast webs of informal relationships. The highest skill for a networker is not presenting, talking, or blabbing, but listening: making room for the other person.

Blaise Pascal, writing during the generation of Isaac Newton, when the science of Europe was just beginning to grasp the vastness of the universe, wrote, "The eternal silence of these infinite spaces terrifies me." (*Le silence éternel de ces espaces infinis m'effraie.*) I like to think of these infinite spaces as a pool from which one may sip when the brain and heart become parched from too much fullness, too much noise.

At 18, there was never enough time in the day to do all there was to do, to say all there was to say, and life seemed to strain against its seams. At three times 18, there is the more humbling sense that perhaps one has said quite a bit already, and a far greater interest in leaving room for comments from the empty spaces.

The Power to Create
or Tear Down
The Words Come First, Then the Phenomenon
September '08

The words you speak have enormous impact on others. Indeed, which words you use and how you use them is one of the most powerful leadership secrets there is. Yet often we don't even realize what it is we're saying.

I recently lost my phone charger and went to the store to buy a replacement. Standing at the register, I held out my debit card and looked uncertainly at the card-swiping gizmo. The man behind the register saw my confusion and said, "Strip down. Facing me."

I paused, then repeated his words back to him. The woman at the next register burst out laughing.

Words. Honestly, they're pretty malleable.

I have a friend who grew up hearing "Silent Night" and thinking that "Round John Virgin" was a character in the story.

When I was 6, I had a friend who used to wet her bed every night. My mom told me she had "a bladder problem." I had no idea what a "bladder" was. I thought she said my friend had "a splatter problem," and that made perfect sense to me.

When my son Nick was very young, he had a problem pronouncing the words "airplane" and "airport." He said "ahhplane" and "ahhport." This went on for a few years. Then one day we drove to the Charlottesville Airport to pick up my dad, who was coming for a visit. We collected the maestro, and as we began driving home, Nick said something about how exciting it was to "come get Grandpa at the *ahh*port." Then he turned to my dad and explained in perfect English, "I can't say *airport*."

"No?" said my dad, intrigued. "What do you say?"

"I say, *ahh*port," Nick replied.

Words often get a bum rap. "We tried to talk it over," says George Benson, "but the words got in the way." I don't think so. I think it's more like this: "We tried to talk it over, but got in the way." People often say of some especially intense experience, "Words cannot describe how I felt." Sure they can. It's a question of how you're using them.

We often don't realize the power our words have to influence others—and ourselves.

There's a scene in the film *American Beauty* where the parents (played by Annette Bening and Kevin Spacey) have just seen their daughter Jane (Thora Birch) in a high school dance number, and the mom says: "Honey, I'm so proud of you! I watched you very closely, and you didn't screw up once!"

What's the real message here? "Honey, I totally expected you to screw up—but for once, you didn't, and boy, was I surprised!"

She could have told Jane how great she looked, how well she moved, how good her timing was and how fantastic the coordination of the whole group was, or any one of a hundred things that would have affirmed something positive about who Jane is and what she accomplished. But Jane's mom was so busy being vigilant about what she saw as Jane's potential to screw up, that was all she could comment on. It's a classic passive-aggressive "left-handed compliment"—the sort of compliment that actually conveys a concealed insult.

If you get a chance to watch the film, pay attention to Thora Birch's expression as her character's mother delivers that line. Does she get the message? She sure does. We all do. We *always* get the message behind the words, even if we're not consciously aware of it.

And by the way, nobody is more expert at giving us left-handed compliments than we ourselves.

Compare that scene to this one in *Julie & Julia*. Julia Child (Meryl Streep) is distraught because a major publisher has once again turned down her manuscript. As her husband Paul (Stanley Tucci) consoles her, he paints a word picture for her of how her book is absolutely going to be published and is going to be a huge success. Then he tells her:

"Your book is genius. Your book is going to change the world."

He was right, of course. It was, and it did. *Mastering the Art of French Cooking* transformed cooking in American households for generations. But would all that have happened if he had not said those words?

Here is what James (Jesus' little brother) had to say about the power of the human tongue (James 3:1 ff.): "Look at ships: they may be huge and driven by fierce winds, but they can be turned by this tiny little rudder in whatever direction the pilot chooses. That's the power of the tongue."

The man ought to know: he was involved in some pretty powerful networking circles and saw both sides of the word-of-mouth coin. In fact, he ended up being hurled off the temple wall and stoned to death because of the propaganda people promulgated about him in their first-century version of the telephone game.

Obi Wan told Luke that the power of The Force could be used for great good, or for great evil. Consider yourself a Jedi Knight of the Force of words.

The fourth gospel-writer claims that words were here before we were: "In the beginning was the Word." Genesis confirms the sequence: God *says* "Light—*be!*" and then light *is*. The words come first, then the phenomenon. Words, in other words, are not mere reporters after the fact, but central players in the drama.

Words create. Words *lead*.

Being in Love
The Number One Criterion
for a Strong Prospect
November '08

Who is a good candidate for joining you in this business?

We say, "someone who is a people-person." Yet we've seen people who are bona fide people-people who don't go far in this business. And people who have gone far in this business who are card-carrying introverts and not people-people at all.

We say, "Look for people who have influence in their community." But the same caveat applies: that correlation often fails to hold.

We say, "Look for people with whom you share a common bond." Hmm. I have close friends who are writers or cellists who are not even remotely interested in joining my business. My two brothers, ditto.

So when you go prospecting, who are you really looking for? I think you're looking for someone who falls in love. How do you know? There are three signs to look for.

They see it.

Beauty is in the eye of the beholder; so is opportunity. You can't *make* someone see the value this business model has to offer. You can show it and explain it, but that goes only so far. They see it, or they don't. There's an expression in networking: "You can't say the right thing to the wrong person, and you can't say the wrong thing to the right person." This is true in courtship, in genuine friendship, and in your business.

They want it.

We like to say, "can succeed in this business," but that isn't accurate. Who can succeed here is anyone *who wants to*, and a lot of people don't. This business is not for everyone. For one thing, it's hard work. (That eliminates quite a few candidates right there.) It also requires resilience in the face of repeated disappointment; a willingness and capacity to work in partnership with others; and faith in human nature. Most of all, it requires a compelling interest in succeeding at this business that borders on obsession. This often has nothing to do with the candidate's financial status. It's not something you can predict or predefine; it's an individual matter.

They do it.

This last should be obvious, but evidence suggests it's not, because I keep seeing leaders and aspiring leaders in this business who persistently chase after, attempt to work with, struggle to figure out how to offer the right support to, and pin hopes upon people in their networks *who clearly are not doing it.* There are people who see it and want it, but just won't take the actions. Puzzling, I know, but there it is. What's missing? They're not in love.

You can't make them see it, nor want it, nor do it. You can't make someone fall in love.

And when they do, watch out: nothing will stop them.

Love and Residual
Network Marketing Is
Royalties for the Rest of Us
January '09

A few weeks ago, I got a check in the mail for $404.79. Before I explain why, I have to digress with a brief story about my dad.

Born in Germany, my dad emigrated to the United States during World War II. Before leaving his homeland at the age of 19, he published his first book, a translation of a classic eighteenth-century text on music composition that was revered by Bach, Haydn, Mozart, Beethoven and scores of illustrious others. The original text was in Latin, which my dad prepared in a German edition.

Upon arriving here, he was soon drafted into the American army and shipped overseas, ending up back in Europe as a counterintelligence agent tasked with debriefing citizens. The war's close found him in a town near the famous mountaintop residence of Richard Strauss, legendary composer of *Also Sprach Zarathustra* (that dramatic music that plays when the apes discover the big thingamajig in the opening of Stanley Kubrick's *2001: A Space Odyssey*).

So my dad goes up the mountain to interrogate Strauss, and finds the old man teaching his own grandnephew composition out of . . . (wait for it) . . . *my dad's book.*

After returning to the States, my dad eventually produced another edition of the book, this time in English, which was published here by W.W. Norton as *The Study of Counterpoint*. He taught me composition from it when I was a teenager. It is still used in schools today.

And by now I'll bet you've guessed how this all ties in. That $404.79 check was from W.W. Norton: my portion of this royalty period's proceeds from a book my dad started working on when *he* was a teenager in the 1930s.

After depositing that check, I went out with my son Chris and bought an LCD monitor he's been wanting. I doubt that my dad ever imagined, when he was 19, that his efforts would someday buy a computer monitor for his 20-year-old grandson. But that's exactly what they did.

Residual income is like that; so is love. They both defy the entropy of time. They *last*.

Of course, most of us will never write a classic textbook on music composition (let alone *Also Sprach Zarathustra*). That's where network marketing comes in. To borrow Apple's old slogan, network marketing is *royalties for the rest of us*.

A few days later, a much larger check arrived, one that has put a roof over Chris's head for the past twenty years: the commission check I've received every month since joining a network marketing company in the summer of 1986—two years before Chris was born.

Residual income. The best investment ever invented.

Being Heard
What an Amazing Thing It Is
March '09

My office is downstairs in our house; directly above me is the living room, at the edge of which is the location of the food and water dishes of our inimitable seven-pound poodle, Ben.

One night while focused on a manuscript at my desk, I heard the *pat-pat-pat-pat-pat* of Ben's tiny feet upstairs as he trotted in from our bedroom (where he had been faithfully guarding Ana while she watched TV) through the kitchen and toward the location of the dishes. From the sound of it, he was popping in for a drink of water.

Cocking my ear, I heard that right-to-left *pat-pat-pat-pat-pat*, followed by a brief pause—too brief for drinking and with no telltale *clink-clink-clink-clink-clink* of his dogtags against the dish signifying his lapping at the dish—and then an immediate about-face left-to-right *pat-pat-pat-pat-pat-pat* receding again toward the hallway, where the stairs are located.

Then about ten seconds of silence.

And then my door slowly swung open. His nose poked through, then his face. He looked at me. I looked back. "What's up, Ben?" I said. "No water? Your dish empty?"

I will never forget the look on his face.

Now Ben's is an awfully expressive face, but I don't think I'd ever seen him register such an unmistakable expression before. He did a visible double-take, right out of a Chuck Jones cartoon, and gaped at me with a look of absolute exuberance, a look of stunned revelation. Then, notching his head forward a full two inches to peer at me with intensity, his face beamed a gaze that said unambiguously: "Yes! Yes! That's *exactly* what I meant! How the hell did you *know?*"

I got up and went upstairs, him trotting excitedly at my heels. Sure enough, we found the water dish empty. Ever since that day, Ben has been palpably more attached to me than he was before.

What an amazing thing it is, whether for dog or for human: to be seen, heard and understood by another.

Gold and Twopence
Thoughts on the Network Marketing Dream
May '09

On January 24, 1848, a young carpenter named James Marshall discovered a bit of shiny yellow metal in Coloma, a sleepy little town in the center of what was about to become the state of California. Within a year some 300,000 men, women and children had poured into the territory in hopes of striking it rich. Only a tiny percentage did so (Marshall himself was forced off his land and died penniless), but the dream endured.

According to Texas A&M professor H.W. Brands, in his fascinating book *The Age of Gold: The California Gold Rush and the New American Dream*, the "California Dream" spread to the rest of the country and in time became the essence of the American Dream.

But that isn't how things started. The original American Dream, says Brands, "was the dream of the Puritans, of Benjamin Franklin's Poor Richard's [Almanack] . . . of men and women content to accumulate their modest fortunes a little at a time, year by year by year."

While George Washington is revered as the "father of his country," it's Franklin who is most closely identified with the roots of the modern American character, a sober mix of practical values—thrift, hard work, self-discipline and a devotion to education—with an Enlightenment zeal for scientific innovation and categorical opposition to authoritarian rule . . . all traits that have a mighty familiar ring to network marketers.

And yet we too have our version of Gold Rush impulse.

This is the internal conflict bred into the American experience, and it is woven through the DNA of the network marketing dream. Franklin versus Marshall; hard work and a frugal appreciation of modest gains, versus the dream of instant wealth won by boldness, pluck and timing.

But wealth, as it turns out, is a highly malleable thing.

Franklin's two Declaration of Independence colleagues, John Adams and Thomas Jefferson, both died on the same day (July 4, 1826, the Declaration's fiftieth anniversary). Adams, a lawyer from a frugal New England farming family, never made much money; Jefferson, a plantation owner, was the picture of wealthy aristocracy. Yet on their deathbeds, Adams had managed to amass a net worth of about $100,000. Jefferson was $100,000 *in debt*.

One of Franklin's most enduring sayings, usually misquoted these days as "A penny saved is a penny earned," actually read, "A penny saved is twopence dear." In other words, if you take some modest earnings and save the money instead of squandering it, you can *double* it; sort of a self-generated gold rush.

Perhaps the dream's reality lies somewhere in between the nugget and the penny: there *is* a bit of gold in them thar hills— but it doesn't have to take much to make you rich.

Compassion
What It Takes to Earn an A+
June '09

Earlier this fine New England summer evening, while my sweet wife Ana was traveling and working in Singapore, I had dinner out on our deck with her sweet mother, Sylvia. As we chatted over salmon and goat cheese, Sylvia recounted a story from her youth.

As a nursing student at Franklin Hospital in Greenfield, Massachusetts, Sylvia had a paper to write. The students in her class each had to pick a patient they had worked with and prepare a detailed paper on the patient's condition, treatment, progress, and the rest.

She chose a young woman who was pregnant, and had all sorts of complications. The pregnancy was not going well, and the woman had a really rough time of it. To make matters worse, there was no husband: Sylvia's patient was an unwed mother.

This was the 1940s, remember: the stigma of unmarried pregnancy loomed large, and unwed mothers had a much tougher time of things than they do today. Sylvia (then all of 18) sympathized with her, but decided that her marital status was not relevant to the matter at hand, and she made a point of leaving it out of her paper.

She did a pile of research, documented the woman's condition and progress carefully, including the birth, which she attended. The birth went well. The woman called her baby Treasure, which no doubt was quite accurate.

When the papers came back graded, Sylvia was nervous. She had really worked hard on it and hoped it had gotten at least a passing grade. With her first glance she saw the big letter A written at the top. Then she looked closer, and realized it didn't say A. It said A+.

Sylvia was flabbergasted. (Also thrilled.) She went to see the instructor and asked, what was so good about the paper that it had earned her an A+?

"You did an excellent job with your research," the woman told her. "The case was documented well. It was clearly work that deserved an A."

She paused.

"And I noticed that you left out any mention of the fact that the young woman was not married. That deserved an A plus."

Building a solid networking business, supporting people consistently, being a standout leader, all that earns you a passing grade, maybe even an A.

What would it take to earn an A+?

To Break or to Bend
Choosing the Value of "No"
July '09

Many years ago, I was teaching an adult class in nutritional philosophy. After class was over and the students picked themselves up and shambled off to their next class, one woman stayed behind. When the room was empty, she came up to me and said, "You've lost a child, haven't you?"

I was stunned. She was right: I had lost my first son to an illness when he was not quite one year old. But how did she know?

My mind raced back over the previous ninety minutes. There was nothing we'd talked about in class that remotely related to the subjects of parenthood, bereavement, infant diseases, or anything else I could think of that would have conveyed even the slightest clues to that buried bit of personal information.

"I just knew," she said, and I realized that, looking at her, I knew that she had lost a child too. How did I know? I don't know how. It just *showed*.

Adversity changes you. It doesn't simply add an experience to your memory banks, it engraves itself onto your being and alters forever who you are. This is true not only of death and bereavement, but also of such experiences as divorce, disappointment, loss of a friendship, discovery of one's own deep error, reversal of fortunes, frustration of an ambition, failure or collapse of an enterprise.

Or having a promising prospect say "no," or a key business partner say "I quit."

I sometimes tell new distributors in this business that I won't consider them truly *in* the business, genuinely committed and in for the long haul, until after they've had their first crushing disappointment. Hearing myself say those words sometimes makes me cringe, because it sounds a bit brutal—but it's the absolute truth. About your business, and about your life.

Losing a child was an experience so terrible I would not wish on anyone. Yet at the same time, now that it's part of who I am, I cannot truly say I would wish it gone, either. It certainly made me less cocky (at least a little) and more capable of empathizing with another's pain.

Loss and failure *shape* you; they tend to carve furrows of compassion, understanding and generosity of spirit. And that was how the woman knew I'd lost a child: she recognized the impact of adversity because it resonated in her, the way an A-440 tuning fork hums when you play A above middle C on the piano.

While it's true that loss and failure *tend* to carve furrows of compassion and understanding, that result is not foreordained. There is choice involved. People respond to suffering in different ways. Adversity *can* deepen character, but sometimes it simply *damages* character. Faced with difficulty that feels too great to bear, the human being has two choices: break, or bend. In the breaking, we simply become bitter; in the bending, we are humbled and stretched.

You have no choice but to suffer loss; it is an inevitable part of the human journey. To break, or to bend: *there* is the choice.

Life Is Like a Box of Tofu
You Decide What It Tastes Like
September '09

While at a party during the 1920s, the young F. Scott Fitzgerald observed a man named Leonard Zelig who had an uncanny ability to take on the demeanor and even physical appearance of those around him. Over the following two decades the chameleonesque man showed up again and again, fitting seamlessly into dozens of different social circles, from Nazi Germany to the White House, always blending in perfectly. *Amazing* . . .

Except that none of it ever happened. The real Fitzgerald never saw or even heard of Leonard Zelig. Because like his heir apparent Forrest Gump, Zelig was a complete fiction.

Zelig—Fitzgerald party, White House appearance and all—was invented by Woody Allen for his 1983 film of the same name. Gump, the creation of novelist/satirist Winston Groom, was brought to life on film in 1994 by Robert Zemeckis. And like the brilliantly clueless Chance the Gardener, created by novelist Jerzy Kosinksi, filmmaker Hal Ashby and actor Peter Sellers in *Being There* (1979), they are fascinating characters precisely because they are not really characters at all but *take on* whatever characters others see.

Something like money.

On a recent radio interview, I was asked to describe the gist of the book Dave Krueger and I had just released, *The Secret Language of Money*. My answer: "Money is like tofu: it has no flavor of its own, but takes on the taste of whatever you put with it."

I might as easily have said, "Money is like Zelig, or Forrest Gump, or Chance the Gardener . . ." Because money has no character of its own: it is a mirror-mirror on the wall, a movie screen onto which we project the desires and fears, prides and suspicions, hopes and ambitions that make up the stories in our heads.

Have you ever been deep in debt? Ever earned a million dollars? Been broke? How much do you earn today: barely enough to live on? Well into the high six figures? Do your debts outweigh your assets? The other way around? And the $64,000 question: What do your answers to these questions *mean*?

Answer: They mean whatever you say they mean. Life, as it turns out, is not a box of chocolates: you not only *know* whatcha gonna git, you *determine* it.

I have earned millions. I have also been so broke a big repo guy named Chris came to my door one night at 11:00 to haul away my car. In both cases, I made the same mistake: I thought it all said something about *who I was*.

But money, or lack of it, does not decide who you are. It's the other way around. You decide what money is. And then, it appears: just as you said.

Who Gets In?
What If We Started Holding
a Higher Standard?
January '10

What is the single strongest factor creating long-term productivity, coherence and strength of your network organization? What one characteristic, more than any other, dictates whether or not you will still be drawing a check from your business ten years, twenty years from now, and how significant that check will be?

Is it your product? Your comp plan's super-duper triple-up back-end bonuses? Your current momentum? Your company's ability to produce really swell DVDs and web sites? I don't think so.

I posed this question ten years ago in an article entitled "Build to Last," and here's how I answered it then:

"There are two major factors to look at: product and company. Making this choice is crucial, because once made, it is fixed in stone: you can't do anything to change product or company. But there is a third factor, and it is one you can do a great deal to change: in fact, you can determine it—and it has everything to do with the health and longevity of your business. That factor is your organization's *culture*."

Ten years later, nothing has convinced me to change that answer.

I recently had an opportunity to talk with the leaders of two extraordinary billion-dollar corporations, Zappos (Tony Hsieh) and Southwest Airlines (Colleen Barrett). Both are companies industry leaders flourishing during times when so many of their competitors are struggling, and both owe a great deal of their success to their unusual approach to creating a culture. When asked how they manage to promulgate and maintain that culture within their huge organizations, Hsieh and Barrett both had essentially the same answer:

"First, we figure out who we are. Then, we screen all our potential newcomers to make sure they fit that description."

How simple! How obvious! How brilliant! But of course, we can't do that in our network marketing organizations, can we? Because we don't exactly interview people to see if we're going to hire them, right? In fact, we pride ourselves on the fact that *anyone* can join our business, right? We don't screen people *out*, we go to any lengths to get them *in* . . . right?

Or should we perhaps be rethinking every one of those assumptions? What if we tossed out that ridiculous old "three-foot rule" that says we're supposed to corner every breathing body within reach to tell them about our business?

What if, rather than pleading, groveling and begging people to join our organizations, we clearly established our own criteria, based on the amazing culture we wanted to create, and then interviewed only the very best candidates—and held them to that standard? What if we brought in only those people who genuinely fit that description?

Who knows. We might start looking a bit like Zappos or Southwest.

How to Start
Make Something Happen—
and Wholeheartedly Embrace Correction
May '10

The other day I gave a talk to a group of college students, about books, business and writing. Just as we were closing our Q&A, one girl raised her hand. "I was just texting a friend, about your talk," she said, "and he wanted to know, can he ask a question about writing?" Okay. "He says, how do you get started? I mean, are there one or two critical essential things to do, or to avoid doing?"

Yes there are, and it later occurred to me that these two critical things apply just as aptly to getting started in your network marketing business.

First: *do something*. (This answer was actually supplied by the day's other speaker, who was sitting next to me. Good answer.)

For a networker, this means *make things happen*. Take initiative. We like to say this business is very systematic: we develop our simple, duplicable systems of clear, concrete steps everyone is meant to follow alike. And that's all well and good. But the truth is this: those who are successful in this business are not those who docilely follow the directions in the manual, they are the people who *make things happen*.

There is a paradox here. The biggest error new networkers

make is to run out and start yapping all over town. Get on the phone, shove CDs into people's hands, effect a frontal assault on the Sunday congregation or gym club membership—talk, talk, talk. This, of course, almost never ends well, which is why we often start out trainings by saying, "Please *do not* go out and present!"

The paradox is that you *do* want to learn how to do this right—but truthfully, learning how to do it right is secondary to *doing* it, period. It is an entrepreneurial business. Here is the definition of an entrepreneur: *you make things happen.* You rely on you. You are the source of action, the origin of opportunity, the reason things start to shake and move.

So that's the first thing: make things happen. Don't get stuck in learning-following mode; *do* stuff. Take risks. Aim at big targets and then pull the trigger like it's a foregone conclusion that you cannot miss.

Which, of course, you will. Hence step two: *wholeheartedly embrace correction.* This may be the biggest single success secret for aspiring writers. Those who cannot stand being corrected or critiqued will never learn to write well. E.B. White said, "The best writing is rewriting." Hemingway put it this way: "The first draft of anything is crap."

Succeeding at writing requires having the courage to put pen to paper and write that misguided first draft—and the humility then not to quit, but to keep reworking it until it gets better. Succeeding at networking is much the same thing.

You Are Not the Boss of Me
On Dogs and Cats and Leadership
July '10

We have a dog named Ben, although I sometimes think of him as Agent Smith because he so closely resembles a Secret Service agent in the way he shadows my wife, Ana. From room to room, household chore to teleconference, day or night—whatever task Ana is involved in, you will find Ben on the job, blending into the background, standing guard with unflagging vigilance.

Know how to spell *devotion*? D-O-G.

Wouldn't dogs make great downlines? Once a dog has identified you as his leader, he'll do anything you say. Got a new group volume target? Easy. "Fetch!" you say—and the whole downline dashes off across the field in dogged search of the stick you threw. Give a little acknowledgment, a little praise, a scratch behind the ears, and they'll follow you anywhere.

Cats . . . not so much.

I grew up with a cat. She was devoted, too: would sleep on my bed, even lick my hair while I slept so that I would wake up spiky-haired, as if I'd time-traveled in my sleep and had pre-cognitive 1961 visions of punk-rock hair styles. In this, she was somewhat doglike. But you could push her only so far.

Care for a cat and she will follow you, but only in the way of cats, which is to say, at a distance and on her own terms.

The truth of people is that they are neither dogs nor cats, but people. Still, Jung said we each embody both animus and anima. My observation: we also contain *aniwoof* and *animeow*.

Which brings us to leadership.

Stephen Covey talks about *structural authority*, the sort of leadership that comes automatically with the position of captain, general or boss; and *moral authority*, that which arises organically from one's own character. Gandhi was a great example of the latter. He held no formal government position yet wielded such formidable gravitational pull that he countermanded the entire British empire, establishing the largest democracy in the world. Yet Gandhi didn't have the "power" to appoint or dismiss a single government employee.

That's the thing about the network marketing relationship: it carries *zero* structural authority. You are not your downline's boss. You don't hire them, can't fire them, and have no way to impel them to do what you want them to do.

There is a fine line between helping someone stay accountable to her goals and commitments, and giving her marching orders. People don't join networks to gain a new boss.

To the degree that you care about people and look out for their interests, you generate a field of moral authority that beckons them to follow, and they do. *Woof.*

But try saying, "Fetch!" and just watch their feline nature emerge. *Meow.*

Are You Found Wanting?
A Case for Gratitude
July '10

I've been thinking lately about Mick Jagger and the Book of Daniel.

it's the eve of their ruin, at least not yet), where this disembodied finger eerily appears and writes on the wall:

Mene, Mene, Tekel, u-Pharsin

It's a prophecy, couched in the language of economics. These are Aramaic terms for various units of currency. (*Tekel*, for example, is an alternate spelling of *shekel*.) Daniel gives the interpretation. It has to do with King Balshazzar, and it is not especially good news: the King's days are over.

"You have been weighed on the scales," explains David, "and found wanting." That very night the kingdom was invaded. Balshazzar didn't live to see the sun rise.

The part of this I've been thinking about is that phrase, "You have been found wanting." Which brings us to Mick Jagger:

You can't always get what you want.

It's that word, *want*. It seems to me that it isn't just that you can't always get what you want. It's that you can't *ever* get what you want. Because *wanting* and *having* are two mutually exclusive states of being.

The word "want" originally meant "to lack," that is, to *not have*. And it meant this for at least a good five hundred years before anyone thought of persuading the word to mean *desire, to wish for*. That's a lot of years. This is in our phonetic DNA. Whether you are consciously aware of it or not, when you say "I want . . ." you are saying "I lack . . . ."

"I want dinner . . ." *I lack dinner.*
"I want to succeed . . ." *I lack success.*
"I want to be loved . . ." *I am not loved, nobody loves me, perhaps I am not lovable.*

You see the trap? We think we're articulating a wish, a desire—and what we're secretly doing is articulating our failings, the emptinesses and unfulfillments of our lives.

This is why the prayer of petition is often so self-defeating. "Lord, won't you buy me a Mercedes Benz?" is really just another way of saying, "Lord, *you won't* buy me a Mercedes Benz!"

I want, I want, I want . . . the perfect way to keep ourselves in poverty. And the alternative?

I'm so grateful for having . . .

Coachability
The Singular Trait for Great Networking Success
September '10

When my parents were young and poor, my mother taught herself to build bookshelves to house our ever-growing inventory of books. I grew up surrounded by my mom's handiwork—not exactly fine finish carpentry, but it worked.

A school teacher, she taught kids by day and herself by night. She became a self-taught gourmet cook. In my twenties, I went macrobiotic; my mom embraced it utterly, learning how to prepare miso soup, seaweed, tempura and all. One year, when my dad conducted a performance of Handel's oratorio *Israel in Egypt*, which dramatizes the story of Moses and Pharaoh, she taught herself to embroider. She attended the concert and after party (which she catered and hosted) in a dress embroidered with scenes depicting all ten plagues: lice, frogs, fire and hail, smiting of the first-born, the whole—and I mean this in a seamstress's literal sense—nine yards.

She loved to learn.

In our business, people often ask what traits to look for in a prospective partner. There are many answers: someone who is hungry, who "has a compelling *why*." Who is personable. Influential. Hard-working. But over the years I've seen so many industrious, personable, motivated, compellingly whyed and otherwise perfectly traited candidates for success in this business wash out—because they were not able or willing to listen and learn. While those other traits are certainly valuable, I've come to see this singular quality as the first and foremost, the *sine qua non*, the one thread which, if missing, will cause the entire fabric to come unraveled: *coachability*.

In our business model, we do a webinar followed by three-way phone calls. I'm on the line with Ed, who just saw the webinar. It's his first exposure to network marketing, and he starts our conversation this way: "Excellent presentation. I understood it all completely, and don't really have any questions."

I already know Ed will not join. Or if he does, he'll be gone within the month. Why? Because he thinks he already knows. (Hey, I've been doing this for a quarter century, and I *still* have a lot of questions.) As the Zen master points out, it's hard to pour tea into a cup that's already full.

A friend I will call Diane recently joined my business. Diane has past experience in network marketing; in fact, she has built a large organization, earned a good deal of money, touched a lot of lives. Now she's doing it again. Here is something I've noticed about her: she asks a *lot* of questions and then she does something as remarkable as it is unusual: *she listens to the answers*. No wonder her network is growing like a spring forest. There is great vitality in genuine curiosity.

"I guess it comes down to a simple choice, really," says *The Shawshank Redemption*'s Andy Dufresne. "Get busy living, or get busy dying."

Only one of those two options involves *learning*.

Creating Caliber
The Magic of Sponsoring Up
November '10

I did something recently that made me nervous. I invited several people whom I respect highly to look at my opportunity.

"No big deal," one might say, "who *else* would you approach?" The answer to that question, though, is exactly what happens in most network marketing invitations.

In the Harold Ramis film *Multiplicity* (1996), Doug Kinney, the Michael Keaton character, clones himself to make his life more manageable. And it works pretty well, until Doug Kinneys #2 and #3 figure out to clone *themselves*. Doug Kinney #4 is decidedly, well . . . not quite right. When Doug's wife pours out her heart to #4, thinking she's talking to her husband, and asks him searchingly, "What do you want?" the best he can come up with is, "I want pizza."

"You know how, when you make a copy of a copy," explains Doug Kinney #3, "and it's not as sharp as the original?"

Yes, we know. Because we've seen it happen too often in network marketing, where it's often termed *sponsoring down*. Here's what sponsoring down looks like:

Looking for people who we think will say yes.

Looking for people who don't make us nervous to approach.

Looking for people we feel confident we can coach.

Looking for people who have a lot of free time on their hands.

Looking for people who "need our product."

Looking for people who "need the income."

Looking for people who are sick, are broke, have lost hope, have no other serious prospects for getting their lives in order or digging out of a hole. In other words, looking for people we're pretty sure will say yes because, hey, what else have they got going on?

It's so easy to sponsor down because it's non-threatening. But here's what happens. Let's say, on a scale of 1 to 10 of competence and general skill sets, you consider yourself a 7, and you go sponsor 6's, 5's and 4's. They sponsor 5's, 4's and 3's, who sponsor 4's, 3's and 2's. You see where this is going. Soon, you're asking someone a few levels deep in your organization about their *why* and hearing, "I want pizza."

What to do?

Sponsor up. Get out your "chicken list." Go invite people who are skilled, competent, successful, disciplined, motivated, forceful, ambitious, accomplished. Invite people who are so busy they don't really have the time, but who know how to *create* the time—and even more importantly, how to productively *use* that time.

Sponsoring up is like marrying up (also a plan I strongly recommend). It's a statement of faith in your own future, a gesture of respect for the institution, and a sure path to creating something great.

Raise the bar. Build an organization of caliber.

The Network Marketing Middle Class
It's the Engine That Drives Our Networks
July '11

In these stringent economic times, we often hear about the "disappearing middle class." Let's make sure we don't let that happen in network marketing.

In fact, the network marketing middle class has actually been getting steadily stronger for years. And this is a good thing, because in network marketing, it is the middle class that makes the whole thing work.

There are three broad groups in network marketing.

At the topmost layer, there are those who earn a full-time income. Call it the six-figure earners, those generating $100,000 annually and up. This group is a very small minority. If "making the big money" were the way we defined success in network marketing, then to be fair, we would have to say that most network marketers are not successful.

But that's not how it is. Most people who are in network marketing will not be part of that topmost layer, and that's okay with them. They cannot live purely off their MLM income, but they don't have to in order to experience success.

Proof? Look at the bottom layer, those who earn little or

nothing. This includes those who make just enough cash to pay for their monthly product usage. For many, that *is* success. They love their products, wouldn't want to live without them. Being part of the program gives them a slight supplemental income stream that allows them to buy these products and break even.

Then there are the people in between, those who take their network marketing business seriously, work at it, and earn anywhere from a few hundred to a few thousand a month. Not enough so they can turn their backs on any other income, but enough to make a significant difference in their household.

For me, these people are the engine that makes the whole thing go. Sure, the top leaders have enormous influence and generate widespread inspiration. But top leaders can't be everywhere at once, having all those person-to-person conversations that are the living fabric of a thriving network. And sure, all those break-even consumer-distributors are the salt-of-the-earth volume blocks that are the bulk of the business—but they are not involved enough in the business to make it grow. So who really drives the network? The committed, involved part-timers.

They are the middle class of network marketing—and practically every one of them does something else for an income, too. In network marketing households, multiple streams of income is the *norm*.

Most network marketers I've known have *always* done something else, alongside their networking business. We do this in part for the income. We also do it because we have many interests. We don't necessarily want to quit our jobs or "fire our bosses." We *like* what we do. We don't want network marketing to *replace* our current lives. We want it to *enrich* them.

Bigger on the Inside
Noticing People's Core
November '11

There's a marvelous phrase that runs through the final chapter of *The Last Battle*, the final book in C. S. Lewis's extraordinary Chronicles of Narnia series. The children (the heroes of the story) are about to achieve passage into Aslan's country, a paradisiacal world that presents an identical version of their normal world, only more real.

And then something weird happens. To get to this sublime, more genuine place, they enter through a narrow door into what appears from the outside to be a small hut—yet the world they find inside the hut is much larger than the world they entered from.

"The further up and further in you go, the bigger everything gets," explains Tumnus the Faun, their tour guide. "The inside is larger than the outside."

The inside is larger than the outside.

This of course flies in the face of conventional physical logic. (Although advances in quantum physics have found that this turns out to be an apt description of the physical world after all: there is more energy on the inside of empty space than there is in all the matter in the known universe.) Yet I think Tumnus's observation is a perfect description not only of the world the children have just entered, but also of the children themselves.

That is what is so mesmerizing, delicious, and inspiring about infants. Even though they cannot communicate their thoughts with words, you can tell just by looking at them: there is *so much going on* in there.

Their world is bigger on the inside than it is on the outside.

In fact, it's not that they cannot communicate their thoughts in words. They don't *have* their thoughts in words. Words are containers into which they have not yet shrunk their sense of it all. Their reality is too big. Only later will they learn to chop it up and place it, item by item, into words. If all goes well and they are able to stay in touch with their interior spaciousness as they age, they eventually will learn to deepen the dimension of their words so that they may hold larger and larger experiences. If all goes well, the wordless wisdom of the infant eventually rediscovers itself in the artfully worded wisdom of the elderly.

My wife likes to point out that each of us has a little boy or little girl inside, alive and well. For some, that little person seems buried deep; for others, he or she seems quite present and close to the surface.

Perhaps the greatest gift we can give to the people we interact with is to notice the part of them that is bigger on the inside, and not simply interact with the part on the outside.

Expectation Is Everything
Regardless of Who Said So
May '12

A friend just sent me a copy of a book entitled *Attitude Is Everything*, by Jeff Keller. The subtitle reads, "Change Your Attitude . . . Change Your Life!" and the book's introduction leads off with this famous quotation:

> "The greatest discovery of my generation is that human beings can alter their lives by altering their attitudes of mind."
> — William James

And right there, the author lost me.

Now, I don't know Mr. Keller, nor anything about him, and have not yet read any further in his book (which I *do* intend to do at some point). And I have no doubt that he has much wisdom, experience, and value to offer the reader. What's more, I strongly think the core idea contained within the twenty words of that famous quotation are wise indeed, and I agree with it completely and wholeheartedly.

It's just that William James never said it.

At least, not as far as I've been able to determine . . . and I've tried. Oh, how I've tried.

I recently wrote a book with someone who happens to adore

that quote, and it played a significant part in the story. I was instantly suspicious: it's a great line, but it just doesn't sound like something an erudite nineteenth-century philosopher and Harvard professor, the man often referred to as the "father of modern psychology," would say. It sounded more like something James Allen (*As a Man Thinketh*) or some other early twentieth-century positive-thinking, self-help writer would have said.

I started searching. And searching. And *searching*. This pithy quote appears in a zillion places on the Internet, commonly attributed to James but rarely with an actual source. I did find one scholarly-seeming paper that quoted the passage and cited James's *The Principles of Psychology* as the source, even providing a specific page number (290) where it was supposed to have appeared, though without identifying which edition it was referring to, making the page number more or less useless.

So I bought a copy of *The Principles of Psychology*—a digital edition, so it would be fully searchable. I fully searched it. No such passage. Nothing even close. I searched as many terms and phrases as I could think of that might express even a remotely similar concept.

Nuttin.

In my online explorations I also noted that the quotation in question is even more frequently attributed to one James Truslow Adams than to William James. Truslow Adams, a turn-of-the-century amateur historian who served as U.S. delegate to the 1918 Paris Peace Talks, was an enthusiastic author who, amateur status notwithstanding, even earned a Pulitzer for his writing. Cool! Truslow Adams seemed like *exactly* the kind of writer who would say something like this.

But I struck out there, too. I couldn't find a single solid, credible Truslow Adams source for the passage.

Then I discovered that James Truslow Adams had written a biography of, guess who? *Williams James*. Bingo! Maybe Adams, in summing up or paraphrasing something James actually *had* said or written at some point, wrote this line in his biography. Could that be where the whole thing started?

So I ordered a copy—long out of print, existing in hard-cover only. The book finally arrived (a 1937 edition, I think it was), and when I ripped the wrapping off the package I found a biography of . . . Henry Adams. Not Henry James. At which point I quoted an expression which I can confidently attribute to a late-twentieth-century nuclear power plant worker named Homer Simpson:

D'oh!

And this, Dear Reader, is where I left off. I don't know if the book was listed wrong on Amazon, or the vendor picked and packed the wrong volume in sending it to me, or what. I declared my quest over. I had a life to get back to (wife, dog, meals, interacting with the rest of humanity, those sorts of things). I ended up providing the quotation in the book and referring to it as "*attributed to* the Pulitzer Prize–winning historian James Truslow Adams."

If you can find a verifiable source for the line, I'm eager to hear about it. Meanwhile, I'm adding it to my pile of excellent quotations that are, at this point, literary orphans.

Meanwhile, here's another quotation that says something roughly similar to the idea in James/Truslow-Adams/Anonymous's wonderful sentence, and this one I *can* verify:

You've heard the expression, "Go looking for trouble and that's what you'll find"? It's true, and not only about trouble. Go looking for conflict, and you'll find it. Go looking for people to take advantage of you, and they generally will. See the world as a dog-eat-dog place, and you'll always find a bigger dog looking at you as if you're his next meal. Go looking for the best in people, and you'll be amazed at how much talent, ingenuity, empathy and good will you'll find.

Ultimately, the world treats you more or less the way you expect to be treated. . . . In fact, you'd be amazed at just how much *you* have to do with what happens *to* you.

These words were spoken by the business guru Pindar, in *The Go-Giver*—and I *know* those words came directly from his mouth, because Bob Burg and I put them there.

The Path of Risk
Choose Wisely
November '12

Twenty-five years ago I had a tough choice to make. I was in-volved in two different network marketing companies. I had to decide which one to stick with and which one to let go of.

Company A had a full line of amazing products, first-class promotional material, blue chip production values. Some of the biggest names in network marketing were there. So were a few big-name Hollywood celebrities. This company was just about the most impressive, professional thing going.

Company B had a total of three products, a few mediocre brochures, and a single, somewhat embarrassing video. To call them a mom-and-pop operation was not a cliché, just accurate reporting. I went out to visit their headquarters; it turned out to be a little trailer in the middle of nowhere. They had a total of three employees: the mom, the pop, and a third person they'd hired to keep the files and answer the phones.

There it was: a choice. I couldn't keep working them both. One had to go, and I would be staking my future on the other.

I chose Company B. Why? To this day, I'm honestly not sure. It just resonated. Felt like the right thing to do.

So here's what happened.

Within the next twelve months, Company A was gone. One

day they sent out a letter saying how much they appreciated all of us, and how great we were, and they were closing down their networking operations and going retail. It was over.

And Company B? They grew, and kept growing. Next year they will celebrate their thirtieth anniversary. I built an organization with them that has earned me several million dollars. They've never missed a single pay period.

This is not to say that *all* risky choices pay off.

Twenty-three years ago, I had another tough choice. I had started a magazine called *Solstice*, reporting on health and environmental issues. It was tiny and self-financed, but it was growing. Another magazine I knew about, *Macromuse*, came available for sale. It was much bigger; buying it would gain us an instant ten-fold increase in visibility and circulation. It would also take financing. It was a risk. I took it. Borrowed the money, bought the magazine, merged the two titles, and just like that, I was on my way to building a publishing empire.

It didn't work. Too much growth, too fast. In a year the business imploded, went belly-up, and dragged me into bankruptcy. As the ancient knight says in Indiana Jones III, "He chose poorly."

Or did I? Because, if I had it over, I'd do it all again. During that year I learned more—about publishing, business, finance, myself—than I could have learned in ten years of business school. I climbed out of bankruptcy. We started *Upline* magazine, and it helped shape and guide a generation of networking leaders.

There is no safe. It's *all* a risk. The question is, what do you learn?

The Science of What Goes Right

What We've Learned About Happiness and Success

July '13

Fifteen years ago, on a mid-August day in San Francisco's massive Moscone Center, thousands of psychologists sat entranced as one of their peers announced the birth of a new field of psychology. Their discipline had learned a great deal about what goes wrong in the human condition, said the speaker, but had up to this point virtually ignored the question of what goes *right*. That was about to change.

The speaker was Martin Seligman, president of the American Psychological Association, and he was addressing the APA's annual convention, announcing an incredibly ambitious new effort he described as a "Manhattan Project for the social sciences"—a *positive psychology*. In layman's terms, a science of happiness.

A decade and a half later, the field of positive psychology has produced an avalanche of new research. Institutions from school systems to the U.S. military have implemented its findings, Fortune 500 corporations hire happiness consultants, and hardly a week goes by without some new book on happiness topping the *New York Times* bestseller list.

And this is no mere fad. Last year the *Harvard Business Review* dedicated its January issue to the topic. "We've learned a lot about how to make people happy," declared the editors. "We'd be stupid not to use that knowledge."

So what is that knowledge? Exactly what have we learned in the past fifteen years?

First, that happiness is *available*. Our level of happiness (much like our brains and nerve pathways, as the neuroscientists have learned over the same period) is far more malleable than we thought. We are not so hardwired—by genetics, upbringing, or past experience—to a fixed range of mood state as science insisted was the case just twenty years ago.

What's more, the factors that can make us significantly and lastingly happier are not the big things we might expect would make the difference, but the little things we so easily overlook. A consistently positive outlook. Expressing gratitude regularly. A habit of savoring little things in the moment. Simple acts of kindness and generosity to others. Greater investment in friendships and engagement in meaningful activities.

And the most radical finding of all: success does not lead to greater happiness—it's the other way around.

People who have higher levels of happiness, the scientists are telling us, also perform better at work, have more successful careers, and earn more; are more resistant to everything from colds and viruses to stroke and heart attack; have better and longer-lasting marriages and more satisfying friendships; are more involved in their communities; and live longer.

Doing the things that make you happier don't just make you happier. They also make your life work better.

I'll take *that* research over the original Manhattan Project any day.

Epilogue
The Zenification of
Network Marketing

By now, you're probably wondering what any of this has to do with Zen. Nothing, really—and everything.

Of course, network marketing has nothing whatsoever to do *directly* with Zen Buddhism or Japanese culture. (Although it's interesting to note that Japan is one of the strongest markets in the world for our profession—some years, *the* strongest.) But there's been a distinct shift in the way we practice this business over these nearly three decades that I've been participating in it. It's a shift I regard with keen interest, and the best way I've found to describe it is to call it "the Zenification of network marketing."

Picture this: you're standing at a long, polished walnut boardroom conference table, upon which sit two objects. On your left: a big 1980s boom box, two and a half feet wide and over a foot tall, complete with chrome trimmings and major amplification that dials all the way up to eleven.

On your right: an iPod.

The boom box weighs thirty pounds and holds an audiocassette that plays about ninety minutes of music. The iPod is the size and weight of a credit card, fits in your pocket, and holds a few *days* of music.

The iPod is what the boom box looks like after Zenification.

What does the Zenified, iPodicated version of network marketing look like? That's what we've been finding out over the last twenty years, and we are in the process still.

Central to the Zen aesthetic is the practice of *kanso*, or simplicity. Here's how Garr Reynolds, an American designer living in Japan, explains this concept:

> In the *kanso* concept, beauty, grace and visual elegance are achieved by elimination and omission. . . Simplicity means the achievement of maximum effect with minimum means. You do not always need to visually spell everything out. You do not need to (nor can you) pound every detail into the head of each member of your audience, either visually or verbally.[28]

Amen. In other words, if you want to keep people's interest, don't spill every bean you've got. If you walk around wielding the "Three-Foot Rule" like a two-by-four and dumping breathy, effusive thirty-minute presentations on everyone you see, you're going to lose friends and influence nobody. (Sort of like being Dale Carnegie, only in reverse.)

Garr goes on to give this brief list of Zen aesthetic values:

> simplicity; subtlety; elegance; suggestion (rather than complete or obvious description); naturalness (nothing artificial or forced); empty space (or silence); stillness and tranquility; elimination of the non-essential.

Simplicity, subtlety, elegance. Elimination of the non-essential. *Silence.* I like the sound of that! Seems to me we could use a bit more *kanso* in network marketing.

And we're starting to get it. In fact, Zenification has emerged as the hallmark not simply of twenty-first century MLM, but of twenty-first century *everything*. Corporations are deconstructing, decentralizing and outsourcing. Why? Because as a way of doing business, the twentieth-century corporation is a boom box. Today's home-based business is an iPod.

The world around us is evaporating into an ever sleeker transformation of itself. Wired is going wireless, stationary going mobile, heavy going light. Everywhere, our technologies are following the trend that architect and futurist Buckminster Fuller long ago dubbed "doing more with less," and nowhere is this shift more in evidence than in network marketing.

Remember that phone call from my friend Bill in early 1986, when I first heard about network marketing? A few months later, I traveled from upstate New York to Arkansas to visit Bill and see what he was up to. It looked like I was entering an ordinary suburban house—but once inside, I realized I had stepped into a full-fledged warehousing-and-fulfillment operations center.

Bill's ample home office was lined with row after row of shelves stocked with inventory of dozens upon dozens of products. In another room there hung a huge, inverted bag of Styrofoam peanuts, ready for pouring into the stacks of cardboard box flats that lined the walls.

And the bookkeeping! The company Bill worked with was a proud holdover from the classic 1960s MLM model: its distributors still bore the tasks of accounting and check-writing for their networks. My friend not only ordered in bulk from the company and then repacked and reshipped to all his distributors (calculating and adding shipping and tax for each locale), he would also receive a commission check from his company for these purchases, then calculate all of *our* commissions and bonuses and then write and mail checks to *us* . . . whereupon those of us with large enough organizations to have people underneath us earning something would turn around and do the same for our people.

This was one very large, very bulky boom box of an operation. It's amazing we ever found any time to hold any actual conversations with our people.

As I soon learned, this way of doing things was already history; Zenification was on the march. During the 1980s, computer technology relieved distributors of these administrative burdens. Toll-free 800-number technology suddenly made it practical for all orders to be placed directly with the home office, and inexpensive long-distance telephone service made it practical to build long-distance business relationships and expand one's group outside the perimeters defined by a day's car ride. (That is to say, *relatively* inexpensive long distance. It's hard to imagine in these days of dirt-cheap flat-rate service, but I remember telling my leaders in the early nineties, "You know your group is in momentum when your long-distance bill exceeds your mortgage," and in those days it was *true*.)

Suddenly, nine-tenths of the actual tasks of the business were taken off our hands. The physical realities of the business were soon Zenified right down to nothing, freeing us up to go into the *information* business.

And boy, did we ever. We became purveyors of information, gobs of it, often suffocating our victims in huge masses of brochures, data and background material. In the mid-to-late 1990s America was very nearly buried in an avalanche of audiocassettes and other network-marketing-generated, mass-promoted prospecting tools. But the avalanche did not last long: the quiet revolution of Zenification was not finished with us. In fact, it had just gotten started. Soon our videotapes and audio cassettes metamorphosed into little plastic slivers called CDs and DVDs, and then these disappeared altogether, evaporating into weightlessness on the Internet.

In the eighties we held gigantic hotel meetings; the pro-
totypical enrolling event was the massive rally. Today we do
our presentations on tablets and smartphones, and the prime
enrolling event is a three-way phone call—which we do on our
wireless earpiece while tromping barefoot through our backyard
garden or sitting with our laptop on our deck.

As our tools have changed, our approach and philosophy
have shifted with them. At some point during the nineties the
entire aesthetic of the business began making a subtle shift to
an ethos of *less*. From dumping information on people to listening. From hopes of "big money" and lavish lifestyles to an
appreciation of *smart* money, simplicity of financial planning
and long-term security: Robin Leach (*Lifestyles of the Rich and
Famous*) to David Ramsey (*Financial Peace*). From presenting to
inviting—a focus on "closing" to one on *opening*.

Today we're getting out of the *information* business and into
the *communication* business—a leap as vast as the one we took
from the industrial age into the information age. Information
is one-way, communication is two-way. Information leads to
overload; communication leads to understanding. Information is
telling; communication is asking. More information means more
noise; more communication means less. In a communication
economy, the way to wealth is through achieving greater clarity.

Elimination of the inessential.

Kanso.

There's another aspect to Zen that is a little harder to define,
a quality of *presence* that is shared alike by the Kendo swords-
man, the Aikido master and the Zen calligrapher. One of the
curious things about a master of martial arts is that he or she is
virtually impossible to push or knock down. Within the silence,
emptiness or understatement of the Zen expression there lies a

grounded core that is unshakable; the best word I can think of to describe it is *certainty*.

It is the certainty that comes with knowing what you know—but it is not "knowledge" in the sense of acquired information. It is the kind of knowing that arises from inside. It is knowing who you are. The more we have been freed of the inessential distractions of the business, the more intimately we have come to grapple with the essentials of the business—the core within the core.

Which is what? What is that "essence"?

Maybe the best way to say it is to point out some things it isn't. It isn't posturing, exaggerating, cajoling, convincing or persuading.

Strip away everything unnecessary, everything that doesn't work, everything that is excessive, that is unproductive, that is inauthentic, that is hyperbole or rings false, that is superfluous to what you truly want and genuinely value.

Let go of all of that, and what's left?

The Zen of MLM.

ENDNOTES

1 Actually, a large proportion of network marketing's ranks join simply for the ability to buy products they love at wholesale cost. They never earn a dime—unless you count wholesale discounts as earned income—because that's not their reason for joining. But I'm speaking here of people who join a networking company with the intention of pursuing it as an income-generating business.

2 "The Economic Expression of the American Revolution," *Networking Times*, Nov/Dec 2006.

3 "Why I Love Network Marketing," *Networking Times*, Mar/Apr 2005.

4 "Smart Networkers Finish Rich," *Networking Times*, Mar/Apr 2005.

5 "Creating a Life of Significance," *Networking Times*, Nov/Dec 2003.

6 "Torch-Bearers of the Young and Successful," *Networking Times*, Jul/Aug 2004.

7 "Champion on the Hill," *Networking Times*, Nov/Dec 2006.

8 "The Economic Expression of the American Revolution," *Networking Times*, Nov/Dec 2006.

9 "The Greatest Act of Faith," *Networking Times*, Sep/Oct 2006.

10 In these digital days, the OGM cassette tape is a thing of the past. A stopwatch or egg timer with a sixty-second setting will do.

11 Reprinted as an *Upline* Special Report, "The $300 Solution" proved to be the single most popular article in *Upline*'s ten-year career, and is still widely circulated on the Internet today.

12 Here in 2014, this reference is admittedly obscure. In the mid-nineties, one of the most popular prospecting audiocassettes in the business was entitled "Dead Doctors Don't Lie."

¹³ "Cheek to Cheek," words and music by Irving Berlin.

¹⁴ Nowadays, of course, email, online video and social media have replaced voice mail and physical mailings, but the principle remains unchanged.

¹⁵ Exodus 17:8–13.

¹⁶ *Network Marketing Lifestyles*, May 2000 (i.e., the same issue in which this editorial appeared).

¹⁷ Hebrews 11:1.

¹⁸ The cover story of the issue of *Network Marketing Lifestyles* in which this piece first appeared (January 2001) was a story on Amway and its legendary lead distributor, Dexter Yager.

¹⁹ The Frank Keefer and Jay Sargeant quotes in these two paragraph were both taken from articles in the September 2001 of *Network Marketing Lifestyles*, in which this piece first appeared.

²⁰ "Due Diligence," *Networking Times*, Nov/Dec 2006.

²¹ Small Business Research Bulletin #RB010-1104, *The Small Business Economy 2004: A Report to the President*, prepared by the Small Business Administration's Office of Advocacy (www.sba.gov/advo).

²² This statement was in reference to the party-plan company Pampered Chef, which was the 2002 purchase. The other two direct selling companies owned by Buffett's investment firm Berkshire Hathaway are Kirby (vacuum cleaners) and World Book (encyclopedias).

²³ 2003 "State of the Industry" address to the DSA (www.dsa.org).

²⁴ *The Next Millionaires*, by Paul Zane Pilzer (Momentum Media, 2006).

²⁵ "Champion on the Hill," *Networking Times*, Nov/Dec 2006.

²⁶ "The Economic Expression of the American Revolution," *Networking Times*, Nov/Dec 2006.

²⁷ "The Greatest Act of Faith," *Networking Times*, Sep/Oct 2006.

²⁸ Garr Reynolds, a former manager of Worldwide USer Group Relations at Apple who now lives and teaches in Japan, in a post entitled "Gates, Jobs & the Zen Aesthetic" on his web site, www.presentationzen.com.

SOURCES

Grateful acknowledgment is made to John Milton Fogg (*It's Time*), Randy Gage (Gage Research & Development), Chris Gross (*Networking Times*), George Madiou (TheNetworkMarketingMagazine.com) and Jan Ruhe (*The Master Presentation Guide*) for permission to use materials that first appeared in their publications.

"Residual Income, Residual Impact" originally appeared in the September 1991 issue of *Upline* and again in the November 2000 issue of *Network Marketing Lifestyles*.

"The One-Minute Networker" originally appeared in the April 1992 issue of *Upline*.

"The Tortoise and the Hare" originally appeared in the August 1993 issue of *Upline*.

"Point, Click, Success!" originally appeared in the December 1993 issue of *Upline*.

"The Ultimate Secret to Handling Objections" originally appeared in the February 1994 issue of *Upline*.

"In Praise of Quesfirmations" originally appeared in the March 1994 issue of *Upline*.

"Selling You on You" originally appeared in the June 1994 issue of *Upline* and again in the June 2002 (inaugural) issue of *Networking Times*.

"Houses of Straw, Houses of Brick" originally appeared in the September 1994 issue of *Upline* as "Who's Afraid of the Big Bad Wolf?"

"Paying for Lunch" originally appeared in the December 1994 issue of *Upline*.

"Getting Stretched" originally appeared in the March 1995 issue of *Upline*.

"The Treacherous Dichotomy" originally appeared in the June 1995 issue of *Upline* and again in the December 2002 ("Philanthropy") issue of *Networking Times*.

"The High Road" originally appeared in the September 1995 issue of *Upline*, and has been on display ever since in the sales room at Lexus of Richmond in Virginia.

"Wemen" originally appeared in the October 1995 issue of *Upline* and again in the January 2003 ("Women in Networking") issue of *Networking Times*.

"You Are Not a Dinosaur" originally appeared in the November 1995 issue of *Upline* and again in the February 2003 ("Technology") issue of *Networking Times*.

"Dancin' Check to Check" originally appeared in the December 1995 issue of *Upline*.

"The Eighth Day of the Week" originally appeared in the January 1996 issue of *Upline*, again in the March/April 2005 ("Financial Freedom") issue of *Networking Times*, and was reprinted in *The Slight Edge*, by Jeff Olson (Momentum Media, 2005).

"Stop, Look, Listen" originally appeared in the February 1996 issue of *Upline* and again in the March 2003 ("Leadership") issue of *Networking Times*.

"It's about the Product... and It's Not about the Product" originally appeared in the March 1996 issue of *Upline*.

"The Great Balancing Act" originally appeared in the April 1996 issue of *Upline* as "How to Not Fall Off Your Horse."

"Ears: An Amazing Communication Technology" originally appeared in the May 1996 issue of *Upline*.

"The Power of Not Resisting" originally appeared in the June 1996 issue of *Upline* as "How to Not Fall Down."

"Curiosity" originally appeared in the July 1996 issue of *Upline* as "The Road Less Traveled."

"In the Wind Tunnel" originally appeared in the September 1996 issue of *Upline*.

"One Way or the Other" originally appeared in the November 1996 issue of *Upline* as "Multiplicity."

"What People Want" originally appeared in the December 1996 issue of *Upline* and again in the August 2002 issue ("Money") of *Networking Times*.

"Increase Your R.Q." originally appeared in the February 1997 issue of *Upline*.

"Residual Leadership" originally appeared in the February 1997 issue of *Upline* as "Don't Let George Do It" and again in the October 2002 ("Personal Growth") issue of *Networking Times* under the present title.

"Build to Last" originally appeared in September 1998 as a portion of a special report entitled "Build to Last," offered by Randy Gage to accompany his audio album *Crafting Your Vision*, published by Gage Research & Development, Inc.

"Don't Present!" originally appeared in September 1998 as another portion of the "Build to Last" special report for Randy Gage's audio album *Crafting Your Vision*, published by Gage Research & Development, Inc.

"The Cello Lesson" originally appeared in the March 2000 issue of *Network Marketing Lifestyles*.

"Leaders Hold a Vision" originally appeared in the May 2000 issue of *Network Marketing Lifestyles*.

"You Are What You Think" originally appeared in the July 2000 issue of *Network Marketing Lifestyles*.

" 'What Have You Done for Me Lately?' " originally appeared in the September 2000 issue of *Network Marketing Lifestyles*.

"Your Words" originally appeared in the September 2000 issue of *Network Marketing Lifestyles* as "Your Voice."

"Reach for the Stars" originally appeared in the November 2000 issue of *Network Marketing Lifestyles*.

"The Myth of the 'Ordinary Person' " originally appeared in the January 2001 issue of *Network Marketing Lifestyles*.

"True Leadership" originally appeared in the March 2001 issue of *Network Marketing Lifestyles*.

"First, Do No Harm" originally appeared in the May 2001 issue of *Network Marketing Lifestyles*.

"Secrets of a Great Presentation" originally appeared in June 2001 as an epilogue to *The Master Presentation Guide*, by Jan Ruhe.

"Telling the Truth" originally appeared in the September 2001 issue of *Network Marketing Lifestyles*.

"Love at First Sight" originally appeared in the November 2001 issue of *Network Marketing Lifestyles*.

"Bright Beams on the Highway" originally appeared in the June 2002 (inaugural) issue of *Networking Times*.

"Gossip" originally appeared in the December 2002 ("Philanthropy") issue of *Networking Times*.

"*No Fair!* . . . or Is It?" originally appeared in the April 2003 ("Money") issue of *Networking Times*.

"Can You Say the B Word?" originally appeared in the May 2003 ("Communication") issue of *Networking Times*.

"Giving Up Your Right to Be Right" originally appeared in the June 2003 ("Teamwork") issue of *Networking Times*.

"Loyalties Beget Royalties" originally appeared in the July 2003 ("Loyalty") issue of *Networking Times*.

"It's Not What You Say" originally appeared in the August 2003 ("Spiritual Networking") issue of *Networking Times*.

"People Do What People Do" originally appeared in the September 2003 ("Learning") issue of *Networking Times*.

"All for One and One for All" originally appeared in the October 2003 ("Community") issue of *Networking Times*.

"The Anonymous Gift" originally appeared in the December 2003 ("Giving") issue of *Networking Times*.

"The Sky's Not the Limit" originally appeared in the January 2004 ("Belief") issue of *Networking Times*.

"Network Marketing at the Oscars®" and the reader response originally appeared in the February/March 2004 ("Women and Freedom") and April 2004 ("Coaching") issues of *Networking Times*.

"Be Careful What You Fish for" originally appeared in the May/June 2004 ("Goals") issue of *Networking Times*.

"Why Not?" originally appeared in the July/August 2004 ("Youth") issue of *Networking Times*.

"The Best Plan" originally appeared in the September/October 2004 ("Systems") issue of *Networking Times*.

"Envisioning" originally appeared in the November/December 2004 ("Mission-Driven Business") issue of *Networking Times*.

"The Art of Presentation" originally appeared in the January/February 2005 ("The Art of Presentation") issue of *Networking Times*.

"Lies, Damn Lies and Statistics" originally appeared in the May/June 2005 ("Duplication") issue of *Networking Times*.

"The Days" originally appeared in the July/August 2005 ("Making Time") issue of *Networking Times*.

"The Core within the Core" originally appeared in the September/October 2005 ("Learning") issue of *Networking Times*.

"The Greatest Contribution" first appeared in the November/December 2005 ("Making a Contribution") issue of *Networking Times*.

"An Opportunity to Communicate" first appeared in the January/February 2006 ("Understanding People") issue of *Networking Times*.

"A Million Little Dollars" and the correspondence that follows originally appeared in the March/April 2006 ("Playing the Game") and May/June 2006 ("Virtual Networking") issues of *Networking Times*.

"When We Will Arrive" originally appeared in the May/June 2006 ("Virtual Networking") issue of *Networking Times* as "The Challenge."

"The Strength of Weak Ties" originally appeared in the July/August 2006 ("Networking from the Inside Out") issue of *Networking Times*.

"A Walk on the Moon" originally appeared in the September 2006 ("The Elements of Greatness") issue of *Networking Times*.

"Ignore the Memo: Fly Anyway" originally appeared in the November/December ("Are You Making a Difference?") issue of *Networking Times*.

"The Light and the Bushel" originally appeared in the January/February 2007 ("I've Run Out of People to Talk to . . . Now What?") issue of *Networking Times*.

"Staring at Blank Paper" originally appeared in the March/April 2007 ("Creating Your Future") issue of *Networking Times*.

A portion of "Cutting a New Path" (a bit more than half) originally appeared in the October 2005 (inaugural) edition of TheNetworkMarketingMagazine. com; it was later expanded for the book *It's Time* (ed. John Milton Fogg, March 2007).

"Trust" originally appeared in the May/June 2007 ("Trust Rules!") issue of *Networking Times*.

"Be Their Beacon" originally appeared in the July/August 2007 ("Teams That Rock!") issue of *Networking Times*.

"A Revolutionary Idea: Ask" originally appeared in the September/October 2007 ("The Web Gets Personal") issue of *Networking Times*.

"A Wealth of Possibilities" originally appeared in the November/December 2007 ("True Wealth") issue of *Networking Times*.

"Without a Net" originally appeared as a blog post on johndavidmann.com on 12-13-07.

"Putting People Together" originally appeared in the March/April 2008 ("Money Matters") issue of *Networking Times*.

"The Networker Doth Protest Too Much" first appeared in the May/June 2008 ("Beyond Belief") edition of *Networking Times*.

"Our Favorite Whats" originally appeared in the July/August 2008 ("Life Purpose") issue of *Networking Times*.

"Shhhhh: The Art of Quiet" originally appeared in the September/October 2008 ("The New Midlife") issue of *Networking Times*.

"The Power to Create or Tear Down" originally appeared as a blog post on johndavidmann.com on 8-5-08.

"Being in Love" originally appeared in the November/December 2008 edition ("The Power of Love in Business") of *Networking Times*.

"Love and Residual" originally appeared in the January/February 2009 ("Expand Your Contact List") edition of *Networking Times*.

"Being Heard" originally appeared as a blog post on johndavidmann.com on 3-16-09.

"Gold and Twopence" originally appeared in the May/June 2009 ("Elevating the Profession") issue of *Networking Times*.

"Compassion" originally appeared as a blog post on johndavidmann.com on 6-22-09.

"To Break or to Bend" originally appeared in the July/August 2009 ("Success through Adversity") issue of *Networking Times*.

"Life Is Like a Box of Tofu" originally appeared in the September/October 2009 ("Financial Peace") issue of *Networking Times*.

"Who Gets In?" originally appeared in the January/February 2010 ("Creating a Culture") edition of *Networking Times*.

"How to Start" originally appeared in the May/June 2010 ("Powerful Beginnings") edition of *Networking Times*.

"You Are Not the Boss of Me" originally appeared in the July/August 2010 ("The Yin and Yang of Business") edition of *Networking Times*.

"Are You Found Wanting?" originally appeared as a blog post on johndavidmann.com on 7-6-10.

"Coachability" originally appeared in the September/October 2010 ("Lifelong Learning") edition of *Networking Times*.

"Creating Caliber" originally appeared in the November/December 2010 ("Global Wealth Building") edition of *Networking Times*.

"The Network Marketing Middle Class" originally appeared in the July/August 2011 ("Multiple Streams of Income") issue of *Networking Times*.

"Bigger on the Inside" originally appeared in the November/December 2011 ("Raising Future Generations") edition of *Networking Times*.

"The Business for the Rest of Us" originally appeared in the January/February 2012 ("Leaving a Legacy") edition of *Networking Times*.

"Expectation Is Everything" originally appeared as a blog post on johndavidmann.com on 5-5-12.

"The Path of Risk" originally appeared in the November/December 2012 ("The Global Rise of Entrepreneurship") edition of *Networking Times*.

"The Science of What Goes Right" originally appeared in the July/August 2013 ("Happiness in Business") edition of *Networking Times*.

ACKNOWLEDGMENTS

As John Donne observed, no man is an island, entire of itself—and the same is true for no Mann, and no book, either. Every piece of fruit (be it book, business or pure idea) is the result of the efforts and good will of all the people who make up the tree that helped produce it, and not only the particular branch from which it happened to pop. My heartfelt thanks go out:

to Randy Gage, for the fabulous title idea;

to Seth Godin, for the generous quote on the cover;

to Richard Brooke, Bob Burg, Art Jonak and Tom Schreiter, who read the manuscript and offered their kind comments;

to John Milton Fogg, for starting it all;

to Chris and Josephine Gross, for their amazing and indefatigable dedication;

to Reed Bilbray, for his friendship and strategic wisdom;

to Luke Melia, for his endless cheer and Zen webmastery;

to Mia Inderbitzen, for her ever-willing esprit de corps and design skills;

to my faithful readers, for the years of waiting with persistent patience for this book to happen;

to my mother and father, Carolyn and Alfred Mann, for giving me so many magnificent examples of how life works;

and most of all to wife, best friend and partner in life, Ana Gabriel Mann, who never tires of encouraging me, and who understands this thing called network marketing better than anyone else I know.

ABOUT THE AUTHOR

JOHN DAVID MANN is one of the United States' preeminent writers on network marketing. He was cofounder and senior editor of the *Upline* journal and editor in chief of *Network Marketing Lifestyles* and *Networking Times*. In 1992 he edited and produced the underground bestseller *The Greatest Networker in the World*, by John Milton Fogg, which became the defining book in its field and sold more than a million copies in eight languages. His books *The Go-Giver* and *The Slight Edge* have been included in the sales kits of multiple networking companies. During the 1990s, John built a multimillion-dollar network organization of over 100,000 people.

John's diverse career has made him a thought leader in several different industries. At age 15 he was recipient of the 1969 BMI Awards to Student Composers and several New Jersey State grants for composition; his musical compositions were performed throughout the U.S. and his musical score for Aeschylus' *Prometheus Bound* (written at age 13) was performed at the amphitheater at Epidaurus, Greece, where the play was originally premiered. At 17 he and a few friends started their own high school in Orange, New Jersey, called Changes, Inc. Before turning to business and journalism, he forged a career as a concert cellist. In 1986 he founded and wrote for *Solstice*, a journal on health, nutrition and environmental issues; his series on the climate crisis (yes, he was writing about this back in the eighties) was selected for national reprint in *Utne Reader*.

John is an award-winning author whose writings have earned the Nautilus Award, the Axiom Business Book Award (Gold Medal), and Taiwan's Golden Book Award for Innovation, and his books are published in more than twenty languages around the world. He is coauthor of the international bestseller *The Go-Giver* with Bob Burg, the *New York Times* bestseller *Flash Foresight* with Daniel Burrus, the *New York Times* bestseller *The Red Circle* with Brandon Webb, *Take the Lead* with Betsy Myers (named Best Leadership Book of 2011 by Tom Peters and *The Washington Post*), and *The Slight Edge* with Jeff Olson.

He is married to Ana Gabriel Mann and considers himself the luckiest mann in the world. You can visit him at www.john-davidmann.com.

Made in the USA
Middletown, DE
09 December 2015